"*Modern Romance* is wicked and witty, slapstick in its silliest moments, but completely serious in its efforts to dissect the intricacies of our romantic lives." —*Shelf Awareness*

"The book is an obsessive exploration of what makes hearts flutter and break across the globe, but most importantly, it dissects those ideas through the lens of a right-and-left swiping society. And as a result, Ansari's final product doesn't only feel complete—it's hilariously executed, even without his unmistakable high-register voice belting the punch lines. At 250 pages, *Modern Romance* is a lean, pithy read that's perfect to reach the tech-obsessed generation it explores." —*Paste* magazine

"An engaging look at the often head-scratching, frequently infuriating mating behaviors that shape our love lives." —*Refinery29*

"This book is essentially an Aziz Ansari stand-up routine in print form. His unique voice is present throughout the book. One reason that people love Aziz is his outlook on life. He has a funny way of refocusing seemingly ordinary things and zeroing in on very small details that most would not notice. He brings all of that and more to the table with this book. This book is informative, presents a lot of thought-provoking topics, and discusses them thoroughly. Paired with Aziz's distinct voice, this book is even more endearing." —*The Source*

"You're not going to find a traditional humor book. And that's a good thing. *Modern Romance* is something a bit more unique: a comprehensive, in-depth sociological investigation into the 'many challenges of looking for love in the digital age.' *Modern Romance* gives an impressive overview of how the dating game has changed with the advent of cell phones and the Internet. But there's also some practical advice peppered in there by Ansari himself." —*Bustle*

"Even comedy phenoms get dumped. But when it was this *Parks and Recreation* star's turn, he channeled the rejection into an extensive (and riotous) investigation of the current state of dating, going as far as recruiting an NYU sociologist to be his collaborator/wingman." —*O, The Oprah Magazine*

"A social-science book that's pleasant to read and a comedy book that actually has something to say." —*Bookforum*

D0210154

"Always-hilarious Aziz Ansari proves you can be smart and funny at the same time. Not only did I laugh my ass off, I really learned stuff. Where was this book when I was twenty-two years old?"

—Steven Levitt, coauthor of the #1 *New York Times*
bestselling *Freakonomics*

"Laughing is my second least-favorite thing in the world after thinking. This book was torture. Not a page passed without an unwanted eruption of giggles or insight. Aziz is funny as hell, and smart as shit."

—Jonathan Safran Foer, author of *Eating Animals*

"It's the voices that will have you reading this remarkable book in one sitting! The voices of old people who married someone who lived in their apartment building or the building next door and the voices of the young people who check out hundreds of romantic possibilities a night, with so much choice that choice becomes impossible. And then there is the voice of Ansari himself, funny, of course, but also deeply compassionate. This book defines serious fun."

—Sherry Turkle, Abby Rockefeller Mauzé Professor of the Social
Studies of Science and Technology, Massachusetts Institute of
Technology, and author of *Reclaiming Conversation*

"*Modern Romance* is just like Aziz Ansari himself—charming, thoughtful, reasonable, and able to distill the madness of the world into something both sane and wildly funny."

—Dave Eggers, author of *Your Fathers, Where Are They?*
And the Prophets, Do They Live Forever?

"Ansari and Klinenberg elegantly capture the entirely new ways that singles communicate, court, and find love today. *Modern Romance* is a captivating read, with deep insight into history, science, and culture, and loads of wit and charm. Along the way, you may even collect some valuable tips for finding a soul mate."

—Helen Fisher, senior research fellow, the Kinsey Institute;
author of *Why Him? Why Her?*

PENGUIN BOOKS

MODERN ROMANCE

Aziz Ansari is a writer, director, stand-up comedian, and actor. He currently stars in, writes, and directs *Master of None*, his own original series for Netflix. The series was called "the year's best comedy straight out of the gate" by the *New York Times*. In 2014, Ansari became the seventh comedian ever to sell out Madison Square Garden in New York. His two sold-out performances at the legendary arena were filmed for his fourth comedy special, *Aziz Ansari: Live at Madison Square Garden*, which was released in March 2015 on Netflix. For seven seasons, he starred as Tom Haverford on the beloved NBC comedy series *Parks and Recreation* with Amy Poehler. He has also appeared in several films, including *This Is the End*, *Funny People*, and *30 Minutes or Less*. He enjoys eating fresh pasta and watching multiple hours of critically acclaimed television dramas in one sitting.

Eric Klinenberg is a professor of sociology and director of the Institute for Public Knowledge at New York University. He's the author of *Going Solo* (Penguin Press), *Fighting for Air*, and *Heat Wave*, and has contributed to *The New Yorker*, *Rolling Stone*, and *This American Life*.

Praise for *Modern Romance*

Winner of the 2015 Goodreads Choice Awards for Nonfiction

A *BuzzFeed* Best Nonfiction Book of the Year

A *National Post* Best Book of the Year

"A sprightly, easygoing hybrid of fact, observation, advice, and comedy."
—*The New York Times*

"A hilarious, often unsettling account of what young singles go through as they search for love in the digital age."
—*Rolling Stone*

"The ever hip and funny comedian and *Parks and Recreation* star embarks on a surprisingly insightful exploration of the complex realities of dating today. . . . Ansari's eminently readable book is successful, in part, because it not only lays out the history, evolution, and pitfalls of dating, it also offers sound advice on how to actually win today's constantly shifting game of love. Often hilarious, consistently informative, and unusually helpful."
—*Kirkus Reviews*

"*Modern Romance* is equal parts cultural investigation, self-help treatise, and celebrity memoir, its various statistical findings illustrated by graphs and tables and leavened with jokes." —*New Yorker* Page-Turner

"*Modern Romance* reads like a CliffsNotes to relationshipping as it is currently experienced by (mostly middle-class, Ansari admits, and mostly straight) Americans. It's the familiar stuff of research and sitcomedy, distilled into a funny, and highly readable, summary." —*The Atlantic*

"Entertaining and illuminating." —*The Guardian* (London)

"A funny and scholarly examination of the twenty-four-hour romance cycle." —*The Boston Globe*

"A lively look at love, marriage, and the oddities of mating in the twenty-first century." —*The Economist*

"With topics like online dating apps to serious social science research, the book is sure to have you laughing if not taking a few notes." —*USA Today*

"Funny, informative, and surprisingly earnest." —*The Daily Beast*

"With his first foray into the literary sphere, Ansari handedly accomplishes what he set out to do. *Modern Romance* provides insight into what people do to find love. He infuses their stories with his sass and parallels their shame with much of his own. On top of that, Ansari's advice is easy to follow and backed with science and research. *Modern Romance* is the pinnacle of romantic guides—at least until a new dating app makes it obsolete." —Vox

"[A] brightly written, insightful, and often surprising book about just how much, and how rapidly, technology has changed our intimate relationships . . . A smart and well-supported examination of the intersection of tech and romance." —*Tampa Bay Times*

"It's hard to think of another celebrity book that also feels like breaking news. . . . Aside from the jokes, the science of *Modern Romance* holds water, and is absolutely fascinating." —*The A.V. Club*

AZIZ ANSARI

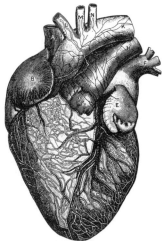

MODERN ROMANCE

With Eric Klinenberg

PENGUIN BOOKS

PENGUIN BOOKS

An imprint of Penguin Random House LLC

375 Hudson Street

New York, New York 10014

penguin.com

First published in the United States of America by Penguin Press,
an imprint of Penguin Random House LLC, 2015
Published in Penguin Books 2016

Image credits appear on page 278.

ISBN 9781594206276 (hc.)
ISBN 9780143109259 (pbk.)

Printed in the United States of America
7   9   10   8

Designed by Walter Green

```
┌─────────────────┐
│    CONTENTS      │
└─────────────────┘
```

MODERN ROMANCE

OH,

shit! Thanks for buying my book. That money is MINE. But I worked really hard on this, and I think you'll enjoy it.

First off, a little about this project. When you have success as a stand-up comedian, you quickly get offers to do a humor book. In the past, I always turned these opportunities down, because I thought stand-up was the best medium for me. In my mind, a book wouldn't be as fun as just using my ideas for stand-up.

So why did I decide to write a book about modern romance?

A few years ago there was a woman in my life—let's call her Tanya—and we had hooked up one night in L.A. We'd both attended a birthday party, and when things were winding down, she offered to drop me off at home. We had been chatting and flirting a little the whole night, so I asked her to come in for a drink.

At the time, I was subletting a pretty nice house up in the Hollywood Hills. It was kind of like that house De Niro had in *Heat*, but a little more my vibe than the vibe of a really skilled robber who takes down armored cars.

I made us both a nice cocktail and we took turns throwing on records while we chatted and laughed. Eventually we started making out, and it was pretty awesome. I remember drunkenly saying something really dumb when she was leaving, like, "Tanya, you're a very charming lady . . ." She said, "Aziz, you're a pretty charming guy too." The encounter seemed promising, as everyone in the room had agreed: We were both charming people.

I wanted to see Tanya again and was faced with a simple conundrum that plagues us all: How and when do I communicate next?

Do I call? Do I text? Do I send a Facebook message? Do I send up a smoke signal? How does one do that? Will I set my rented house on fire? How embarrassed will I be when I have to tell the home's owner, actor James Earl Jones, that I burned his house down trying to send a smoke signal?

Oh no, I just revealed whose sick house I'd rented: King Jaffe Joffer himself, the voice of Darth Vader, film legend James Earl Jones.

Eventually I decided to text her, because she seemed to be a heavy texter. I waited a few days, so as not to seem overeager. I found out that the band Beach House, which we listened to the night we made out, was playing that week in L.A., so it seemed like the perfect move.

Here was my text:

> Hey - don't know if you left for NYC, but Beach House playing tonight and tomorrow at Wiltern. You wanna go? Maybe they'll let you cover The Motto if we ask nicely?

A nice, firm ask with a little inside joke thrown in. (Tanya was singing the Drake song "The Motto" at the party and, impressively, knew almost all the lyrics.)

I was pretty confident. I wasn't head-over-heels in love with Tanya, but she seemed really cool and it felt like we had a good connection.

As I waited for her response, I started picturing our hypothetical relationship. Perhaps next weekend we would go see a movie at the cool outdoor screening series they do at the Hollywood Forever Cemetery? Maybe I could cook Tanya dinner later this week and try out that brick chicken recipe I'd been eager to attempt? Would Tanya and I go vacation in Ojai later in the fall? Who knew what our future would be? This was going to be great!

A few minutes went by and the status of my text message changed to "read."

My heart stopped.

This was the moment of truth.

I braced myself and watched as those little iPhone dots popped up. The ones that tantalizingly tell you someone is typing a response, the smartphone equivalent of the slow trip up to the top of a roller coaster. But then, in a few seconds—*they vanished*. And there was no response from Tanya.

Hmmm . . . What happened?

A few more minutes go by and . . .

Nothing.

No problem, she's probably just crafting her perfectly witty response. She started a draft, didn't feel good about it, and wanted to get back to it later. *I get it.* She also probably didn't want to seem overeager and be writing back so fast, right?

Fifteen minutes go by . . . Nothing.

My confidence starts going down and shifting into doubt.

An hour goes by . . . Nothing.

Two hours go by . . . Nothing.

Three hours go by . . . Nothing.

A mild panic begins. I start staring at my original text. Once so confident, now I second-guess it all.

> Hey - don't know if you left for NYC, but Beach House playing tonight and tomorrow at Wiltern. You wanna go? Maybe they'll let you cover The Motto if we ask nicely?

I'm so stupid! I should have typed "Hey" with two y's, not just one! I asked too many questions. What the fuck was I thinking? Oh, there I go with another question. Aziz, WHAT'S UP WITH YOU AND THE QUESTIONS?

I'm struggling to figure it out but trying to keep calm.

Okay, maybe she's busy with work. No big deal.

I'm sure she'll get back to me as soon as she can. We had a connection, right?

A fucking day goes by.

A FULL DAY!

Now my thoughts get crazier:

What has happened?! I know *she held my words in her hand!!*

Did Tanya's phone fall into a river/trash compactor/volcano?

Did Tanya *fall into a river/trash compactor/volcano?? Oh no, Tanya has died, and I'm selfishly worried about our date. I'm a bad person.*

I shared my dilemma with a friend.

"Aww, come on, man, it's fine. She'll get back to you. She's probably just busy," he said optimistically.

Then I look on social media. I see her logged onto Facebook Chat. Do I send a message? *No! Don't do that, Aziz. Be cool. Be cool . . .*

Later I check Instagram, and this clown Tanya is posting a photo of some deer. Too busy to write me back, but she has time to post a photo of some deer she saw on a hike?

I'm distraught, but then I have a moment of clarity that every idiot has in this situation.

MAYBE SHE DIDN'T GET THE TEXT!

Yes, that's what's happened, right? There was a glitch in her phone of some sort. Of course.

This is when I contemplate a second text, but I'm hesitant due to the fact that this scenario has never happened with my friends:

"Hey, Alan. I texted you to go get dinner and you didn't write back for a full day. What happened?"

"Damn! I didn't see the text. It didn't go through. Glitch in my phone. Sorry about that. Let's grab dinner tomorrow."

Back to the Tanya situation. At this point it's been more than twenty-four hours. It's Wednesday. The concert is *tonight*. To not even write back and say no, why would she do that? At least say no so I can take someone else, right? Why, Tanya, why? I start going nuts thinking about it. How can this person be rude on so many levels? I'm not just some bozo. She's known me for years.

I kept debating whether I should send anything, but I felt it would just be too desperate and accepted that she wasn't interested. I told myself that I wouldn't want to go out with someone who treats people that way anyway, which was somewhat true, but I was still beyond frustrated and insulted.

Then I realized something interesting.

The madness I was descending into wouldn't have even existed twenty or even ten years ago. There I was, maniacally checking my phone every few minutes, going through this tornado of panic and hurt and anger all because this person hadn't written me a short, stupid message on a dumb little phone.

I was really upset, but had Tanya really done anything that rude or malicious? No, she just didn't send a message in order to avoid an awkward situation. I'd surely done the same thing to someone else and not realized the similar grief I had possibly caused them.

I didn't end up going to the concert that night. Instead I went to a comedy club and started talking about the awful frustration, self-doubt, and rage that this whole "silence" nonsense had provoked in the depths of my being. I got laughs but also something bigger, like the audience and I were connecting on a deeper level.

I could tell that every guy and girl in the audience had had their own Tanya in their phone at one point or another, each with their own individual problems and dilemmas. We each sit alone, staring at this black screen with a whole range of emotions. But in a strange way, we are all doing it together, and we should take solace in the fact that no one has a clue what's going on.

I got fascinated by the questions of how and why so many people have become so perplexed by the challenge of doing something that people have always done quite efficiently: finding romance. I started asking people I knew if there was a book that would help me understand the many challenges of looking for love in the digital age. I found some interesting pieces here and there, but not the kind of comprehensive, in-depth sociological investigation I was looking for. That book simply didn't exist, so I decided to try to write it myself.

When I started the project, I thought the big changes in romance were obvious—technological developments like smartphones, online dating, and social media sites. As I dug deeper, however, I realized that the transformation of our romantic lives cannot be explained by technology alone; there's much more to the story. In a very short period of time, the whole culture of finding love and a mate has radically changed. A century ago people would find a decent person who lived in their neighborhood. Their families would meet and, after they decided neither party seemed like a murderer, the couple would get married and have a kid, all by the time they were twenty-two. Today people spend years of their lives on a quest to find the perfect person, a soul mate. The tools we use on this search are different, but what has really changed is our desires and—even more strikingly—the underlying goals of the search itself.

The more I thought about these changes, the more I had to write this book. But I also knew that I, bozo comedian Aziz Ansari, probably couldn't tackle this topic on my own, and I decided to reach out to some very smart people to guide me. I teamed up with the sociologist Eric Klinenberg, and we designed a massive research project, one that would require more than a year of investigation in cities across the world and involve some of the leading experts on love and romance.

Before we get into things, I want to tell you more about our project, so you know what we did—and didn't—do. The primary source of data for this book is the research that Eric and I did during 2013 and 2014. We conducted focus groups and interviews with hundreds of people in New York City, Los Angeles, Wichita, Monroe (NY), Buenos Aires, Tokyo, Paris, and Doha. These weren't ordinary interviews. First, we assembled diverse groups of people and wound up having incredibly personal conversations about the intimate details of their romantic lives. Second, and even more intriguing, many of the people who participated in our research volunteered to share their phones with us, so we could track their interactions through text messages, e-mails, online dating sites, and swipe apps like Tinder. This information was revelatory, because we could observe how actual romantic encounters played out in people's lives and not just hear stories about what people remembered. Since we asked people to share so much personal information, we promised them anonymity. That means all the names of people whose stories we tell here are pseudonyms, as is standard practice in qualitative social science research.

To expand our reach beyond just those cities, we created a Modern Romantics subreddit forum on the website Reddit to ask questions and essentially conduct a massive online focus group receiving thousands of responses from around the world. (I want to give huge thanks to everyone who participated in these sessions, as the book would not have been possible without them.) So in the book, when we mention "the subreddit," this is what we are referring to.

We also spent a long time interviewing some incredibly smart people, including eminent sociologists, anthropologists, psychologists, and journalists who have dedicated their careers to studying modern romance—and who were very generous with their time. Here's a list that I'm terrified I'm going to leave someone off of: danah boyd of Microsoft; Andrew Cherlin of Johns Hopkins University; Stephanie Coontz of Evergreen State College; Pamela Druckerman of the *New York Times*; Kumiko Endo of the New School, who also assisted us with our research in Tokyo; Eli Finkel of Northwestern University; Helen Fisher of Rutgers University; Jonathan Haidt of NYU; Sheena Iyengar of Columbia University; Dan Savage; Natasha Schüll of MIT; Barry Schwartz of Swarthmore College; Clay Shirky of NYU; Sherry Turkle of MIT; and Robb Willer of Stanford, who also helped us design some research questions and analyze our data.

In addition to these interviews, we got access to some amazing quantitative data that we use extensively here. For the past five years, Match.com has sponsored the largest survey of American singles around, a nationally representative sample of about five thousand people with questions about all kinds of fascinating behaviors and preferences. Match generously shared it with us, and we, in turn, will share our analysis of it with you. We've also benefited from the goodwill of Christian Rudder and OkCupid, which has collected a treasure trove of data on how its users behave. This information has been incredibly useful, because it allows us to distinguish between what people say they want and what people actually do.

Another great source of data was Michael Rosenfeld at Stanford University, who shared material from the "How Couples Meet and Stay Together" survey, a nationally representative survey of 4,002 English-literate adults, three quarters of whom had a spouse or romantic partner. Rosenfeld, as well as another researcher, Jonathan Haidt of NYU, gave us permission to use charts that they'd developed in this book. Big thanks to them both.

With the help of all these people, Eric and I managed to cover a vast set of issues related to modern romance, but we didn't cover everything. One thing that I definitely want you to know up front is that this book is primarily about heterosexual relationships. Early in the process Eric and I realized that if we tried to write about how all the different aspects of romance we address applied to LGBT relationships, we simply wouldn't be able to do the topic justice without writing an entirely separate book. We do cover some issues relating to love and romance among gays and lesbians, but not at all exhaustively.

The other thing I want to say here is that most of the research we did involved speaking with middle-class people, folks who had gone to college and put off having kids until their late twenties or thirties and now have quite intense and intimate relationships with their expensive smartphones. I know that love and romance work differently in very poor and very rich communities, both in the United States and in the other countries we visited for our research. But again, Eric and I felt that studying all the variations related to class would overwhelm us, so that's not in the book.

Okay, that's pretty much what you need to know by way of introduction. But before we begin, I do want to give a sincere thanks to you—the reader.

You could have bought any book in the world if you wanted. You could have picked up a copy of *Unruly: The Highs and Lows of Becoming a Man* by Ja Rule. You could have bought *Rich Dad, Poor Dad*. You could have even bought *Rich Ja, Poor Ja: Ja Rule's Guide to Sensible Finance*.

You could have bought all of those books (and maybe you did!), except for the last one, which, despite my repeated e-mails, Ja Rule continues to refuse to write.

But you also bought mine. And for that I thank you.

Now, let's begin our journey into the world of . . . *modern romance*!

CHAPTER 1

SEARCHING FOR YOUR SOUL MATE

**any** of the frustrations experienced by today's singles seem like problems unique to our time and technological setting: not hearing back on a text. Agonizing over what really is your *favorite* movie for your online dating profile. Wondering whether you should teleport over some roses to that girl you had dinner with last night. (REALLY SKEPTICAL THAT THEY WILL FIGURE OUT TELEPORTATION BY BOOK RELEASE IN JUNE 2015 AS I WAS TOLD BY MY SCIENCE ADVISERS. EDITOR, PLEASE REMOVE IF TELEPORTATION KINKS HAVEN'T BEEN WORKED OUT.)

These kinds of quirks are definitely new to the romantic world, but as I investigated and interviewed for this book, I found that the changes in romance and love are much deeper and bigger in scale than I realized.

Right now I'm one of millions of young people who are in a similar place. We are meeting people, dating, getting into and out of relationships, all with the hope of finding someone we truly love and with whom we share a deep connection. We may even want to get married and start a family too.

This journey seems fairly standard now, but it's wildly different from what people did even just decades ago. To be specific, I now see that our ideas about two things—"searching" and "the right person"—are completely different from what they used to be. Which means our expectations about how courtship works are too.

DOUGHNUTS FOR INTERVIEWS:

A VISIT TO A NEW YORK RETIREMENT COMMUNITY

If I wanted to see how things have changed over time, I figured that I should start by learning about the experiences of the older generations still around today. And that meant talking to some old folks.

To be honest, I tend to romanticize the past, and though I appreciate all the conveniences of modern life, sometimes I yearn for simpler times. Wouldn't it be cool to be single in a bygone era? I take a girl to a drive-in movie, we go have a cheeseburger and a malt at the diner, and then we make out under the stars in my old-timey convertible. Granted, this might have been tough in the fifties given my brown skin tone and racial tensions at the time, but in my fantasy, racial harmony is also part of the deal.

So, to learn about romance in this era, Eric and I went down to a retirement community on the Lower East Side of New York City to interview some seniors.

We came armed with a big box of Dunkin' Donuts and some coffee, tools that the staff had said would be key to convincing the old folks to speak with us. Sure enough, when the seniors caught a whiff of doughnuts, they were quick to pull up chairs and start answering our questions.

One eighty-eight-year-old man named Alfredo took to the doughnuts very quickly. About ten minutes into the discussion, to which he'd contributed nothing but his age and name, he looked at me with a confused expression, threw up his doughnut-covered hands, and left.

When we came back a few days later to do more interviews, Alfredo was back. The staff explained that Alfredo had misunderstood the purpose of the previous meeting—he thought we wanted to talk to him about his time in the war—but he was now fully prepared to answer questions about his own experiences in love and marriage. Once again, he was pretty quick to take down a doughnut, and then, faster than you could wipe the last few crumbs of a French cruller off your upper lip, Alfredo was gone-zo.

I can only hope that a similarly easy way to scheme free doughnuts presents itself to me when I go into retirement.

Thankfully, others were more informative. Victoria, age sixty-eight, grew up in New York City. She got married when she was twenty-one—to a man who lived in the same apartment complex, one floor above her.

"I was standing in front of my building with some friends and he approached me," Victoria said. "He told me he liked me very much and asked if I'd like to go out with him. I didn't say anything. He asked me two or three more times before I agreed to go out with him."

It was Victoria's first date. They went to a movie and had dinner at her mom's house afterward. He soon became her boyfriend and, after a year of dating, her husband.

They've been married for forty-eight years.

When Victoria first told me her story, it had aspects I expected to be common among the group—she married very young, her parents met her boyfriend almost immediately, and they shifted into marriage fairly quickly.

I figured that the part about marrying someone who lived in her same building was kind of random.

But then the next woman we spoke with, Sandra, seventy-eight, said she got married to a guy who lived just across the street.

Stevie, sixty-nine, married a woman who lived down the hall.

Jose, seventy-five, married a woman who lived one street over.

Alfredo married someone from across the street (probably the daughter of the neighborhood doughnut shop owner).

It was remarkable. In total, fourteen of the thirty-six seniors I spoke with had ended up marrying someone who lived within walking distance of their childhood home. People were marrying neighbors who lived on the same street, in the same neighborhood, and even in the same building. It seemed a bit bizarre.

"Guys," I said. "You're in New York City. Did you ever think, *Oh, maybe there's some people outside of my building?* Why limit yourself so much? Why not expand your horizons?"

They just shrugged and said that it wasn't what was done.

After our interviews we examined whether this spoke to a larger trend. In 1932 a sociologist at the University of Pennsylvania named James Bossard looked through five thousand consecutive marriage licenses on file for people who lived in the city of Philadelphia. Whoa: *One-third* of the couples who got married had lived within a five-block radius of each other before they got married. One out of six had lived within the same block. Most amazingly, one of every eight married couples had lived in the *same building* before they got married.[1]

Maybe this trend of marrying locally held in big cities but not elsewhere? Well, a lot of sociologists in the 1930s and 1940s were

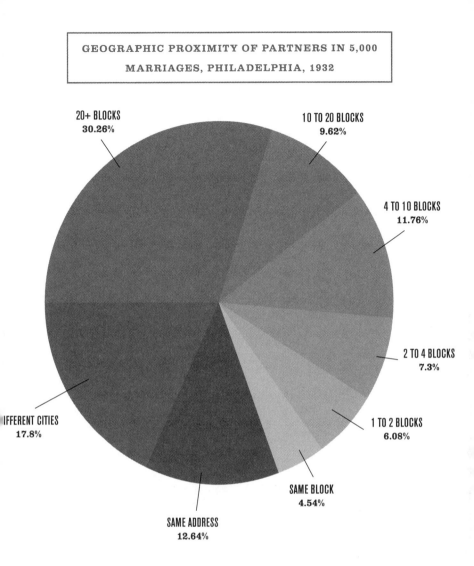

GEOGRAPHIC PROXIMITY OF PARTNERS IN 5,000
MARRIAGES, PHILADELPHIA, 1932

20+ BLOCKS
30.26%

10 TO 20 BLOCKS
9.62%

4 TO 10 BLOCKS
11.76%

2 TO 4 BLOCKS
7.3%

1 TO 2 BLOCKS
6.08%

SAME BLOCK
4.54%

SAME ADDRESS
12.64%

DIFFERENT CITIES
17.8%

wondering that same thing, and they reported their findings in the leading social science journals of the time. Yep, their findings were remarkably similar to Bossard's in Philadelphia, with a few variations.

For instance, people in smaller towns also married neighbors when they were available. But when they weren't, because the pool was too small, people expanded their horizons—but only as far as was necessary. As the Yale sociologist John Ellsworth Jr. said after a study of marriage patterns in Simsbury, Connecticut (population 3,941): "People will go as far as they have to to find a mate, but no farther."[2]

Things are obviously very different today. I found out sociologists don't even do these sorts of studies on the geography of marriage at the city level anymore. Personally, I can't think of even one friend who married someone from their neighborhood, and hardly anyone who married a person from their home city. For the most part my friends married people they'd met during their postcollege years, when they were exposed to folks from all over the country and in some cases all over the world.

Think about where you grew up as a kid, your apartment building or your neighborhood. Could you imagine being married to one of those clowns?

EMERGING ADULTHOOD:
WHEN GROWN-UPS GROW UP

One reason it's so hard to imagine marrying the people we grew up with is that these days we marry much later than people in previous generations.

For the generation of people I interviewed in the New York City retirement community, the average age of marriage was around twenty for women and twenty-three for men.

Today the average age of first marriage is about twenty-seven for women and twenty-nine for men, and it's around thirty for both men and women in big cities like New York and Philadelphia.

Why has this age of first marriage increased so dramatically in the past few decades? For the young people who got married in the 1950s, getting married was the first step in adulthood. After high school or college, you got married and you left the house. For to-

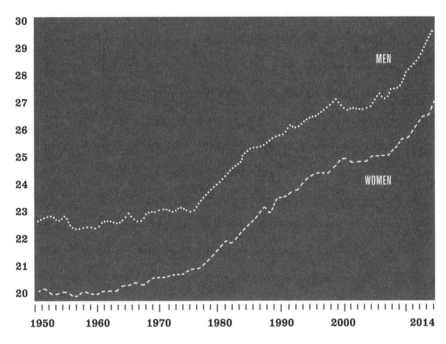

AVERAGE AGE OF FIRST MARRIAGE
IN THE UNITED STATES

Source: U.S. Census Bureau, Decennial Censuses, 1890 to 1940, and Current Population Survey, Annual Social and Economic Supplements, 1947 to 2014.

day's folks, marriage is usually one of the later stages in adulthood. Now most young people spend their twenties and thirties in another stage of life, where they go to university, start a career, and experience being an adult outside of their parents' home before marriage.

This period isn't all about finding a mate and getting married. You have other priorities as well: getting educated, trying out different jobs, having a few relationships, and, with luck, becoming a more fully developed person. Sociologists even have a name for this new stage of life: emerging adulthood.

During this stage we also wind up greatly expanding our pool of romantic options. Instead of staying in the neighborhood or our building, we move to new cities, spend years meeting people in college and workplaces, and—in the biggest game changer—have the infinite possibilities provided by online dating and other similar technologies.

Besides the effects it has on marriage, emerging adulthood also offers young people an exciting, fun period of independence from their parents when they get to enjoy the pleasures of adulthood—before becoming husbands and wives and starting a family.

If you're like me, you couldn't imagine getting married without going through all this. When I was twenty-three, I knew nothing about what I was going to be as an adult. I was a business and biology major at NYU. Would I have married some girl who lived a few blocks from me in Bennettsville, South Carolina, where I grew up? What was this mysterious "biology business" I planned on setting up, anyway? I have no clue. I was an idiot who definitely wasn't ready for such huge life decisions.*

The seniors we spoke with simply did not have such a life stage, and many seemed to regret the lack of it. This was especially true for the women, who didn't have much chance to pursue higher education and start careers of their own. Before the 1960s, in most parts of the United States, single women simply didn't live alone, and many families frowned upon their daughters moving into shared housing for "working girls." Until they got married, these women were pretty much stuck at home under fairly strict adult supervision and lacked basic adult autonomy. They always had to let their parents know their whereabouts and plans. Even dating had heavy parental involvement: The parents would either have to approve the boy or accompany them on the date.

At one point during a focus group with older women, I asked them straight out whether a lot of women their age got married just to get out of the house. Every single woman there nodded. For women in this era, it seemed that marriage was the easiest way of acquiring the basic freedoms of adulthood.

Things weren't a breeze after that, though. Marriage, most

---

* My Bubba Sparxxx tattoo is a constant reminder.

women quickly discovered, liberated them from their parents but made them dependent on a man who might or might not treat them well and then saddled them with the responsibilities of homemaking and child rearing. It gave women of this era what was described at the time by Betty Friedan in her best-selling book *The Feminine Mystique* as "the problem that has no name."*

Once women gained access to the labor market and won the right to divorce, the divorce rate skyrocketed. Some of the older women I met in our focus groups had left their husbands during the height of the divorce revolution, and they told me that they'd always resented missing out on something singular and special: the experience of being a young, unencumbered, single woman.

They wanted emerging adulthood.

"I think I missed a stage in my life, the stage where you go out with friends," a woman named Amelia wistfully told us. "I was never allowed to go out with friends. My father wouldn't allow it. He was that strict. So I tell my granddaughters, 'Enjoy yourself. Enjoy yourself. Then get married.'" Hopefully this doesn't lead to Amelia's granddaughters doing a ton of ecstasy and then telling their mom, "Grandma told me to enjoy myself! Leave me alone!!"

This sentiment was widely shared. Everyone, including the women who said they were happily married, said they wanted their daughters and granddaughters to approach marriage differently from how they had. They wanted the young women they knew to date a lot of men and experience different relationships before they took a husband. "My daughter, I told her go out, get an education, get a car, enjoy yourself," said Amelia. "Then, at the end, choose someone."

Even Victoria, who had been married for forty-eight years to the man who grew up in the apartment above her, agreed. She emphasized that she loved her husband dearly but hinted that, given another chance, she might have done something else.

"My husband and I, we understand each other," she said. "But

---

* In her first draft Friedan named the problem Hampton, but her editors told her it wasn't catchy enough.

we're very different. Sometimes I wonder, if I had married someone who had the same interests as me . . ." She trailed off.

Maybe she was interested in doughnuts and was thinking about a life with Alfredo?

THE LUXURY OF HAPPINESS:

FROM COMPANIONATE TO SOUL MATE MARRIAGE

The shift in when we look for love and marriage has been accompanied by a change in what we look for in a marriage partner. When the older folks I interviewed described the reasons that they dated, got engaged to, and then married their eventual spouses, they'd say things like "He seemed like a pretty good guy," "She was a nice girl," "He had a good job," and "She had access to doughnuts and I like doughnuts."*

When you ask people today why they married someone, the answers are much more dramatic and loving. You hear things along the lines of "She is my other half," "I can't imagine experiencing the joys of life without him by my side," or "Every time I touch her hair, I get a huge boner."

On our subreddit we asked people: If you've been married or in a long-term relationship, how did you decide that the person was (or still is) the right person for you? What made this person different from others? The responses were strikingly unlike the ones we got from the older people we met at the senior center.

Many were filled with stories that illustrated a very deep connection between the two people that made them feel like they'd found someone unique, not just someone who was pleasant to start a family with.

One woman wrote:

---

* Yep. Alfredo.

The first moment I truly remember falling in love with my boyfriend was when I was singing Whitney Houston's "Greatest Love of All" under my breath to myself while we were studying near each other and then he started singing it at the top of his lungs. And we sang the whole song just laughing and dancing around the room. Moments like those where I feel so free and goofy and loved make me know he is the right person. Also I feel like since we've been together, I have become the best version of myself. I push myself to try different things and keep learning even though I'm out of school. It's so much for myself but having his support in my corner has made all the difference.

Another woman wrote:

He makes me laugh, and if I don't feel like laughing, he stops and takes the time to find out why. He makes me feel beautiful and loved in my most ugly and <u>unlovable moments</u>. We also share the same faith, morals, work ethic, love of movies and music, and the desire to travel.

And one said:

He's different from everyone because: He's a one-of-a-kind human being. There is no one in this world like him. He is stunning, and I am amazed by him every single day. He's made me a better person for having known and loved him. 5 years going strong and I'm still obsessed with him. He is my best friend.

All of these people had found someone truly special. From the way they described things, it seemed like their bar for committing to someone was much higher than it had been for the older folks who settled down just a few generations ago.

To figure out why people today use such exalted terms when they explain why they committed to their romantic partner, I spoke with Andrew Cherlin, the eminent sociologist of the family and author of the book *The Marriage-Go-Round*. Up until about fifty years ago, Cherlin said, most people were satisfied with what he calls a "companionate marriage." In this type of marriage each partner had clearly defined roles. A man was the head of his household and the chief breadwinner, while a woman stayed home, took care of the house, and had kids. Most of the satisfaction you gained in the marriage depended on how well you fulfilled this assigned role. As a man, if you brought home the bacon, you could feel like you were a good husband. As a woman, if you kept a clean house and popped out 2.5 kids, you were a good wife. You loved your spouse, maybe, but not in an "every time I see his mustache, my heart flutters like a butterfly" type of way.

You didn't marry each other because you were madly in love; you married because you could make a family together. While some people said they were getting married for love, the pressure to get married and start a family was such that not every match could be a love match, so instead we had the "good enough marriage."

Waiting for true love was a luxury that many, especially women, could not afford. In the early 1960s, a full *76 percent* of women admitted they would be willing to marry someone they didn't love. However, only 35 percent of the men said they would do the same.[3]

If you were a woman, you had far less time to find a man. True love? This guy has a job *and* a decent mustache. Lock it down, girl.

This gets into a fundamental change in how marriage is viewed. Today we see getting married as finding a life partner. Someone we love. But this whole idea of marrying for happiness and love is relatively new.

For most of the history of our species, courtship and marriage weren't really about two individuals finding love and fulfillment. According to the historian Stephanie Coontz, author of *Marriage, a History*, until recently a marital union was primarily important for establishing a bond between two families. It was about achieving security—financial, social, and personal. It was about creating conditions that made it possible to survive and reproduce.

This is not ancient history. Until the Industrial Revolution, most Americans and Europeans lived on farms, and everybody in the household needed to work. [Considerations about whom to marry were primarily practical.]

In the past, a guy would be thinking, *Oh, shit, I gotta have kids to work on my farm. I need four-year-old kids performing manual labor ASAP. And I need a woman who can make me clothes. I better get on this.* A woman would think, *I better find a dude who's capable on the farm and good with a plow so I don't starve and die.*

Making sure the person shared your interest in sushi and Wes Anderson movies *and* made you get a boner anytime you touched her hair would seem far too picky.

Of course, people did get married because they loved each other, but their expectations about what love would bring were different from those we hold today. For families whose future security depended on their children making good matches, passion was seen as an extremely risky motivation for getting hitched. "Marriage was too vital an economic and political institution to be entered into solely on the basis of something as irrational as love," writes Coontz.[4]

Coontz also told us that before the 1960s most middle-class people had pretty rigid, gender-based expectations about what each person would bring to a marriage. Women wanted financial security. Men wanted virginity and weren't concerned with deeper qualities like education or intelligence.

"The average couple wed after just six months—a pretty good sign that love was still filtered through strong gender stereotypes rather than being based on deep knowledge of the other partner as an individual," she said.

Not that people who got married before the 1960s had loveless marriages. On the contrary, back then couples often developed increasingly intense feelings for each other as they spent time together, growing up and building their families. These marriages may have started with a simmer, but over time they could build to a boil.

But a lot of things changed in the 1960s and 1970s, including our expectations of what we should get out of a marriage. The push for women's equality was a big driver of the transformation. As more women went to college, got good jobs, and achieved economic independence, they established newfound control over their bodies and their lives. A growing number of women refused to marry the guy in their neighborhood or building. They wanted to experience things too, and they now had the freedom to do it.

According to Cherlin, the generation that came of age during the sixties and seventies rejected companionate marriage and began to pursue something greater. They didn't merely want a spouse— they wanted a soul mate.

By the 1980s, 86 percent of American men and 91 percent of American women said they would not marry someone without the presence of romantic love.[5]

The soul mate marriage is very different from the companionate marriage. It's not about finding someone decent to start a family with. It's about finding the perfect person whom you truly, deeply love. Someone you want to share the rest of your life with. Someone with whom, when you smell a certain T-shirt they own, you are instantly whisked to a happy memory about the time he or she made you breakfast and you both stayed in and binge-watched all eight season of *Perfect Strangers*.

We want something that's very passionate, or boiling, from the get-go. In the past, people weren't looking for something boiling; they just needed some water. Once they found it and committed to a life together, they did their best to heat things up. Now, if things aren't boiling, committing to marriage seems premature.

But searching for a soul mate takes a long time and requires enormous emotional investment. The problem is that this search for the perfect person can generate a lot of stress. Younger generations face immense pressure to find the "perfect person" that simply didn't exist in the past when "good enough" was good enough.

When they're successful, though, the payoff is incredible. According to Cherlin, the soul mate marriage has the highest potential for happiness, and it delivers levels of fulfillment that the generation of older people I interviewed rarely reached.

Cherlin is also well aware of how hard it is to sustain all these good things, and he claims that today's soul mate marriage model has the highest potential for disappointment. Since our expectations are so high, today people are quick to break things off when their relationship doesn't meet them (touch the hair, no boner). Cherlin would also like me to reiterate that this hair/boner analogy is mine and mine alone.

The psychotherapist Esther Perel has counseled hundreds of couples who are having trouble in their marriages, and as she sees things, asking all of this from a marriage puts a lot of pressure on relationships. In her words:

> Marriage was an economic institution in which you were given a partnership for life in terms of children and social status and succession and companionship. But now we want our partner to still give us all these things, but in addition I want you to be my best friend and my trusted confidant and my passionate lover to boot, and we live twice as long. So we come to one person, and we basically are asking them to give us what once an entire village used to provide: Give me belonging, give me identity, give me continuity, but give me transcendence and mystery and awe all in one. Give me comfort, give me edge. Give me novelty, give me familiarity. Give me predictability, give me surprise. And we think it's a given, and toys and lingerie are going to save us with that.[6]

Ideally, though, we're lucky, and we find our soul mate and enjoy that life-changing mother lode of happiness.

But a soul mate is a very hard thing to find.

FINDING YOUR SOUL MATE

Okay, so no one said searching for a soul mate would be easy. Still, in many ways it seems like today's generation of singles is better off because of the changes in modern romance. Taking time to develop ourselves and date different people before we get married helps us make better choices. For instance, people who marry after the age of twenty-five are far less likely to divorce than those who get married young.[7]

We also don't even *have* to get married if we don't want to. Getting married and starting a family was once seemingly the only reasonable life course. Today we've become far more accepting of alternative lifestyles, and people move in and out of different situations: single with roommates, single and solo, single with partner, married, divorced, divorced and living with an iguana, remarried with iguana, then divorced with seven iguanas because your iguana obsession ruined your relationship, and, finally, single with six iguanas (Arturo was sadly run over by an ice cream truck).

There are no longer any predetermined life paths. Each of us is on our own.

When we do marry, we are marrying for love. We are finding our soul mates. And the tools we have to find our soul mates are incredible. We aren't limited to just the bing-bongs who live in our building. We have online dating that gives us access to millions and millions of bing-bongs around the world. We can filter them any way we want. When we go out, we can use smartphones to text any number of suitors while we are out barhopping. We aren't constrained by landlines and relegated to whomever we have made firm plans with.

Our romantic options are unprecedented and our tools to sort and communicate with them are staggering.

And that raises the question: Why are so many people frustrated?

For the book, Eric and I wanted to see what would happen if we were able to gather groups from different generations to discuss dating past and present. We organized a large focus group of two hundred people.

We sent out an invite and said that anyone who attended had to bring one or two parents to the event. Then, when people showed up, we split the families into two different sections—young folks on the left and parents on the right. We spent an hour going back and forth between the sides, asking people to explain how they met new people to date, asked each other out, and made decisions about marriage and commitment.

When we talked to the older people who were in happy, successful marriages, the way they had met sounded quaint and simple, with much less stress than singles go through today. Sure, they met at a young age and probably weren't as sophisticated then as they later became, but as one woman told me: "We grew up and changed together. And here we are in our sixties, still together."

People from the older generation there that night had almost always asked each other out immediately over the phone or in person. This is how a gentleman named Tim described the first time he asked out his future wife: "I saw her at school, and I said, 'You know, I have these tickets to see the Who at Madison Square Garden . . .'"

That sounds infinitely cooler than texting back and forth with a girl for two weeks only to have her flake on seeing a Sugar Ray concert.

When I talked to the people about dating back in the day, they said they'd go to one bar or a mixer, which was like a community dance, usually put on by a church or college or other local institution, where young people could talk and meet. They'd stay there the whole night and have one or two drinks.

That seems more pleasant than what I see out in bars today, which is usually a bunch of people staring at their phones trying to find someone or something more exciting than where they are.

What about all our options? We can find the perfect person now, right? The old folks actually saw all this choice as a *disadvantage*. They expressed sympathy and concern about their children's situation—and gratitude that things had been simpler, albeit far from perfect, when they were young.

"Something I have to say in defense of the young folks today is that there's just so many choices out there," one mom said. "When I was growing up, there was a mixer and there was a bar, and that was about it. But now—my god. I would really hate to be single nowadays."

"Why do you think it's so bad for them?" I asked. "Think about all the options young people have now, all the doors that are there for them to open."

The older folks weren't buying it. They understood that they had had fewer options when they were growing up, but, intriguingly, they didn't seem to regret having fewer choices. As one woman explained, "You didn't think about the choices you had. When you found someone you liked, you jumped into a relationship. I don't think we thought, *Well, there are another twelve doors or another seventeen doors or another four hundred and thirty-three doors*," she said. "We saw a door we wanted, and so we took it."

Now, look at my generation. We're in a hallway with *millions* of doors. That's a lot of doors. It's nice to have all those options.

But—a hallway with *millions* of doors? Is that better? Is it terrifying?

On the one hand, you have so many doors to try. And that sounds better than being shoved into a door when you are really young and maybe not quite ready to be an adult. On the other hand, maybe people in those earlier generations were ready to open a door on their own. After all, think of Amelia, Victoria, and all those other women who were dying to get out of their parents' houses for good and pretty happy to race into the first door they saw. Sometimes the marriages they raced into wound up being lonely and difficult. But often they blossomed into something loving and fulfilling.

Today we want a bunch of doors as options and we are very cautious about which one we open. The emerging adulthood phase of life is basically a pass society gives you to hang out in the hallway and figure out what door is really right for you. Being in that hallway might be frustrating at times, but ideally you grow and mature, and you find a door that really works for you when you're ready.

People who are looking for love today have an unprecedented set of options in the search for an amazing romantic partner or, ideally, soul mate. We can marry pretty much whomever we want to, regardless of their sex, gender, ethnicity, religion, or race—or even location. We're more likely than the generations that came before us to have relationships in which both partners are equals. And, unlike many in prior generations, nearly all of us will only marry someone we love.

The thing is, with all these new possibilities, the *process* of finding that person can be seriously stressful. And, unlike the days when most everyone got married by their midtwenties, today the search for love can go on for decades.

No more marrying the upstairs neighbor or the girl next door.

No more going steady (forever) with your high school sweetheart.

No more "Hey, Mom and Dad, that person in the living room seems nice. Cool if we get married in three months?"

Instead we have a whole new romantic culture based on an epic search for the right person. A search that can take us through college and various career stages. A search that also takes new forms, because in today's romantic climate a lot of the action happens on our screens.

PHONE WORLD

In 2014 the average American spent 444 minutes per day— nearly 7.5 hours—in front of a screen, be it a smartphone, tablet, television, or personal computer. That's higher than the numbers in most European countries, where people spend "only" 5 to 7 hours per day with screens, yet it's not nearly enough to put the United States in the top five nations: China, Brazil, Vietnam, the Philippines, and, in first place, Indonesia, where people spend 9 hours per day staring at a screen.[8]

That 7.5 hours number is really high, but I charted my own use and it doesn't seem too implausible. Today is a fairly normal Sunday morning in Los Angeles for me. I woke up and spent a while texting with my friends Nick and Chelsea about a potential brunch destination. I then hopped on my laptop to research the suggested restaurants. I went on Yelp and the restaurant pages to peep the menus and did random browsing in between (reading whatever silly headlines caught my eye on Reddit* and watching highlights from the previous night's *Saturday Night Live*), then eventually, after about twenty back-and-forths that lasted an hour and seven minutes, Chelsea and Nick decided they just wanted to go to a casual diner nearby. I didn't feel like going there. We didn't even end up getting brunch together.

Instead I went to another place, Canelé, with another brunch crew. During that brunch, a Nelly song came on and I researched the Nelly Wikipedia page, as one must do anytime Nelly-related questions plague one's mind. After brunch, on the way home, I texted with a few other people about potential dinner plans.[†] And now I'm at home on a laptop again, typing out stuff for this chapter that you are reading right now, possibly on a screen as well!

The way I spent the day trying to plan brunch is remarkably similar to how my tenure in the single world went as well: making or attempting to make plans on my phone with whoever was in my dating orbit at the time. Like my brunch with Chelsea and Nick, many times these plans would eventually fall through. And in the

---

* The highlight being a video of a group of kids who turned their door into a "door monster" that gave out Halloween candy. The door was old-timey and had two smaller shutters in the upper left and right that opened, and they put eyes in them and then put a brown felt–covered arm that poked out through another opening so it was a "door monster" giving out candy. It was pretty cute.

† This experiment has made it very clear that the majority of my day is spent on my phone or laptop trying to figure out both *where* and with *whom* I am dining.

same way I cautiously researched these restaurants, young singles are researching one another—on dating sites or social media sites or even just doing general Googling to get a better sense of a potential date.

As I've come to see it, we're spending so much time with our digital devices because we've all developed our own personal "phone worlds."

Through our phone world we are connected to anyone and everyone in our lives, from our parents to a casual acquaintance whom we friend on Facebook. For younger generations, their social lives play out through social media sites like Instagram, Twitter, Tinder, and Facebook as much as through campuses, cafés, and clubs. But in recent years, as more and more adults have begun spending more and more time on their own digital devices, just about everybody with the means to buy a device and a data plan has become a hyperengaged participant in their phone world.

Phone world is the place you go when you want to find someone to see a movie with. It's where you go to decide what movie to go see. It's where you buy the tickets. It's where you let your friend know you have arrived at the theater. It's where your friend tells you, "Shit, I'm at the wrong theater," and where you say, "What the fuck, man? You always do this. Fine. I'm off to see *G.I. Joe: Retaliation* alone, AGAIN."

And now that our phone worlds are integral to even the most mundane of tasks, of course, they are also a big part of where we live our romantic lives.

Today, if you own a smartphone, you're carrying a 24-7 singles bar in your pocket. Press a few buttons at any time of the day, and you're instantly immersed in an ocean of romantic possibilities.

At first, swimming through that ocean may seem amazing. But most modern singles quickly realize that it takes a ton of effort to stay afloat, and even more to find the right person and get to shore together.

There's so much going on in those waters, so many quick decisions and difficult moves to make. And of all the challenges, there's none more daunting than figuring out what to do when you find someone who interests you.

As we saw in my example with Tanya, no matter how simple it may seem, the initial ask can be plagued with stress and frightening ramifications.

CHAPTER 2

THE INITIAL ASK

sking someone out on a date is a simple task that frequently becomes a terrifying conundrum of fear, self-doubt, and anxiety. It's full of tough decisions: How do I ask? In person? Phone call? Text? What do I say? Could this person be the person I end up spending the rest of my life with? What if this is the only person for me? What if I fuck it all up with the wrong message?

Though technology has added a few new, modern quirks to this dilemma, asking a new person to go on a romantic outing has never been easy. It means declaring your attraction to someone and putting yourself out there in a huge way, while risking the brutal possibility of rejection—or, in the modern era, even an unexplained, icy-cold silence.

For the modern dater the first decision is picking the medium to use: call or text. Some people even throw e-mail or social media messaging into the mix. Just a generation ago the landline or even a newspaper classified ad would have been a first stop to finding romance. Today, though, we look at our screens almost immediately. In fact, for many daters a large chunk of their romantic world lives in their phone world.

A quick note: The numbers show that men are still overwhelmingly the ones expected to initiate the first ask. In 2012 only 12 percent of American women had asked anyone out in the previous year. So when discussing this, I use the situation of a guy asking a girl out. The issues discussed generally translate both ways (minus the issue of girls hating dudes initiating with penis photos).

All right, let's see what the overall trends are.

In 2013 the Match.com survey researchers asked Americans: "If you were asking someone out on a first date, which method of communication would you be most likely to use to get in contact?" Here's what they found:

Method of Asking	Over 30	Under 30
PHONE CALL	52%	23%
FACE TO FACE	28%	37%
TEXT MESSAGE	8%	32%
E-MAIL	7%	1%

Two things to note here. First, the drop in phone calls as a preferred method when you change age groups (52 percent to 23 percent) is stark. Among teenagers the percentage who use text messaging is even higher. In a 2012 textPlus survey, 58 percent of

Americans between ages thirteen and seventeen said they'd ask someone out with a text message.[1] It's clear that younger people, who are growing up in a more text-heavy culture, are much more comfortable living their romantic lives via text.

Second, over time, so are all of us.

In 2010 only 10 percent of young adults used texts to ask someone out for the first time, compared with 32 percent in 2013. Asking out someone via text is on course to be the new norm: The phone call is quickly being phased out.

It's worth pausing here to note that this is an insanely fast transformation in how we communicate. For many generations young people used telephone calls to reach out to possible romantic partners. It was a harrowing experience that we all could relate to. Before the initial ask, you would hear terrifying rings and then an answer. It could be the object of your desire or a roommate or even a parent. At that point you would ask to speak with the person you wanted to ask out.

If they were around, the person would finally say, "Hello," and a mild panic would ensue. You would have to spend some time chatting them up, trying to form a bond while also setting things up for a possibly awkward segue into a date ask.

"Hey, so yeah, anyway, I lost the pie-eating contest . . . You wanna see a movie sometime?"

This phone-call ask required some bravery to initiate and some skills to execute properly, but over time you'd get better at it and you would strategize these calls.

Let's say you were a young man named Darren. At first, your calls might be something like this:

DARREN: *Hey, Stephanie. It's me . . . Darren.*
STEPHANIE: *Hey, Darren, how are you?*
DARREN: *I'm good.*
DARREN: *[long pause]*
DARREN: *Okay . . . Bye.*

But soon you'd get better. With time, you'd realize how to be confident on these kinds of calls. You'd have a funny anecdote or conversation piece ready. Witty banter would be at the tip of your tongue, and soon you and Stephanie would be two verbal fencers parrying and riposting it up like this:

> **DARREN**: *Hey, Stephanie. It's me, Darren! [confident, energetic]*
> **WOMAN**: *Hey, Darren. This is Stephanie's mom. One second . . .*
> **DARREN**: *Shit. [quiet]*
> **DARREN**: *You got this, Darren. You got this. [quiet]*
> **STEPHANIE**: *Hello?*
> **DARREN**: *Hey, Stephanie. It's me, Darren! [back to confident, energetic]*
> **STEPHANIE**: *Oh, hey, Darren. What's up?*
> **DARREN**: *I just got an umbrella!*
> **STEPHANIE**: *Cool . . .*
> **DARREN**: *All right, bye!*

Well. You'd get better than that.

The skill that went into making a phone call to a romantic interest is one that younger generations may never need or want to build.

As our technology becomes more prevalent in our lives, romantic behavior that seems strange or inappropriate to one generation can become the norm for people in the next one.

For instance, in a recent survey 67 percent of teens said they'd accept an invitation to prom by text.[2] For older generations the idea of getting invited to something as special as prom by a text message may sound cold and impersonal. It seems inappropriate for the occasion. But younger folks live in a text-heavy environment and this shapes their perception of what is appropriate. For example, in a topic we'll revisit in more depth later, breaking up with someone via text seems pretty brutal to people of my generation, but when we interviewed younger people, several said their breakups happened exclusively by text. For younger generations, who knows what texts lie ahead?

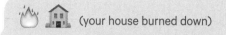 (your house burned down)

I'm pregnant but . . . it's not yours, the dad is this dude I met in Miami a few weeks ago. Really sorry. Let's discuss when you get home?

Hey its Dr. Sampson, bad news— you got cancer in your testicles :(

THE RISE OF THE TEXT MESSAGE

Texting, otherwise known as Short Message Service (SMS), was thought up by Friedhelm Hillebrand, a German engineer, in 1984 and achieved for the first time by Neil Papworth, a young British engineer who messaged his friend "Merry Christmas" in 1992. Alas, his friend didn't reply, because his mobile phone didn't allow him to input text.[3]

Sure it didn't. That's the same shit I hear from friends who don't respond to my mass "Merry Christmas" text. I even throw in a custom image every year; peep this one from 2012.

That said, can you imagine how insane that must have been—to get *the first text of all time?* When no one knew what a text was? It would have

Happy Holidays
From the Ansari Family
(Technically Just Aziz)

been like "WHY ARE THERE WORDS ON MY PHONE??? PHONES ARE FOR NUMBERS!!"

In 1997 Nokia introduced a mobile phone with a separate keyboard, setting things up for the BlackBerry epidemic that would soon afflict most of the global yuppie community, but it wasn't until 1999 that text messages could cross from one phone network to another, and after that usage began to rise. In 2007 the number of texts exchanged in a month outnumbered the number of phone calls made in the United States for the first time in history. And in 2010 people sent 6.1 trillion texts across the planet, roughly 200,000 per minute.

Technology companies have introduced all kinds of new services to help us exchange short messages, and we've responded by tapping away like never before. And of course, this has translated to a vast increase in the number of romantic interactions that are being carried out over text.

One reason for the spike in asking people out by text is that far more of us have smartphones with big screens that make messaging fun and easy. According to consumer surveys, the portion of all American adults who owned a smartphone went from 17 percent in 2010 to 58 percent in 2014, and they're most prevalent among those emerging adults between ages eighteen and twenty-nine, 83 percent of whom carry a smartphone wherever they go.[4] When we're not doing traditional texting, we now have apps like WhatsApp, Facebook Messenger, iMessage, and direct messaging on Twitter, which allow us to message for free. Throughout the world a growing number of people are using SMS for basic communications, and young people in particular have adopted texting at the expense of old-fashioned phone calls.

That said, we haven't given up our old habits altogether. Many people, including young adults, enjoy an occasional phone call and even think that it can signal something special in a budding relationship. But when we first started talking to people about how they ask one another out, we learned that with all these technological transitions, our feelings about when to use which medium have gotten pretty mixed up and confused. How do we figure out when to call, when to text, and when to just drop everything, stand outside someone's window, and serenade them with your favorite nineties R&B tune, perhaps "All My Life" by K-Ci & JoJo?

For that we had to investigate.

CALLING VERSUS TEXTING

"A phone call? The WORST."
—FEMALE FOCUS GROUP PARTICIPANT

"If you want to talk to me, you're going to have to call me."
—ANOTHER FEMALE FOCUS GROUP PARTICIPANT

[Dumbfounded]
—EVERY GUY IN THAT FOCUS GROUP

The issue of calling versus texting generated a wide variety of responses in our focus groups. Generally, younger dudes were *fucking terrified* of calling someone on a phone. This didn't surprise me that much, but I was surprised that younger women also expressed terror at the thought of a traditional phone call. "Phone calls suck and they give me anxiety," said one twenty-four-year-old woman. "Since texting started, an actual phone call feels like an emergency," said another. Other girls thought it was just too forward for someone to call as the first move and said that a text would be more appropriate in general.

However, other women said receiving a phone call from a guy showed he had confidence and helped separate those men from the pack of generic "Hey wsup" texts that normally flood their messaging programs. To these women, the guys who call seem brave and mature. The phone conversations helped create a rapport that made them feel comfortable and safe enough to go out with a person they didn't know all that well.

A woman who came to one of our focus groups discussed how she got so fed up with text messaging that she cut off her texting service and could only be reached by phone calls. This woman never went on a date with a man again. No, she actually started dating someone soon afterward. She also claimed the guys who did work up the courage to call her were a better caliber of man and that she was, in effect, able to weed out a lot of the bozos.

But with some women who loved phone calls, things weren't that simple. In a rather inconvenient twist for would-be suitors, many said they loved phone calls—but had no interest in answering. "I often don't answer, but I like receiving them," said one woman, who seemed oblivious to how ridiculous this statement sounded.

For this group, voice mails provided a screening system of sorts. When they explained this, it made sense to me. If the message was from someone they'd met briefly at a bar, it let them hear the guy's voice and made it easier to sort out the creeps. One girl raved about a nice voice mail a guy had recently left her. I kindly requested she play it and heard this gem: "Hey, Lydia. It's Sam. Just calling to say what's up. Gimme a ring when you get a chance."

THAT WAS IT.

I pleaded to know what was so great about this. She sweetly recalled that "he remembered my name, he said hi, and he told me to call him back."

Never mind the fact that what she described was the content of LITERALLY EVERY VOICE MAIL IN HISTORY. Name, hello, please call back. Not really a boatload of charm on display. To fail this test, a guy would have to leave a message that said: "No greeting. This is a man. I don't remember you. End communication."

When you look at overall numbers on communication, you see that we are generally texting more and calling less. According to Nielsen, Americans' use of phones for voice calls peaked in 2007; we've been calling less, and speaking for fewer minutes, ever since.[5]

This change in communication may have some side effects, though. In her book *Alone Together*, MIT social psychologist Sherry Turkle convincingly makes the case that younger people are so used to text-based communications, where they have time to gather their thoughts and precisely plan what they are going to say, that they are losing their ability to have spontaneous conversation. She argues that the muscles in our brain that help us with spontaneous conversation are getting less exercise in the text-filled world, so our skills are declining.

When we did the large focus group where we split the room by generation—kids on the left, parents on the right—a strange thing happened. Before the show started, we noticed that the parents' side of the room was full of chatter. People were talking to one another and asking how they had ended up at the event and getting to know people. On the kids' side, everyone was buried in their phones and not talking to anyone around them.

It made me wonder whether our ability and desire to interact with strangers is another muscle that risks atrophy in the smartphone world. You don't need to make small talk with strangers when you can read the *Beverly Hills, 90210* Wikipedia page anytime you want. Honestly, what stranger can compete with a video that documents the budding friendship of two baby hippopotamuses? No one, that's who.

At a minimum, young people are growing anxious about real-time phone conversations with people they don't know well, and particularly with potential dates. "I have social anxiety, and having to respond or react on the spot to a phone call or in person would make me overanalyze everything and put myself in a tizzy," one young woman told us. "I would want to take my time and think of a response that is genuine."

The obvious advantage of a text is that a guy can text someone without having to gather the courage needed for a phone call. If you accept Turkle's notion that men are also in general getting worse at spontaneous conversation, it makes sense that this trend will continue to climb.

I discussed this change in communication with Turkle in Los Angeles, and she brought up an interesting thought about getting asked out over the phone back in the day. "When a guy called and asked you out back then, it was a very special thing. You felt special and it was very flattering that he gathered the courage to do it."

When I discussed what I had heard from the interviews with young people today, Turkle said that being asked out through a text message has become so banal that it no longer gives women that sense of flattery. As far as they know, the guy who has sent the message is hitting up lots of women and waiting to see who writes back. Unless he has sent something truly distinctive and personal, a text just isn't all that meaningful.

After many conversations with women in the single world, I must concur.

THE MODERN BOZO

One firm takeaway from all our interviews with women is that most dudes out there are straight-up bozos. I've spent hours talking with women and seeing the kind of "first texts" they get from guys, and trust me, it's infuriating. These were intelligent, attractive, amazing women and they all deserved better.

Some people say that it doesn't matter what you text someone. If they like you, they like you. After interviewing hundreds of singles, I can scientifically confirm that this is total bullshit.

For those who doubt me, here is an example from a show I did at the Chicago Theatre in the spring of 2014.

During that tour, after doing material about texting, I would ask if anyone in the audience had recently met someone and had been texting back and forth. If they had, they would come up to the stage and I would pick a few people and read, analyze, and ask them about what was happening in their messages.

At this particular show I was speaking with Rachel, who had

met a guy at a good friend's wedding. As it happened, the guy was also a friend of her sister's, so he had a pretty good shot at a first date with her. She was single. She was interested. All he had to do was send her a simple message introducing himself and asking her to do something.

Here's what happened.

He sends his first message:

> Hi Rachel! Since I never got a chance to ask you to dance at Marissa and Chris's wedding (I'm Chris's old roommate from Purdue . . .), he and your sister gave me your number. I wanted to say hi and sort of "texty" introduce myself. Haha. :-)
> Hope you had a great weekend . . . hope to chat with you soon!

As soon as I said "texty," it was clear that no one sitting in the 3,600-seat Chicago Theatre would ever fuck this dude in a million years. "Texty," for whatever reason, seemed to be unequivocally disgusting to every one of us there.

He might as well have added: "BTW I have a really disgusting next-level STD! Haha :-) but for real I do."

Rachel wrote back ten minutes later:

> Hey! Great to "meet" you! :) Currently enjoying my birthday weekend with lots of good Mexican food. (It happens when your birthday is Cinco de Mayo.) Hope you had a great weekend too!

He wrote back shortly:

> I toooooootally realized upon reading my last message . . . I didn't include my name. Hahaha. I'm Will. :-) Feliz Cumpleaños as well! And totally digging on the Cinco de Mayo theme.

Rachel never met Will. After a few messages of this nature, Rachel stopped responding. None of us know Will. He may be a kind, handsome man with a heart of gold. But all we have to go on is those messages. And those messages have shaped in our minds a very dorky, terrifyingly Caucasian weirdo. Everything from "texty" to "toooootally" to "Feliz Cumpleaños as well!" had destroyed all chances of Rachel's wanting to meet Will in real life. So please, don't let anyone tell you what you text someone doesn't matter. If they don't believe you, "texty" introduce them to Will and they'll toooootally change their mind.

The interesting thing about text is that, as a medium, it separates you from the person you are speaking with, so you can act differently from how you would in person or even on the phone. In *Alone Together* Sherry Turkle tells the story of a young boy who had a standing appointment for a Sunday dinner with his grandparents. Every week, he'd want to cancel and his mom would tell him to call his grandparents and tell them he wasn't coming. However, he never would, because he couldn't bear to hear the disappointment in their voices. If it were text, though, he probably wouldn't have thought twice about it. As a medium, it's safe to say, texting facilitates flakiness and rudeness and many other personality traits that would not be expressed in a phone call or an in-person interaction.

Beyond flakiness, as far as dating goes, I've observed many men who, while hopefully decent human beings in person, become sexually aggressive "douche monsters" when hiding behind the texts on their phone. The messages being sent are inarguably inappropriate and often quite offensive, but, again, over text the consequences of the recipient's being offended are minimal. You don't see their face. You don't hear their voice. And they aren't there in person to look horrified or throw a heavy object at your dumb head.

On the other hand, on the tiny off chance they are interested, you are all set. It's this dim hope that many dumb dudes are clinging to when they send these painfully obnoxious texts.

A website called Straight White Boys Texting has become a

hub for women to submit these horrifying (and often hilarious) texts that guys have sent them.

As described on the site, the blog came about due to the phenomenon in which a guy texts an inept sexual advance like "hey what's your bra size ;)" or "what would you do if you were here haha lol ;)" apropos of nothing, in order to try to hook up with someone.

This was known as a "straight white boy text," hence the name of the blog, but, to be clear, the site is inclusive of douchey dudes of all races, ethnicities, and sexual orientations.

Here are a few favorites of mine:

••ooo T-Mobile LTE   12:06 AM   @ ✈ 🔋 49% 🔋 ⚡

← ⬤⬛⬛⬛⬛⬛   •••

Jul 16, 2014, 10:44 AM

⬤ Afternoon sex?;)

Message   Send

This gentleman wastes no time. What's interesting to me, though, is would this guy ever act this way in real life? Doubtful that he'd just go up to a woman and say, "Afternoon sex?" and wink at her—unless he was some kind of R&B superstar, in which case he'd be doing it all the time and it would possibly be quite successful.

Here's another:

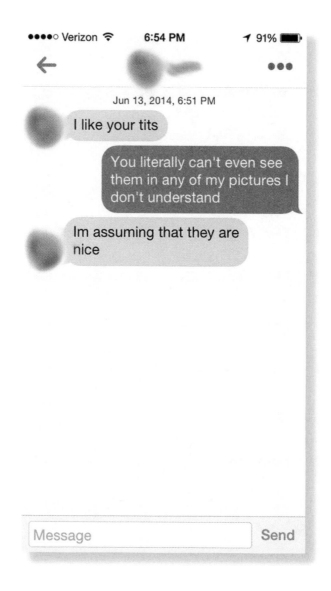

Again, I have to assume if this guy met this woman at a bar, his introduction would be something better than "I like your tits."

The site, and women's phones everywhere, are filled with cringeworthy exchanges like this. And clearly, these are extremely horrible messages. But from our interviews we learned that even for men who don't write such blatantly disgusting nonsense, the smallest changes in what they text on a screen can make a huge difference in their dating success face-to-face.

Sometimes guys who have made a good impression in person and are on the verge of a true connection decide to send something dumb and awful and totally screw things up. Sure, there are extremes, like the woman who immediately lost interest after a guy asked her to Snapchat a photo of "just one boob."

However, the mistakes people make are not always so egregious. We repeatedly found that one text can change the whole dynamic of a budding relationship. In a certain context, even just saying something as innocuous as "Hey, let's hang out sometime" or spelling errors or punctuation choices can irritate someone. When I spoke with Sherry Turkle about this, she said that texting, unlike an in-person conversation, is not a forgiving medium for mistakes.

In a face-to-face conversation, people can read each other's body language, facial expressions, and tones of voice. If you say something wrong, you have cues to sense it and you have a moment to recover or rephrase before it makes a lasting impact. Even on the phone you can hear a change in someone's voice or a pause to let you know how they are interpreting what you've said. In text, your mistake just sits there marinating on the other person's screen, leaving a lasting record of your ineptitude and bozoness.

The fact that your interactions on your phone can have such a profound effect on people's impression of you as a person makes it clear that you basically have two selves now—your real-world self and your phone self.

The phone self is defined by whatever it is you communicate

onto the other person's screen. I interviewed many women who told me that they didn't always have sharp memories of guys to whom they gave their numbers after a conversation in a bar or over drinks at a party. In that context, the first message they get can be a huge factor in whether they reach back, and the phone self that's presented makes all the difference. As you saw with the example with Rachel, even small tweaks of a text message can make the difference between being perceived as nice or mean, smart or dumb, funny or boring.

In our interviews and focus groups, people in all parts of the world generously opened up the secret world in their phones. I've probably scrolled through more text message conversations than anyone and asked men and women what we all are wondering: What was going on in your head when you read/wrote that? What did you think of this guy/girl when you read this message? It was so fascinating to see how people's words could evoke such a wide range of reactions.

Let's first look at the things that irritated people the most.

THE GENERIC "HEY" TEXT

After seeing hundreds and hundreds of messages in women's phones, I can definitely say that most of the texts women receive are, sadly, utterly lacking in either thought or personality. Want to know what's filling up the phones of nearly every single woman? It's this: "Hey," "Hey!" Heyyy!!" "Hey what's going?" "Wsup," "Wsup!" "What's going on?" "Whatcha up to?"

It seems like a harmless message to send, and I've surely sent a good number of them in my own dating life. I and all the others who have sent similar messages surely meant no offense. However, seeing it from the other side is eye-opening. When your phone is filled with that stuff, generic messages come off as super dull and lazy. They make the recipient feel like she's not very special or important to you.

Oh, and in case you're a dude and you've never seen what your "Hey" texts look like when you send them, serially, here's another post from Straight White Boys Texting:

THE SECRETARY PROBLEM

Another irritating situation that plagues both men and women is the endless texting banter that never leads to a meet in the real world. So many people trying to make a connection wind up spending so much time typing and typing and trying to schedule things that eventually whatever spark may have been there diminishes. At our focus groups we heard countless variations of an interaction that goes something like this:

Four days later.

Hey - want to come with to see the new exhibit at the Getty on Saturday?

I would but have to go to Disneyland with my family :(

Hey, well tell Donald Duck I said hello

Will do!

Nine days later.

Sushi on Thursday?

Shit. I can't Thursday, Friday?

Nah, I can't do Friday. Let's talk next week.

Six days later.

Hey! You out tonight?

At this point the conversation ends. It's amazing to see·this exchange go from its fun and flirtatious opening to just plain fizzling out. And you can see how it happens: They go from enjoying the banter to trying to schedule something concrete, and all of a sudden they're acting like secretaries.

The other annoying thing about this scheduling banter is that both parties are sometimes left wondering whether the person is actually busy or pretending to be busy, leading to more confusion and frustration. When you're involved in this kind of back-and-forth, it's hard not to wonder whether the other person even has interest.

THE ENDLESS BACK-AND-FORTH

Scheduling chatter is merely one of the many forms of useless banter that makes dating in the digital age so frustrating, especially for women over twenty-five, since they have less patience for constant text exchanges. Another form, which is especially common among the younger gentlemen out there, emerges when a dude is just too shy to actually ask the other person to do something. Instead of negotiating times and places, they wind up exchanging meaningless texts ad nauseam.

I can't tell you how many girls I met who were clearly interested in a guy who, instead of asking them out, just kept sucking them into more mundane banter with gems like "So where do you do your laundry" What follows are ten back-and-forths about laundry detergent. ("Yeah, I recently switched to fragrance-free detergent. It's been FANTASTIC.")

At a stand-up show I did in Tulsa, I met a young man named Cody. He came onstage and we read through his text messages. There were literally twenty messages of useless, nervous banter. It was clear this woman was interested, but poor Cody simply wasn't asking her to do anything. I told Cody he should just ask her out. He texted her, "Hey Ally. Have you been to Hawaiian Brian's? Let me know if you want to go this week?" Within two hours she said yes, and they enjoyed a delicious meal at Hawaiian Brian's the next week.

On a side note, is there any place on earth that sounds like it has a more chill vibe than Hawaiian Brian's? Or for that matter, is there a chiller name than "Hawaiian Brian"? "Damnit! Hawaiian Brian just stole my debit card and liquidated all my bank accounts!" I can't ever see someone having to utter that sentence.

This is not important (handwritten note)

GRAMMAR/SPELLING

In any interviews we did, whenever bad grammar or spelling popped up, it was an immediate and major turn-off. Women seemed to view it as a clear indicator that a dude was a bozo. Let's say you are a handsome, charming stud who really made a great first impression. If your first text is "Hey we shud hang out sumtimez," you may just destroy any goodwill you have built up.

On our subreddit we were told a story about a man who was dating a spectacular woman but eventually broke up with her. He said it went downhill once he texted her asking if she had heard about a party at a mutual friend's house. Her response was "Hoo?" Not "Who," but "Hoo." He kept trying to force the word "who" into conversation to make sure this beautiful woman could spell a simple three-letter word. Every time, she spelled it "hoo." He said it ruined everything. (**NOTE:** We did confirm that this was a woman and not an owl.)

ARE WE "HANGING OUT" OR GOING OUT ON A DATE?

Another thing that really pisses women off is when dudes ask them to "hang out." The lack of clarity over whether the meet-up is even an actual date frustrates both sexes to no end, but since it's usually the guys initiating, this is a clear area where men can step it up.

"It's becoming too common for guys to ask girls to 'hang out' rather than directly asking them on a date," said one woman. "I'm not sure if it's because guys are afraid of rejection or because they want to seem casual about it, but it can leave one (or both) people unsure about whether or not they're even on a date."

When you are forward in this regard, it can really help you stand out from the crowd. A girl from our subreddit recalled meeting a guy at a loud party: "After I left he texted me, 'Hi [name redacted], this is [first name, last name], we're going on a date.' His confidence, straightforwardness, and refreshingly gentlemanly approach (vs. skirting around 'lets hang out some time') made for an incredible first impression and had a lasting effect."

THE GOOD TEXTS

Not all guys are bozos. We also found some really great texts that gave me hope for the modern man. While a phone call may be great, the advantage of texting is that it can allow a guy or girl to craft a great, thoughtful message that can build attraction.

We were also able to spot some specific traits these successful texts shared. After speaking with hundreds of men and women, the following three things seemed most important.

A FIRM INVITATION TO SOMETHING SPECIFIC AT A SPECIFIC TIME

There is a monumental difference in the fortunes of the guy who texts a girl, "Hey wuts goin on?" versus "Hey Katie, it was great meeting you on Saturday. If you're around next week, I would love to take you to dinner at that restaurant we were talking about. Let me know if you're free."

These two guys could have the same intentions and feelings

in their hearts, but the girl they're texting will never know that. She's going to decide whom to go out with based in part on how she interprets the short little messages that pop up on her phone. The lack of specificity in "Wanna do something sometime next week?" is a huge negative to women. The people interviewed overwhelmingly preferred to have a very specific (and ideally interesting and fun) thing presented with a firm invitation.

SOME CALLBACK TO THE LAST PREVIOUS IN-PERSON INTERACTION

This proves you were truly engaged when you last hung out and seemed to go a long way with women. One guy remembered that a girl was moving and in his text said, "I hope your move went well." The woman we interviewed brought this up and said it had happened *years* ago but she still remembered it.

Another gentleman shared a story on the subreddit where he met a girl at a bar and they talked for a while and at some point he brought up the band Broken Bells and recommended she check it out. The next morning he received a text saying, "I think October is my favorite song on the Broken Bells album." "October" was also *his* favorite song on the album. "Not only did she listen to my recommendation, but we connected in a very strong way. That was the beginning of the conversation, and we've been talking since," he said.

There was also this story from a young woman: "One time, I met a guy at a party. When I got home, he texted me, 'good night little Audrey.' That's not my name. I figured he was just too drunk to remember. After I confronted him about this, he said that he called me Audrey because I told him that I looked up to Audrey Hepburn. It was actually pretty sweet."

I hope you aren't holding an ice cream cone against your chest, 'cause your heart just warmed—and your ice cream just melted.

A HUMOROUS TONE

This is dangerous territory because some dudes go too far or make a crude joke that doesn't sit well, but ideally you both share the same sense of humor and you can put some thought into it and pull it off. And when it's pulled off well, the attraction to a similar sense of humor can be quite strong.

Here's a story from the subreddit: "I met her at a bar in town, 2–3 AM after getting her number I drunkenly text her, 'I'm that tall guy you made out with.' In the morning I woke up to a message that said, 'which tall guy?' I was incredibly impressed with her sense of humor and we're still together 2.5 years later."

THIS IS JUST THE BEGINNING . . .

So this is what I've learned about initial asks, but that's just the beginning. Even if you put out a solid ask, you are subject to a mountain of confusion. The person could be busy—or are they just pretending to be busy? They could give you silence, like I got! The adventure is just starting. Since everyone now has an entire social world in their phone, they're carrying around a device that's loaded with all kinds of back-and-forth, drama, and romance. Navigating that world is interesting, and what happens when you explore someone else's phone world is nuts.

AFTER THE ASK . . .

So you've fired off a successful text, or maybe you've just received one. If you are one of the growing number of people evaluating and making plans with potential romantic partners via text messages, the games are just beginning. Unlike phone calls, which bind two people in real-time conversations that require at least some shared interpretation of the situation, communication by text has no predetermined temporal sequencing and lots of room for ambiguity. Did I just use the phrase "predetermined temporal sequencing"? *Fuck yeah, I did.*

In one of our first focus groups, a young woman, Margaret, told us about a gentleman she'd met at work. He sounded charming and she was definitely interested in him. I asked to see her text exchanges and immediately noticed that his name, according to her iPhone, was "Greg DON'T TXT TIL THURSDAY."

So it was clear why these texts were important. These early communications could be the determining factor in whether she would one day become Margaret DON'T TXT TIL THURSDAY and make a family of little DON'T TXT TIL THURSDAYs of their own.

Margaret later explained that the last name she gave this guy was *not* his name but, in fact, an extreme step she was taking to avoid sending this dude a message for a few days, so as not to seem too eager and to ultimately make herself more desirable. The fear of coming off as desperate or overeager through texting was a common concern in our focus groups, and almost everyone seemed to have some strategy to avoid this deadly pitfall. There is no official guidebook anywhere on texting yet, but a cultural consensus has slowly formed in regard to texts. Some basic rules:

- Don't text back right away. You come off like a loser who has nothing going on.
- If you write to someone, don't text them again until you hear from them.
- The amount of text you write should be of a similar length to what the other person has written to you.
- Carrying this through, if your messages are in blue and the other person's messages are green, if there is a shit ton more blue than green in your conversation, this person doesn't give a shit about you.
- The person who receives the last message in a convo WINS![6]

THE SCIENCE OF WAITING

The one area where there was much more debate was the amount of time one should wait to text back. Depending on the parties involved, it can become a very complicated and admittedly somewhat silly game with many different viewpoints on how to play—and win. As one woman told us, "There is this desire, for me at least, to have the upper hand. I have to have it. So if I text someone, and they wait ten minutes to text me back, I wait twenty. Which sounds stupid, but the way I see it, he and I both know the other is glued to their phone. Everyone is. So if you're gonna play the game, that's fine, but I'll play it better. Very competitive."

DAMN.

Several people subscribed to the notion of doubling the response time. (They write back in five minutes, you wait ten, etc.) This way you achieve the upper hand and constantly seem busier and less available than your counterpart. Others thought waiting just a few minutes was enough to prove you had something important in your life besides your phone. Some thought you should double but occasionally throw in a quick response to not seem so regimented (nothing too long, though!). Some people swore by waiting 1.25 times longer. Others argued they found three minutes to be just right. There were also those who were so fed up with the games that they thought receiving timely responses free of games was refreshing and showed confidence.

But does this stuff work? Why do so many people do it? Are any of these strategies really lining up with actual psychological findings?

These notions about waiting and playing hard to get have been around for ages. According to Greek historian Xenophon, a prostitute once went to Socrates* for advice and he told her: "You must

---

* To be clear, this was not a pimp named Socrates but the esteemed philosopher—that said, Socrates is kind of a good pimp name.

prompt them by behaving as a model of propriety, by a show of reluctance to yield, and by holding back until they are as keen as can be; for then the same gifts are much more to the recipient than when they are offered before they are desired." Conversely, Socrates knew that people tend to discount and sometimes even reject the things that are always available.

I personally find the idea that this stuff works very frustrating. If someone is really into me and showing interest, shouldn't I just appreciate that and welcome those advances? Why do we want what we can't have and sometimes have more attraction to people when they seem a little distant or disinterested?

THE POWER OF WAITING

In recent years behavioral scientists have shed some light on why these waiting techniques can be powerful. Let's first look at the notion that texting back right away makes you less appealing. Psychologists have conducted hundreds of studies in which they reward lab animals in different ways under different conditions. One of the most intriguing findings is that "reward uncertainty"—in which, for instance, animals cannot predict whether pushing a lever will get them food—can dramatically increase their interest in getting a reward, while also enhancing their dopamine levels so that they basically feel coked up.[7]

If a text back from someone is considered a "reward," consider the fact that lab animals who get rewarded for pushing a lever every time will eventually *slow down* because they know that the next time they want a reward, it will be waiting for them. So basically, if you are the guy or girl who texts back immediately, you are taken for granted and ultimately lower your value as a reward. As a result, the person doesn't feel as much of an urge to text you or, in the case of the lab animal, push the lever.

Texting is a medium that conditions our minds in a distinctive way, and we expect our exchanges to work differently with messages than they did with phone calls. Before everyone had a cell phone, people could usually wait awhile—up to a few days, even—to call back before reaching the point where the other person would get concerned. Texting has habituated us to receiving a much quicker response. From our interviews, this time frame varies from person to person, but it can be anywhere from ten minutes to an hour to even immediately, depending on the previous communication. When we don't get the quick response, our mind freaks out.

MIT anthropologist Natasha Schüll studies gambling addiction and specifically what happens to the minds and bodies of people who get hooked on the immediate gratification that slot machines provide. When we met in Boston, she explained that unlike cards, horse races, or the weekly lottery—all games that make gamblers wait (for their turn, for the horses to finish, or for the weekly drawing)—machine gambling is lightning fast, so that players get immediate information.

"You come to expect an instant outcome, and you stop tolerating any delay." Schüll drew an analogy between slot machines and texting, since both generate the expectation of a quick reply. "When you're texting with someone you're attracted to, someone you don't really know yet, it's like playing a slot machine: There's a lot of uncertainty, anticipation, and anxiety. Your whole system is primed to receive a message back. You want it—you *need* it—right away, and if it doesn't come, your whole system is like, 'Aaaaah!' You don't know what to do with the lack of response, the unresolved outcome."

Schüll said that texting someone is very different from leaving a message on a home answering machine, which we used to do in the days before smartphones. "Timewise, and also emotionally, leaving a message on someone's machine was more like buying a lottery ticket," she explained. "You knew there would be a longer waiting period until you found out the winning numbers. You weren't expecting an instant callback and you could even enjoy that suspense, because you knew it would take a few days. But with texting, if you don't hear back in even fifteen minutes, you can freak out."

Schüll told us that she has experienced this waiting distress firsthand. Several years ago she was texting with a suitor, someone she'd starting dating and was really into, and he gave every indication that he was really into her too. Then, out of nowhere, the guy went silent. She didn't hear back from him for three days. She got fixated on the guy's disappearance and had trouble focusing or even participating in ordinary social life. "No one wanted to hang out with me," she said, "because I was just obsessed, like, *What the fuck? Where the fuck is this guy?*"

Eventually the guy reached out and she was relieved to find out that he'd actually legitimately lost his phone, and since that's where he'd stored her number, he had no other way of getting in touch with her.

"With a phone call, three days of silence probably wouldn't drive you that crazy, but with my mind habituated to texting, the loss of that reward . . . Well, it was three days of pure hell," she said.

Even people in relationships experience this anxiety with texting. In my own relationship, which is a committed, loving partnership, I've experienced several instances of a delay in text causing uneasiness. Here's an example:

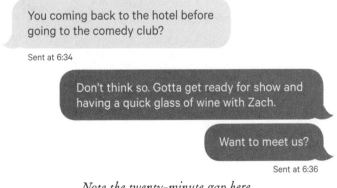

Note the twenty-minute gap here.

In the gap after "Want to meet us?" I was sure she was mad about something. Her responses had been pretty immediate, and it seemed like her pause was an indicator that something was wrong and that I should have been going to the hotel or something.

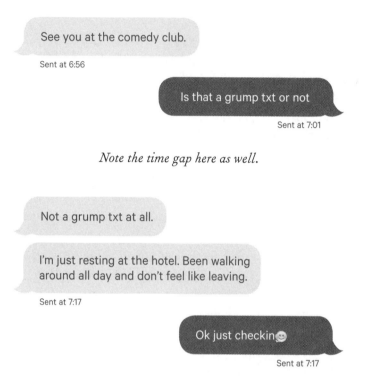

See you at the comedy club.

Sent at 6:56

Is that a grump txt or not

Sent at 7:01

Note the time gap here as well.

Not a grump txt at all.

I'm just resting at the hotel. Been walking around all day and don't feel like leaving.

Sent at 7:17

Ok just checkin😊

Sent at 7:17

Again, when she didn't respond after "Is that a grump txt or not" I was certain she was grumpy, because why wait so long to tell me she's not grumps? All of this change in my perception of her feelings and my own mood was purely because of the temporal differences in texting.

Even in nonromantic situations, waiting has caused uneasiness. I texted an acquaintance about reading a draft of this very book. I wrote: "Hey would you have any interest in reading an early draft of my modern romance book? Just want to get some eyes on it and I feel like you'd get the tone I'm going for and have good feedback. If you're too busy etc, no offense taken."

The text was sent at 1:33 P.M. on a Wednesday and got an immediate "Read 1:33 P.M." But I didn't hear back until 6:14 P.M. the next day. During the time that passed, I worried that maybe I'd overstepped my bounds in our friendship, that it wasn't proper for me to ask, etc. In the end I'd worried for nothing and he wrote back, "yeah, of course! sounds like fun . . ."

If the effect is this powerful for people in committed relationships and friendships, it makes sense that all the psychological principles seem to point to waiting being a strategy that works for singles who are trying to build attraction.

For instance, let's say you are a man and you meet three women at a bar. The next day you text them. Two respond fairly quickly, and one of them does not respond at all. The first two women have, in a sense, indicated interest by writing back and have, in effect, put your mind at ease. The other woman, since she hasn't responded, has created uncertainty, and your mind is now looking for an explanation for why. You keep wondering, *Why the fuck didn't she write back? What's wrong? Did I screw something up?* This third woman has created uncertainty, which social psychologists have found can lead to strong romantic attraction.

The team of Erin Whitchurch, Timothy Wilson, and Daniel Gilbert conducted a study where women were shown Facebook profiles of men who they were told had viewed their profiles. One group was shown profiles of men who they were told had rated their profiles the best. A second group was told they were seeing profiles of men who had said their profiles were average. And a third group was shown profiles of men and told it was "uncertain" how much the men liked them. As expected, the women preferred the guys who they were told liked them best over the ones who rated them average. (The reciprocity principle: We like people who like us.) However, the women were *most* attracted to the "uncertain" group. They also later reported thinking about the "uncertain" men the most. When you think about people more, this increases their presence in your mind, which ultimately can lead to feelings of attraction.[8]

Another idea from social psychology that goes into our texting games is the scarcity principle. Basically, we see something as more desirable when it is less available. When you are texting someone less frequently, you are, in effect, creating a scarcity of *you* and making yourself more attractive.

WHAT WE DO WHEN WE ARE INTERESTED

Sometimes there's another reason that people take so long to text you back: They aren't playing mind games or busy. They're just GOOGLING THE FUCK OUT OF YOU.

In one 2011 survey, more than 80 percent of millennials admitted to doing online research on their partner before a first date.[9] And why not? With our expanded dating pools, we're meeting people we hardly know, including total strangers with no existing social ties to us. Fortunately, the same technology that allows us to connect with them also helps us figure out whether they post cute pictures of baby elephants or something more malicious, like a blog chronicling their latest elephant-poaching expedition in Botswana.

Usually Internet research turns up little more than some basic biographical information and a smattering of photographs from Facebook and Instagram. Some singles said even this relatively minimal content is helpful, because it gives them clues about people's interests and character before meeting them. That makes sense to me, since you could argue that the photos posted on an Instagram page offer a more compelling and realistic representation of someone than their carefully crafted online dating profile.

Others see the process as harmful, though, because reading too much of a person's online history can deprive them, and their date, of the fun of discovering someone new. Some singles we spoke with described meeting a person and being unable to enjoy the date because they already had all kinds of preconceived notions that were difficult to block out.

One gentleman I met told me that the personal information we can so easily obtain online often causes him to be too harsh on people. "I'll go through and look at their entire timeline of tweets. I'll see one dumb thing I don't agree with, and then I kind of mentally check out on the date," he said.

It may be harsh to judge someone's personality off a tweet or two, but if you're serious about your research, the Internet offers a whole lot more information than that. When we posed the question of first-date Internet research to the subreddit, we heard some serious horror stories.

One woman recounted canceling a date after a brief bit of research:

I googled my date who had a very distinctive name. According to a weekly synagogue newsletter, he and his wife were hosting a Torah class for children in their home the same day as our date.

This has also been recorded as the only time in history someone has said, "Whew, I'm glad I read that weekly synagogue newsletter."

Other stories were even more horrific.

One woman wrote:

[A] friend from work met a firefighter in a bar a few months ago. They talked a lot that night/exchanged numbers and were texting back and forth for the next week while setting up a first date. He told her he didn't have a facebook and when she mentioned that to some other people, they told her she should be concerned that he might be lying and actually have a girlfriend or be married. So she google searched his name + LA fire department and found that there was a news story on him (with a video!) about how he AND HIS MOTHER beat up an elderly woman who was feeding stray cats on their street. She immediately stopped talking to him.

This is why I always say: If your mother asks you to come beat up an elderly woman on the street for feeding stray cats—JUST SAY NO. It'll always come back to haunt you.

WHAT WE DO WHEN WE AREN'T INTERESTED

If you are just plain not interested in someone, you have a whole other conundrum to deal with. How should you let this person know you aren't interested? From our interviews, it seems there are three big approaches: pretend to be busy, say nothing, or be honest.

In every stop on my tour, from San Francisco to London to Wichita, I asked audiences which method they used. In total, this was more than 150,000 people, and in every audience, a sample size of a few thousand, the response was always the same. Overwhelmingly, most people practice the "pretend to be busy" and "silence" methods. Only a small sliver of the crowd would say they were honest.

However, when I flipped the situation and said, "Okay, now pretend the situation is reversed. Someone else is dealing with *you*. How do you prefer *they* handle the situation? Clap if you prefer *they* pretend to be busy."

A smattering of claps.

"Clap if you prefer they say nothing, that they give you silence."

A smaller smattering.

"And finally, clap if you prefer that they are honest with you."

Basically, the whole audience would applaud.

Why do we all say we prefer honesty but rarely give that courtesy to others? Maybe in our hearts we all want to give others honesty, but in practice it's just too damn hard. Honesty is confrontational. Crafting the "honest" message takes a lot of time and thought. And no matter how delicately you do it, it feels cold and mean to reject someone. It's just easier on many levels to say nothing or pretend to be busy until people get the picture.

Do we really prefer to get the cold, hard truth when someone is rejecting us, though? We don't respond well to rejection, especially when we've put ourselves out there and shown interest in another person, and it's painful to read a message saying that someone doesn't want to date you.

If we're honest with ourselves, we realize that, however bizarre, we actually prefer to be lied to. If someone lies and says they are dating someone or they are moving to another town soon, you don't feel rejected, because it's no longer about *you.*

This way, our feelings aren't hurt *and* we aren't left confused or frustrated by silence or "pretend to be busy" issues. So I guess what I'm saying is the next time someone asks you out and you aren't interested, the nicest thing you can do is write back: "Sorry, can't do dinner tomorrow. I'm leaving on a secret mission with the space program! When I return to earth, I will have barely aged at all, but you'll be seventy-eight years old. I just don't think it's a good time for me."

WHAT HAPPENED WITH TANYA, THOUGH?

The thing to remember with this nonsense is, despite all your second-guessing about the content or timing of your message, sometimes it's just not your fault and other factors are at play. When I was dealing with the Tanya situation, one friend gave me the best advice, in hindsight. He said, "A lot of times you're in these situations and you second-guess the things you said, did, or wrote, but sometimes it just has to do with something on *their* end that you have no clue about."

A few months later I ran into Tanya. We had a lot of fun together and she eventually told me that she was sorry she didn't get back to me that time. Apparently at the time she was questioning her entire sexual identity and was trying to figure out if she was a lesbian.

Well, that was definitely not a theory that crossed my mind.

We ended up hooking up that night, and this time she said there would be no games.

I texted her a few days later to follow up on this plan.

Her response: silence.*

---

* To be clear, Tanya and I are still friends and she's a very nice person.

CHAPTER 3

ONLINE DATING

s a public figure, I have never considered doing any online dating. I always figured there was a chance someone who was a stalker type would use it as an opportunity to kidnap and murder me.

I'm not sure how the scenario would go. Maybe my stalker (probably an Indian dude) sees my profile and thinks, *Oh, here's that comedian guy on OkCupid. FINALLY, I have a way to reach out to him and slowly plot his murder.* He sends me a message pretending to be a woman. I see the profile. "She" likes tacos and *Game of Thrones*. I'm very excited.

What I imagine my Indian dude stalker looks like.*

We plan a date. I'm nervous, but in a fun way. I go to pick "her" up. He, wearing a wig, answers the door. I immediately realize this is wrong, but he knocks me out before I can react. When I wake up, I'm in a dark basement filled with dolls, and a creepy song like "The Chauffeur" by Duran Duran is playing. He then performs a face-off surgery and takes over my life.

I scream in agony and think, *I knew this would happen.*

Okay, this is probably a highly unlikely scenario, but still, you understand my hesitation. The truth is I've always thought online dating is great.

I once met someone who found his wife by using Match.com and searching—and this is a direct quote—"Jewish and my zip code." I joked that that's how I would go about finding a Wendy's. "I'd type

---

* **NOTE:** Since this is just a stock image of an Indian guy, I'm legally required to mention that though I have said this is what my stalker would probably look like, this guy is *not* actually a stalker. He's just an Indian guy who sometimes gets paid to pose with a laptop for stock photography.

Wendy's and my zip code and then I'd go get some nuggets." It is a little silly that that's how this guy found his wife, but to me it honestly is a beautiful and fascinating thing that this goofy search led to him finding the person with whom he will share his life.*

It's an amazing series of events: He types in this phrase, all these random factors and algorithms come together, this woman's face comes up, he clicks it, he sends a message, and then eventually that woman becomes the person he spends the rest of his life with. Now they're married and have a kid. A life. A *new life* was created because one moment, years ago, he decided to type "Jewish 90046"† and hit "enter."

Connections like this are now being made on a massive scale. OkCupid alone is responsible for around forty thousand dates of new couples every day. That's eighty thousand people who are meeting one another for the first time daily because of this website. Roughly three thousand of them will end up in long-term relationships. Two hundred of those will get married, and many of them will have kids.[1]

THE RISE OF ONLINE DATING . . .

Online dating has its origins in the 1960s, with the emergence of the first computer dating services. These services claimed that they could leverage the new power of computers to help the luckless in love find their soul mate in a rational, efficient manner. They asked clients to fill out long questionnaires, the answers to which they would enter into computers the size of living rooms. (Well, not all the services did this. Apparently one, Project Flame at Indiana University, got students to fill out computer punch cards and then, rather than put them in the computer, the

---

* Less beautiful but equally fascinating: "Jewish + zip code" is also a popular search phrase on aryanhousehunters.com, the real estate site for anti-Semites.

† Jewish 90046 is also the name of the least intimidating Terminator model of all time.

scientists shuffled the deck and created a faked match.) The computer would chew on the data and, based on whatever primitive algorithm had been entered into it, spit out two theoretically compatible clients, who would then be sent on a date.[2]

These services hung around in various forms throughout the 1980s, but they never really caught on. There were a few good reasons for their failure. One was pretty simple: Not many people had personal computers at home, or even at work, and the idea that some strange machine was going to identify the perfect partner was just weird. After thousands of years of dating and mating without electronic assistance, most people resisted the idea that the answer to finding true love was to consult a bulky IBM. There was also another big reason people didn't flock to computer matchmakers: The companies that ran them couldn't show that they knew what made two people good romantic partners, and no one had evidence that the systems actually worked. Finally, there was a strong stigma attached to computer dating, and most people considered using machines for this purpose a sign of romantic desperation.

Classified ads, not matchmaking machines, were the medium of choice for singles looking for new ways to connect during the 1980s and early 1990s. The genre was actually invented in the 1690s, and by the eighteenth century matrimonial advertising had become a flourishing part of the newspaper business.[3] The ads really took off after the sexual revolution of the 1960s, when men and women alike were emboldened to seek new ways to meet people. Decades before Craigslist, the "Personals" sections of daily and, especially, weekly newspapers were full of action, particularly in the "thin markets" such as among LGBT folks and middle-aged (usually divorced) and older straight people.

The ads were very brief, generally under fifty words, and would lead with a bold, all-caps heading that would attempt to grab people's attention, anything from STRAWBERRY BLONDE to LONELY GUY! to SURPRISE ME or even just MY NAME IS WILLIE!

Then the person would quickly describe themselves and what they were looking for or in search of (ISO). In order to save space, people used abbreviations, like SWM (single white male), SJF (single Jewish female), SBPM (single black professional male), and, of course, DASP (divorced Asian saxophone player.)

You would usually get a certain amount of space for free and then would have to pay for more space. For instance, in the *L.A. Times* you got four lines for free and then paid eight dollars per line afterward.

Here are some ads from the *Beaver County Times* in December 1994, just months before the first online dating site emerged:

are looking for a loving and caring relationship, please call BOX 23520

I'M YOUR ANGEL
Attractive, intelligent, black Christian woman. Seeking a friendship with a Christian male. I love movies, and many other things. Call me and let's talk. BOX 17600

SELECTIVE LADY
Single white blonde, in my mid 40's. I have blue eyes. In search of a single or divorced white gentleman, age 40 to 60. Honesty and sincerity a must. Want a non smoker with a sense of humor. Like good conversation, movies, walks and jazz. BOX 23516

SINCERE WHITE FEMALE
Divorced female, 42, 5ft 8in, brown hair and eyes, enjoys, VCR movies, & pets. I am happy, honest and enjoy life, any height, weight, color or handicap welcome. Only marriage minded. BOX 23517

SINGLE WHITE FEMALE
23, with brown hair, brown eyes, looking for single white male 23 to 30. Slim to medium build, has a job, likes to dance, go to the movies, and out to eat. Hoping for a possible relationship and later on, possible marriage. BOX 23519

LIVING FOR HOLIDAYS
Divorced, white female, blond hair and blue eyes, seeking single or divorced black male, over 6' is a plus, medium to large build must enjoy R & B music, dancing and quiet evenings at home. If you want to spend the holidays with someone please call. BOX 17508

BEAVER COUNTY AREA
Sensitive, single black female, age 34. Looking for a single, very tall, kind of witty, charming male, age 40 and over. Only a serious person need ap-

lions, walking, dancing, and eating out at times BOX 17590

BEAVER COUNTY AREA
Single white female age 46. Stand 5'4" tall with blue eyes and blond hair; full figured. Likes country music, dining out, movies, and craft shows. Seeking a single white male age 46 to 56. for a relationship; possibly more. BOX 17585

IT'S ALL GOOD
Hour-glass shape, single black female, 19, 135lbs., 5ft. 6in. I enjoy dancing, going to clubs, movies, hanging out, and listening to Rap and R & B. Looking for a single male, 19 to 25, who has the same interests. Give me a call BOX 17584

MEN SEEKING WOMEN
Call 1-900-680-7755
$1.99 per min.

A RARE BREED
Widower, Christian, 60, non smoker, non drinker, likes most music, walks, evenings out as well as in. 5'7", brown hair and brown eyes. Seeking single white female, 40 to 62, with similar values BOX 23599

LONELY PUPPY
Single white male, looking for single white female. 21 to 25, to take me home, out of the cold. I'm loveable, house broken and know how treat a woman. call Buzz BOX 23595

MAN SEEKING WOMAN
Single white male. 42, looking for someone to have fun with, going to movies. grabbing a bite, talking, spending evenings watching videos, eve walks. friendship and possible relationship. Alcoholics, junkies, and margees need not apply BOX 23518

LETS KICK IT

... to medium build, to enjoy the holiday spirit with. If you enjoy the holiday spirit and want romance, call... BOX 23547

BEAVER CO. AREA
28 year old male, 5'9", 150lbs. I'm very active, creative and educated. Enjoy snow skiing and sports. Non smoker seeking a single white female age 21 to 33 with similar interests. Want someone slim to medium build, for dating and possibly more. BOX 17552

CARING CHRISTIAN MAN
46, brown hair, blue eyes, 5ft 11in, attractive, huggable teddy bear. Enjoys slow dancing, movies, tennis, long walks. Seeks attractive non smoker, average build, single or divorced white lady. Age not important. BOX 23549

LOOKING FOR YOU
Single white male in search of single white female. 30 to 50. I am 42, brown/gray hair, brown eyes. 5ft 9in, 140 pounds, with many varied interests, mainly kareoke singing. dancing. If you are interested, please call. BOX 23551

BEAVER COUNTY AREA
Single white male age 50. 6'2". big man with a big heart. with some physical disabilities. Love the outdoors, travel, quiet evenings, music and cooking. Seeking companionship? Relationship? Age not important. BOX 23544

RELATIONSHIP SOUGHT
Single white male age 23, 5'7", 240 pounds, with black hair. Searching for a single or divorced white female age 18 to 23, for friendship; maybe a relationship. Must have a good sense of humor BOX 23538

ATTENTION LADIES
Nice looking professional, single

WARM AND CARING
Attractive single white male, age 20, 5'6", 123 pounds, brown/blonde hair, brown eyes. I'm a college student and computer tech., who is tired of relationships that stop on a dime. Looking for an attractive female age 20 to 25, to become good friends with and possibly have a relationship. Non smoker BOX 17596

BROKEN HEARTED MAN
24, white single male, 5'10", 160 pounds. Searching for white single female. 21-25, with some build to share good times with. Friendship definitely, relationship possible. Drinker's and smoker's not important. BOX 17589

SEEKING MISS RIGHT
Single white male, non drinker, 28, 6ft 3in., attractive, employed ex-partier. Enjoys adventure, travel, beaches, outdoors, scuba, and boating. In search of single white female, who is attractive, petite, adventurous, casual drinker OK. Weekends to burn. If possible, get wild and see the world BOX 17583

THE NICE GUY
34 year old, 5'10", 180lb., male. Enjoy going out and having fun, staying in and sharing relaxing evenings with special lady. If you are sincere, and between 21 and 40...call. BOX 17582

MUSTANG
18 yrs. old, 5'11", long blond hair, blue eyes. 137lbs., smoker, like quiet evenings. going out at night and having lots of fun. Seeking white female, same interest, ages 18 to 20. BOX 17572

WANTED OLDER WOMAN
White male, 47, seeking older wom-

After the ads were placed, interested parties would call a toll-based 900 number and leave a message in that person's mailbox. The cost of leaving these messages hovered around $1.75 per minute, and the average call lasted about three minutes. You would listen to the person's outgoing message and then leave your voice mail, and you even had the option to listen and rerecord if you wanted. The person who placed the ad would go through the messages and contact those people they were interested in.

With no photos and so little information to go off of, finding love through personals could be a frustrating experience. That said, occasionally newspaper personals really did lead to love connections. As it happens, Eric's dad, Ed, was an active user of classified newspaper personal ads in Chicago during the 1980s and early 1990s, and he remembers his experiences well. Ed published his ads in the *Chicago Reader*, the local alternative weekly. Fortunately for us, he saved the last, most successful one he ever posted:

SEEKING ADVENTURE??

Divorced Jewish male, 49, enjoys sailing, hiking, biking, camping, travel, art, music, French and Spanish. Seeking a woman who's looking for a long-term relationship and who shares some of these interests. Be bold—call right now! Chicago Reader Box XXXXX.

There's a lot in this ad that will look familiar to today's online daters. Ed gives his status, religion, age, and personal interests. We get a sense that he's pretty cosmopolitan, and there's even a promise of adventure if we dare to be bold. (Nice move, Ed!)

The ad above generated responses from about thirty-five women, he recalls. Those who responded had to call the designated 900 number and type in his mailbox code. When they did, they heard his personal greeting, which he reconstructed for us:

Hello! If you're seeking adventure and fun, you've come to the right ad! My name is Ed. I'm a forty-nine-year-old divorced Jewish man with two adult children. I have my own house in Lincoln Park and I've owned my own advertising and public relations company since 1969. I'm a longtime recreational sailor and I have a boat in Monroe Harbor. I also enjoy bike riding, hiking, running, camping, and photography. I graduated from the University of Michigan with an English degree, and after graduating from college I worked for six months, saved all my earnings, and attended the Sorbonne College. During the summer vacation I hitchhiked ten thousand miles through Europe and parts of the Middle East. Obviously, world travel is a big interest of mine! I'm active in two French-language groups and I also speak Spanish. If I've caught your attention and you'd like to talk to me on the phone, please respond to this message and leave a number where I can reach you. I look forward to hearing from you soon!

Damn, Ed sounds pretty badass in this greeting. Dude owns a boat and is active in not one but *two* French-language groups. Ed told us that he'd call in to check the messages about once a week—a far cry from today's online daters, many of whom check for matches every few hours or even get instant push notifications on their phone. "I listened to each of them several times, making notes about key items of information. Then I called the women who sounded most interesting, and that time, one really stood out."

Hello, my name is Anne and I really like your Reader *ad as well as your voice introduction when I called you just now. I'm a divorced thirty-seven-year-old woman with no children, and yes—I am seeking adventure! I enjoy many of the activities you listed. I lived in Colombia and in Peru for a short time, so I speak Spanish, as you do. If you'd like to meet in person, please call me. I hope you do!*

Ed made the call and invited Anne to meet for coffee. Often, he explained to us, these first encounters went badly, because with newspaper ads you had no idea what the other person looked like, and you were basically going off how they sounded on the phone. But he and Anne had a good vibe right away, and things quickly took off. They dated for six years before he proposed to her on a sailing trip by hoisting a self-made sail that said, "Dear Annie, I love you—Will you marry me?" She said yes, and before long they'd sailed off to California to start a new life together.

Now, the idea of meeting through a newspaper personals ad makes for a pretty great story, but for many years Anne never told it.

She's a high-achieving professional with a fancy degree from an elite university and a straitlaced family, and she knew there was a stigma attached to couples who met through newspaper ads. Anne made up a decoy story about her and Ed's meeting being a setup, for the inevitable moments when people asked how they had met. Her own friends and family didn't know the truth until her wedding day, when she confessed during her toast, at which point her family disowned her for being such a loser. Okay, that didn't happen, but wouldn't that have been nuts?

A few years before Ed and Anne found love through a newspaper ad, some entrepreneurs tried to bring cutting-edge technology to matchmaking by introducing video dating services, which gave singles a more dynamic sense of their prospective partners, including a much-needed visual component. With video dating, someone like Ed or Anne would go to a small studio, sit before a small crew, and spend a few minutes introducing themselves on camera. Every so often, they'd get a VHS cassette with short videos of prospects in the mail, and if they liked someone they saw, they could try to arrange a date.

Video dating never really caught on, but if you do some YouTube searching, you can observe some fantastic archived footage. One guy, Mike, led with this amazing notice:

Hi, my name's Mike, and if you're sitting there watching this tape smoking a cigarette, well, hit the fast-forward button, 'cause I don't smoke and I don't like people who do smoke.

In addition to that, most of the clips I watched contained guys setting themselves up as enjoying "having fun" and looking for "someone to have fun with." They also shared a little bit about themselves. "I like pizza," said one gentleman. "No fatties, no alcoholics," proclaimed another. "I'm currently cleaning up toxic waste" is how one man described his professional life, while another described himself as "an executive by day, a wild man by night," and a third proclaimed, "I'm interested in all aspects of data processing."

One gentleman declared no "Donna Juanitas," which sounded like a horrifying racial slur against Hispanic women. However, I did some Internet research and found out it was actually the female equivalent of a Don Juan. Basically, he didn't want a woman who was sleeping around. That said, if that's the goal, shouldn't the term be "Donna Juan" instead of "Donna Juanita"? Where does the "Juanita" come from? Why does her last name change? Seems like the person who came up with this term is under the impression that last names in Spanish have gender-specific conjugations. So a man named Jorge Lopez would be married to a woman named Ana Lopezita? My Spanish is horrible, but even I know that makes no sense. Okay, this was quite a tangent—look for my other book, *Donna Juan: The Etymology of Racial Slurs*, sometime in 2023.*

---

* UPDATE: I showed this passage to my friend Matt Murray, who brought up a great point. After reading this section, he wrote me this eye-opening note: "In this case, isn't 'Don' an honorific, like 'Don Julio' or 'Don Corleone'? So, I think the guy would be right to change 'Juan' to 'Juanita.' Weirdly the part he got wrong was the 'Donna' part, which should, I believe, be 'Doña.'" Wow. Thanks Matt. Who could have ever guessed how deep this rabbit hole would go?

After each clip, the suitor's stats would be flashed on the screen, like this:

First Name:
Code: DE 105M
Home:
Religion:
Education: B.A.
Occupation: Own Company
Age: 25   Height: 6'2" Weight: 190
Age Range of Partner: 21- 28
Max. Distances of Partner: 80 Mi.
Times Married: 0   No. of Children: 0
Interests: Sailing. Dancing. Adventure

In a way, I'm kind of bummed video dating died out, because the clips I explored were really great. Peep the dude above. One of his interests is "adventure"!

The failure of video dating did not scare off the entrepreneurs who recognized how another new technology, the Internet, might revolutionize matchmaking. And in the mid-1990s, when personal computers and modems that connected users to the Internet were becoming more popular, online dating began to take off.

Match.com launched in 1995, and it wasn't just an updated version of computer dating services; it had one crucial innovation: Instead of matching up clients with an algorithm, Match.com let its clients select one another, in real time. Most people were skeptical that the service would change anything. But not Gary Kremen, who founded the company and served as its first CEO. During his first big television interview, Kremen wore a tie-dyed shirt, sat on a brightly colored beanbag chair, and boldly told the camera: "Match .com will bring more love to the planet than anything since Jesus Christ."[4]

But first it required some tinkering. Initially Match.com was hampered by the same stigma that had kept people away from previous computer dating services. During the Internet boom of the late 1990s, though, people's relationship to computers and online culture changed dramatically, and more and more people were getting comfortable using computers for basic tasks. Over time, e-mail, chat rooms, and ultimately social media would require people to develop online personas. And the idea of using a computer to find dates became completely acceptable. By 2005 Match.com had registered forty million people.

However, once it was clear that there was a market for online dating services, competing companies sprang up everywhere, seeking out new niches and also trying to chip away at Match .com's client base. Each new site had its own distinctive branding—eHarmony was for people looking for serious relationships, Nerve was for hipsters, JDate for Jewish folks, and so forth.

But most sites shared a basic template: They presented a vast catalog of single people and offered a quasiscientific method of filtering through the options to find the people most likely to match. Whether these algorithms were more effective than the algorithms of the computer dating services is a matter of some controversy, but as computers became dazzlingly fast and sophisticated, people seemed more inclined to trust their matchmaking advice.

ONLINE DATING TODAY

I always knew online dating was popular, but until recently I had no idea just how massive a force it is in today's search for a romantic partner.
According to a study by the University of Chicago psychologist John Cacioppo (not to be confused with John Cacio e Pepe, a fat Italian guy who loves pasta with pecorino and black pepper), between 2005 and 2012 more than *one third* of couples who got married in the United States met through an online dating site. Online dating was *the* single biggest way people met their spouses. Bigger than work, friends, and school *combined*.[5]

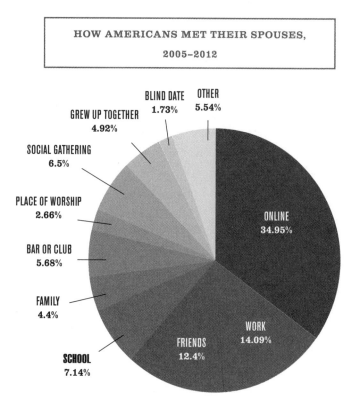

HOW AMERICANS MET THEIR SPOUSES,
2005–2012

OTHER 5.54%

BLIND DATE 1.73%

GREW UP TOGETHER 4.92%

SOCIAL GATHERING 6.5%

PLACE OF WORSHIP 2.66%

BAR OR CLUB 5.68%

FAMILY 4.4%

SCHOOL 7.14%

FRIENDS 12.4%

WORK 14.09%

ONLINE 34.95%

Cacioppo's findings are so shocking that many pundits questioned their validity, or else argued that the researchers were biased because they were funded by an online dating company. But the truth is that the findings are largely consistent with those of Stanford University sociologist Michael Rosenfeld, who has done more than anyone to document the rise of Internet dating and the decline of just about every other way of connecting.

His survey, "How Couples Meet and Stay Together," is a nationally representative study of four thousand Americans, 75 percent married or in a romantic relationship and 25 percent single. It asked adults of all ages how they met their romantic partners, and since some of the respondents were older, the survey allows us to see how things varied among different periods.[6]

It's especially instructive to compare things from 1940 to 1990, right before the rise of online dating, and then again from the 1990s until today.

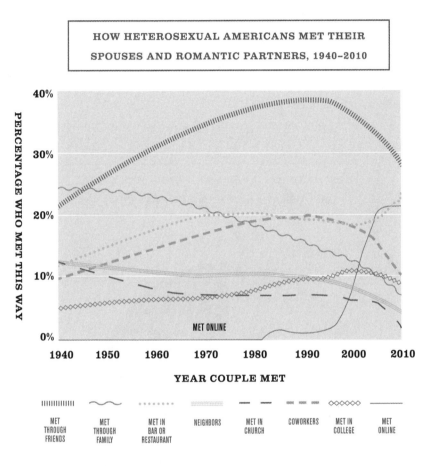

HOW HETEROSEXUAL AMERICANS MET THEIR
SPOUSES AND ROMANTIC PARTNERS, 1940–2010

First let's look at the difference between 1940 and 1990—just before online dating arrived. In 1940 the most common way to meet a romantic partner was through the family, and 21 percent met them through friends. About 12 percent met through church or in the neighborhood, and roughly the same portion met in a bar or restaurant or at work. Just a handful, about 5 percent, met in college, for the simple reason that not many people had access to higher education.

Things were different in 1990. The family had become a far less influential matchmaker, pairing up only 15 percent of singles, as did the church, which had plummeted to 7 percent. The most popular route to romance was through friends, which is how nearly 40 percent of all couples met.

The portion of people who met in bars had also increased, going up to 20 percent. Meeting someone in college had gone up to 10 percent, while meeting in the neighborhood was just a bit less common than it had been in 1940.

Another popular way partners found each other in 1990 was

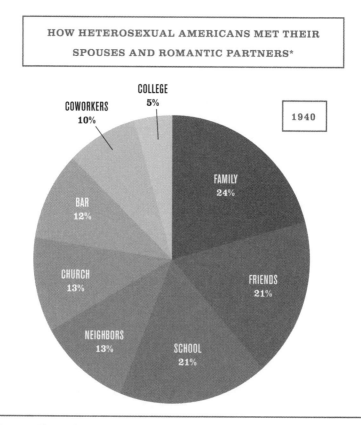

HOW HETEROSEXUAL AMERICANS MET THEIR
SPOUSES AND ROMANTIC PARTNERS*

COLLEGE 5%
COWORKERS 10%
1940
BAR 12%
FAMILY 24%
CHURCH 13%
FRIENDS 21%
NEIGHBORS 13%
SCHOOL 21%

* **NOTE:** The numbers here add up to more than 100 percent because many people reported meeting their spouse in more than one of these categories—for instance, family connections who met in school, college students who met in a bar—and they checked more than one answer.

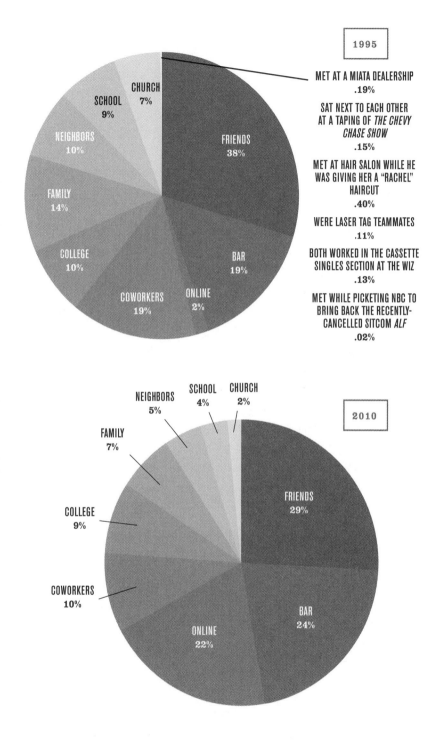

MET AT A MIATA DEALERSHIP
.19%

SAT NEXT TO EACH OTHER
AT A TAPING OF *THE CHEVY
CHASE SHOW*
.15%

MET AT HAIR SALON WHILE HE
WAS GIVING HER A "RACHEL"
HAIRCUT
.40%

WERE LASER TAG TEAMMATES
.11%

BOTH WORKED IN THE CASSETTE
SINGLES SECTION AT THE WIZ
.13%

MET WHILE PICKETING NBC TO
BRING BACK THE RECENTLY-
CANCELLED SITCOM *ALF*
.02%

CHURCH
7%

SCHOOL
9%

NEIGHBORS
10%

FRIENDS
38%

FAMILY
14%

COLLEGE
10%

BAR
19%

ONLINE
2%

COWORKERS
19%

NEIGHBORS
5%

SCHOOL
4%

CHURCH
2%

2010

FAMILY
7%

COLLEGE
9%

COWORKERS
10%

FRIENDS
29%

ONLINE
22%

BAR
24%

ONLINE DATING   83

when a man would yell something to the effect of "Hey, girl, come back here with that fine butt that's in them fly-ass acid-washed jeans and let me take you to a Spin Doctors/Better Than Ezra concert." The woman, flattered by the attention and the opportunity to see one of *the* preeminent musical acts of the era, would quickly oblige. This is how roughly 6 percent of couples formed. To be clear, this is just a guess on my part and has nothing to do with Mr. Rosenfeld's research.

The advent of online dating sites has transformed the way we begin romantic relationships. In 2000, a mere five years after Match .com was invented, 10 percent of all people in relationships had met their partners on the Internet, and by 2010 nearly 25 percent had. No other way of establishing a romantic connection has ever increased so far, so fast.[7]

In 2010 only college and bars remained roughly as important as they had been in 1995. In contrast, the portion of people who met through friends had dropped precipitously, from 40 percent to 28 percent, and meeting through the family, work, or the neighborhood became even less common, each around 10 percent or well below. And churches went the way of the Spin Doctors and Better Than Ezra, all but totally out of the game.

Now online dating is almost a prerequisite for a modern single. As of this writing, 38 percent of Americans who describe themselves as "single and looking" have used an online dating site.[8]

ONLINE DATING AND THIN MARKETS

Internet dating has changed the game even more dramatically in what Rosenfeld calls "thin markets," most notably people interested in same-sex relationships, but increasingly older and middle-aged straight people too. The reason is pretty obvious: The smaller the pool of potential romantic partners, the lower the odds of finding romance face-to-face, whether through friends, in schools, or in public places. Sure, there are booming gay neighborhoods in some cities, but the people who live and hang out there see a lot of one another. After a while those who are single have moved through their options and they're looking for something new. That's one reason why today meeting in bars or in the neighborhood is far less common among LGBT couples than it used to be, and why nearly 70 percent of LGBT couples meet online. (BLT couples—bacon, lettuce, and tomato couples—are inanimate objects and are not engaging in romantic pursuits.)

Back to LGBT folks: Rosenfeld's research shows that online dating is "dramatically more common among same-sex couples *than any way of meeting has ever been for heterosexual or same-sex couples in the past.*" (Emphasis ours.) And recent trends suggest that as more old people go online, Internet dating will start to dominate their world too.

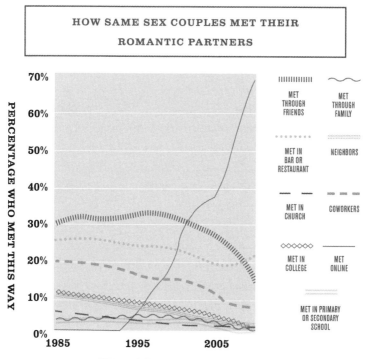

HOW SAME SEX COUPLES MET THEIR ROMANTIC PARTNERS

PERCENTAGE WHO MET THIS WAY

YEAR COUPLE MET

MET THROUGH FRIENDS
MET THROUGH FAMILY
MET IN BAR OR RESTAURANT
NEIGHBORS
MET IN CHURCH
COWORKERS
MET IN COLLEGE
MET ONLINE
MET IN PRIMARY OR SECONDARY SCHOOL

SOCIAL STIGMA

There can still be a social stigma with online dating sites, and people are sometimes afraid to admit that's how they met their partner. Their fear is that using an online site means they were somehow not attractive or desirable enough to meet people through traditional means, but in recent years this concern seems to be declining. Occasionally we interviewed people who felt embarrassed that they had met their mates online and crafted "decoy stories" for their friends and family. I hope the prevalence of online dating that we're reporting here will destroy the fears any readers have about it not being accepted. No matter what your friends and family say when they hear you met your special person through a website, you have plenty of company in finding your mate through these means. If you are still uneasy about it, though, and you need help crafting a decoy story, I can suggest a few for you to try:

It was a rainy Sunday winter afternoon and I decided to go the movies. Everything was sold out except for a special Christmas screening of the Arnold Schwarzenegger film Jingle All the Way. *I looked over and I saw one other person in the theater. It was Janine. I sat next to her and we started chatting. By the time Arnold had finally secured a "Turbo Man" doll for his son, Jamie, we had already boned it out TWICE.*

I was in the hallway of my apartment building throwing out a bag of trash when a small puppy walked up to me. We looked at each other, and then I turned around. He then tapped me with his paw. I turned around to face him. The puppy spoke, in a voice that sounded old and raspy, with a strong Southern accent not unlike the one Kevin Spacey does in House of Cards, *and said, "Katherine . . . Katherine, listen to me . . . You must go and find Dan-*

iel Reese. He will be your husband." I never saw the puppy again and I never met a Daniel Reese, but that night I met Dave at a bar downtown.

I was attending a boxing match in Atlantic City, when suddenly gunshots rang out and the secretary of defense, whom I was assigned to protect, was killed. Of course, I ordered the arena to be locked down and then, using my expert detective skills, determined that the mastermind of the whole plan was none other than my own partner, Kevin Dunne. That bastard. After fighting one of the boxers myself, I was able to escape just as Hurricane Jezebel hit the boardwalk. Yup, you know what that means. Tidal wave. Eventually Dunne shot himself in front of the TV cameras once he realized his plan had failed, and that's where I met Cindy.

NOTE: Use this story only if you're sure your audience has not seen the Nicolas Cage movie *Snake Eyes.*

It's easy to see why online dating has taken off so much. It provides you a seemingly endless supply of people who are single and looking to date. You have the tools to filter and find exactly what you are looking for. You don't need a third party, like a friend or coworker, to facilitate an intro. The sites are on all the time and you can engage whenever and wherever you want.

Let's say you're a girl who wants a twenty-eight-year-old man who's five foot ten, has brown hair, lives in Brooklyn, is a member of the Baha'i faith, and loves the music of Naughty by Nature. Before online dating, this would have been a fruitless quest, but now, at any time of the day, no matter where you are, you are just a few screens away from sending a message to your very specific, very odd dream man. But, of course, there are downsides with online dating as well.

THE PROBLEMS WITH ONLINE DATING

So far I've painted a pretty nice picture of millions of people finding love with a few clicks. In theory, online dating should be a big improvement over traditional methods of meeting people. It's infinitely larger, more efficient, more precise, and always readily available. Of the successful relationships in the Rosenfeld study, 74 percent of the people started as total strangers, meaning had it not been for online dating, they would never have met.

However, despite the undeniable success that the numbers above represent, the research I've done and read makes it clear that the new dating technology has created its own new set of problems. To get a real sense of the world of online dating, we had to look beyond the numbers. So we set out to try to understand the real-life experiences people were having as online daters.

One of the most enlightening ways we found to learn about online dating was when, in a move that I still can't believe we were able to pull off, Eric and I hooked up a computer to a projector and asked young singles to log on to their accounts to show us what it was really like to be an online dater. They showed us their inboxes and what they would generally do upon logging in.

The first time we did this, at a live show in Los Angeles, an attractive woman pulled up her OkCupid account and let me project it onto a large screen that everyone in the house could see. She was receiving fifty new messages a day and her inbox was clogged with literally hundreds of unread solicitations. As she scrolled and scrolled through message after message, the guys in the audience looked on in horror. They couldn't believe the sheer volume of it all. The woman said she felt bad that a lot of the messages would probably just be deleted because she would never have time to respond to them all. The men in the audience collectively let out a pained groan. Throughout all our interviews, this was a consistent finding: In online dating women get a ton more attention than men.

In his book *Dataclysm*, OkCupid founder Christian Rudder

illustrates this stark difference in attention with the following graph of user data from OkCupid. This is a chart of messages received per day plotted against attractiveness based on user ratings.

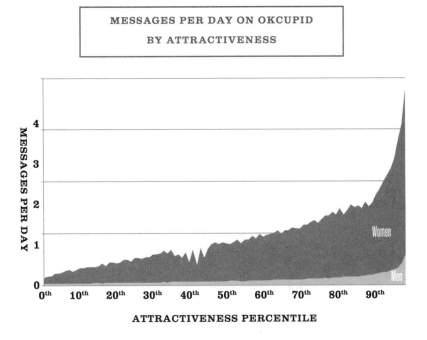

MESSAGES PER DAY ON OKCUPID
BY ATTRACTIVENESS

Even a guy at the highest end of attractiveness barely receives the number of messages almost all women get.

But that doesn't mean that men end up in the online equivalent of standing alone in the corner of the bar. Online there are no lonely corners. Everywhere is filled with people looking to connect.

A guy who may have had very little luck in the bar scene can have an inbox filled with messages. The number of messages may not be as high relative to that of the most attractive women on the sites, but relative to the attention they'd get in more traditional social environments, it's huge.

Basically, every bozo can now be a stud.

Take Derek, a regular user of OkCupid who lives in New York. What I'm about to say is going to sound very mean, but

Derek is a pretty boring white guy. Medium height, thinning brown hair, nicely dressed and personable, but nothing immediately magnetic or charming. He isn't unattractive, but he wouldn't necessarily turn heads if he walked into a bar or party.

At our focus group on online dating in Manhattan, Derek got on OkCupid and let us watch as he went through his options. These were women whom OkCupid had selected as potential matches for him based on his profile and the site's algorithm. The first woman he clicked on was very beautiful, with a witty profile page, a good job, and lots of shared interests, including a love of sports. After looking it over for a minute or so, Derek said: "Well, she looks okay. I'm just gonna keep looking for a while."

I asked what was wrong, and he replied, "She likes the Red Sox."

I was completely shocked. I couldn't believe how quickly he just moved on. Imagine the Derek of twenty years ago, finding out that this beautiful, charming woman wanted to date him. If she was at a bar and smiled at him, Derek of 1993 would have melted. He wouldn't have walked up and said, "Oh, wait, you like the Red Sox?! No thank you!" and put his hand in her face and turned away. But Derek of 2013 just clicked an *X* on a Web browser tab and deleted her without thinking twice, like a J.Crew sweatshirt that didn't live up to his expectations upon seeing a larger picture.

Derek didn't go for the next one either, despite the fact that the woman was comparably attractive. For ten or fifteen minutes Derek flipped his way around the site without showing even a hint of enthusiasm for any of the numerous extremely compelling women who were there looking for romance, until finally he settled on one and typed out a simple message, leaving the others to die in his browser history.

Now, let me say that I liked Derek. He was a nice person and I feel horrible about calling him a boring white guy. My point is that he did not strike me as a stud. But wow, when you watched him comb through those profiles, he had a stud mentality. I couldn't help thinking that he and who knows how many other people like him are doing a lot better with online dating than they would in other forums. Derek and all online daters, men and women, are being presented with more romantic possibilities than ever before, and it is clearly changing their whole approach to finding a potential mate.

There was another amazing example of this phenomenon on our subreddit. One young man wrote in to say how shocked he was to see how an attractive female friend of his fared on Tinder. "She had a 95% match rate," he reported. "Close to 150 matches in 20 minutes. She is insanely attractive in person but I was not expecting that. She could get as many matches in one hour as I could in 4 months." In part, this guy is complaining about the problems of being a man in the world of online dating: There's lots of competition for attractive women, and women get much higher hit rates than men. Granted. But in the midst of this he also said something incredible: "I got approximately 350 matches in 5 months." That's seventy people a month. Twenty years ago, if you met a guy who said he'd met seventy women who'd expressed interest in him in the past month, you'd assume he was quite a stud. Today he can be any guy with a smartphone and a thumb to swipe right.

EXHAUSTION:
ARPAN VERSUS DINESH

Derek and all the other people like him have vastly increased their dating options, but at what price? I learned all about the toll online dating can take when I met two very different and interesting men in a focus group in Los Angeles.

It was a Saturday morning and we were conducting our interviews in an office building on the west side. I walked in from the parking garage and got into the elevator, and I saw two Indian dudes. One was Arpan. The other was Dinesh. At first I was scared: Was one of these guys my Indian stalker? Nah, they seemed cool.

If I had to guess who had the better dating life based just on our initial hellos, I would have easily said Arpan. He was dressed a little more fashionably, he had a confidence and charm to him, and he seemed comfortable with all these strangers. Dinesh was a bit shy, not as hip in his dress, and just not as jovial. When the focus group started, though, a different picture emerged.

We began the discussion by just asking what people were looking for. Arpan slouched down in his seat and told his story.

"I'm Arpan. I'm twenty-nine and I live in downtown L.A.," he began. "I'm looking for something serious. I've been single for a few years. And you know, at the initial stages, especially when I was a little younger, like, twenty-six, it was cool. There are so many options!" For a while having easy access to a world of single women who lived nearby was exciting, and he'd spend hours online checking out profiles or casually flirting. He went out a lot too, and gradually honed his technique.

Arpan then described his descent into darkness. He said that initially he would spend a lot of time crafting enticing personal notes to women, his logic being that women receive so many messages that he had to do something to stand out from the crowd in their inboxes. Eventually, though, the return on investment was too low to justify all that time and energy. He would spend all this time being thoughtful but then felt like the women would just dismiss him based on looks or some other variable.

And even if the girl responded, it wasn't always easy. "Then finally she responds. You're like, *Yay!* A euphoric moment," he said. Then he'd be drawn into a back-and-forth exchange with this person that could last quite a while and then, as he described it, "either it fades out, or you meet up with them and it's horrible, and you just wasted all that time."

This all started taking a toll on Arpan and he became a different person. He decided he was going to stop with the thoughtful messages because it just wasn't worth the time. He started mass mailing what he admittedly described as "douchebag" messages.

"I'm so jaded and so tired of it that I don't actually take the time anymore. I will send a stupid message like 'Hey, you're pretty. Want to grab a drink?' Literally mass message, like, twenty, thirty people because I'm so tired. They're going to base [their response] on looks anyway." The lack of thoughtfulness in his messages made things easier and more effective. "There's no work," he said. "And I get more response rate, which is so weird."

Weird, yes, but also true. In *Dataclysm*, Christian Rudder used actual user data from OkCupid to show that writing a standard message and then copying and pasting it to initiate conversations is 75 percent as effective as writing something more original. Since it's also way less demanding, Rudder says that "in terms of effort-in to results-out it always wins."[9]

So Arpan did game the system to his advantage a little, but he didn't just standardize his initial messages; he also developed a template for his dates. When he started online dating he would often take women out to dinner, but at a certain point he decided this was a "rookie mistake." If he didn't hit it off with this person, he was in for the long haul, stuck in a seemingly endless dinner, so he decided to switch to drinks. He also felt that investing time in picking a fun place to go was too much effort considering that most of the dates ended up being a bust, so he narrowed his date spots to a few bars that were walking distance from his apartment.

So: just drinks, minimal effort on his part, *and* you have to travel to him. Ladies, are you getting sexually excited just reading this?!

We asked him where he took his last two dates, both of whom he found through online sites. "Volcano, five blocks away from my house." And the other? "Lucky Strike Lanes, six blocks away from my house." Any potential ladies that got excited about a bowling date quickly would have their dreams crushed, though. According to Arpan, "It's actually bowling, but there's a lounge/bar area, so I don't do the bowling." Ouch. Quite a bait and switch. "Hey! Let's go bowling! Just kidding, let's just get a drink at the lounge."

On that note, it is fairly common knowledge that nothing gets a girl more turned on than a bowling lounge. Between watching fat guys tossing bowling balls and the dulcet tones of *The Simpsons* arcade game, I can't imagine those encounters not ending in a marathon boning session.

"Dating is tiring, without a doubt," Arpan told us. "It's a lot of work. And you know, now I'm so jaded and, like, so tired of it that I don't actually take the time anymore. I'm at the point where it's just like, 'Find me somebody! Make it happen!'" But as far as I could tell, his techniques were not working out.

Arpan, who at first glance comes off as a vibrant, confident guy, has been so beaten down by dating that the very mention of the topic leads him to slouch down and spin tales like a weary war veteran. The rigors of the online dating world transformed this once-excited young single man into a sad lug whose idea of a date is to not bowl at a bowling alley that he can get home from as quickly as possible.

Others in our focus groups commiserated over the fact that sorting through this new sea of options available through online dating was almost becoming a second job. The word "exhausting" came up in every discussion we had, and after hearing people's experiences, it made sense.

All the work that went into finding even one date—reading through messages, finding a message you like, clicking the profile, sorting through the profile, and then, after all that, STILL having to engage in a series of back-and-forths to gauge rapport and then plan a real-world meet-up—was taking its toll.

Some had even reached a breaking point. Priya, twenty-seven, said she'd recently deleted her Tinder and OkCupid accounts. "It just takes too long to get to just the first date. And I feel like it's way more effective utilizing your social groups," she said. "It's like I would rather put myself in those social situations than get exhausted."

For Priya, as for so many of the online daters we met in different cities, the process had morphed from something fun and exciting into a new source of stress and dread.

Now, what about Dinesh, the other Indian guy?

Dinesh had a completely different approach to dating. "I'm not on any dating sites," he announced to our group that morning, looking a bit perplexed by the conversation.

"What was the last first date you went on?" I asked.

"I met a girl at church and we went to a movie just recently," he said.

The way he said it was so confident and badass. Compared with what Arpan had just said, Dinesh's "church and a movie" sounded like "motorcycle race and some sport fucking."

"What about the last girl before that who you met?" I continued.

"I met her at a volunteer thing," Dinesh replied.

The guys in the room seemed mesmerized by the fantasy of dating a beautiful girl who also does heartfelt charity work.

Before that, he reported, he'd met a girl at a holiday party. "I have a bunch of really good groups of friends, kind of across L.A., so I meet tons of people."

The key, Dinesh said, is to have friends who hang out in different groups in different places, and to mix up the nights so that you're spending some time with all of them. Whether it's in church, with volunteer groups, at office parties, or on a sports field, it's always a place where people meet organically.

"There's a lot of cool stuff going on in L.A. at all times," he explained. "I think it's fun and interesting to meet new people, and if I meet people in person, they're more willing to open up their schedules. I am too. I'm more willing to, like, go to work super early and then be home by, like, five or six to make something happen." He looked over to consider Arpan and then turned back to us. "And no, I'm not exhausted." Fortunately, Arpan at this point was so slumped in his chair that it blocked his ears and he didn't even hear this.

Dinesh had a Zen vibe to him that wasn't matched by anyone else in the room. While the other singles assembled that morning seemed jaded and frustrated, Dinesh seemed more comfortable and at ease with dating. Was it because he avoided online dating? Or was it that those who were dating online were actually pretty bad at it?

After several lengthy conversations with experts, I would guess the latter was a significant factor.

MOST PEOPLE STINK AT ONLINE DATING

Online dating is like a second job that requires knowledge and skills that very few of us have. In fact, most of us have no clue what we're doing. One reason is that people don't always know what they're looking for in a soul mate, unlike when they're picking something easier, like laundry detergent (big ups to Tide Mountain Spring—who doesn't want their clothes to smell like a fresh mountain spring?!).

While we may think we know what we want, we're often wrong. According to Dan Slater's history of online dating, *Love in the Time of Algorithms*, the first online dating services tried to find matches for clients based almost exclusively on what clients said they wanted. The client would usually fill out a survey indicating certain traits they were looking for in a partner. For example, if a man said he was looking for a tall, blond woman with no kids and a college degree, the company showed him everyone who fit this description. But pretty soon online dating companies realized that this wasn't working. In 2008 Match.com hired Amarnath Thombre as its new "chief of algorithms." Thombre set about figuring out why a lot of couples that Match.com's algorithm said were a perfect fit often didn't make it past the first date. When he began digging into the data, he discovered something surprising: The kind of partner people said they were looking for didn't match up with the kind of partner they were actually interested in.

Thombre discovered this by simply analyzing the discrepancy between the characteristics people said they wanted in a romantic partner (age, religion, hair color, and the like) and the characteristics of the people whom they actually contacted on the dating site. "We began to see how frequently people break their own rules," he told Slater. "When you watch their browsing habits—their actual behavior on the site—you see them go way outside of what they say they want."[10]

When I was writing stand-up about online dating, I filled out the forms for dummy accounts on several dating sites just to get a sense of the questions and what the process was like. The person I described that I wanted to find was a little younger than me, small, with dark hair. The person I'm currently dating, whom I met through friends, is two years older, about my height—OKAY, SLIGHTLY TALLER—and blond. She wouldn't have made it through the filters I placed in my online dating profile.

A big part of online dating is spent on this process, though— setting your filters, sorting through many profiles, and going through a mandatory "checklist" of what you think you are looking for. People take these parameters very seriously. They declare that their mate "must love dogs" or that their mate "must love the film *Must Love Dogs*," which stars Diane Lane as a newly divorced woman who's encouraged by her friend to start an online dating profile that states her dates "must love dogs." (Shout-out to the *Must Love Dogs* Wikipedia page for helping me recall the plot.)

But does all the effort put into sorting profiles help?

Despite all the nuanced information that people put up on their profiles, the factor that people rely on most when preselecting a date is looks. Based on the data he has reviewed, Rudder told us that he estimates that photos drive 90 percent of the action in online dating.

PROFILE PHOTOS:
WHY YOU NEED TO GO SPELUNKING WITH A PUPPY ASAP

If 90 percent of your fate as an online dater depends on the photos you pick, this is an important decision. So what works? Rudder examined which kinds of images proved most and least successful on the dating site OkCupid, and he made some surprising discoveries.[11]

First let's examine what works for women. Most women (56 percent) choose to go with a straightforward smiling pic. But the 9 percent who opt to go with a more "flirting to the camera" vibe are slightly more successful. See the examples below:

THE STRAIGHTFORWARD SMILING PIC

THE FLIRTING TO CAMERA PIC

Now, those results are not very surprising, but what's weird is that men actually fare better when they are *not* smiling and are looking *away* from the camera. Whereas women did worse when they didn't make eye contact, for guys, looking away was much more effective. This seems really counterintuitive. These are good photos? What are they looking at?

THE NOT SMILING, LOOKING AWAY PIC

"Oh shit, is that a raccoon in my kitchen?"

"I'm staring at my brother, whose leg I just ate. I've been lost in the desert for three weeks without food or water. Also, I like photography and playing guitar."

"Just grab a photo of me in front of this bridge—oh whoa, is that a bee? Quick! I didn't pack my EpiPen!"

The second thing Rudder discovered is that, for women, the most effective photo angle is a straightforward "selfie," shot down from a high angle with a slightly coy look.

When scanning through profiles, we saw a trend of people picking certain templates for their photos—hanging with friends drinking, outdoors near a mountain, etc. Rudder's data shows that for women, the high-angle selfie is by far the most effective. Second is in bed, followed by outdoor and travel photos. At the lower end, the ones that are least effective are women drinking alcohol or posing with an animal.

Oddly enough, for men the most effective photos are ones with animals, followed by showing off muscles (six-packs, etc.), and then photos showing them doing something interesting. Outdoor, drinking, and travel photos were the least effective photo types.

Most intriguing to me, though, was when Rudder looked at the data of what photos led to the best conversations. Whereas "cleavage" shots of women got 49 percent more new contacts per month than average, the images that resulted in the most conversation showed people doing interesting things. Sometimes faces didn't even need to appear. A guy giving a thumbs-up while scuba diving. A woman standing in a barren desert. A woman playing a guitar. These photos revealed something deeper about their interests or their lives and led to more meaningful interactions.

OPTIMAL PROFILE PHOTOS

So based on these data, the answers are clear: If you are a woman, take a high-angle selfie, with cleavage, while you're underwater near some buried treasure.

If you are a guy, take a shot of yourself holding your puppy while both of you are spelunking.

MESSAGING STRATEGY

So let's say the person is intrigued by your photos. Now what? The messages begin.

As with text messages, there are all sorts of strategies people use when communicating on a dating site. Unlike with SMS texts, though, with these messages we actually have data on what works.

According to Rudder, the messages that get the best response rate are between forty and sixty characters. He also learned something by analyzing how long people spent on the messages. The ones that received the highest response rate took only around two minutes to compose. If you overthink it and spend too much time writing, the response rate goes down.

What about the Arpan strategy of copying and pasting? The problem with Arpan's message is that it's clearly a copy-and-paste message with little thought and no personal touch. What really seems to be effective is taking the time to compose a message that seems genuine and blasting it out en masse. Here's a message that one guy blasted out to forty-two people:

I'm a smoker too. I picked it up when backpacking in may. It used to be a drinking thing but now I wake up and fuck, I want a cigarette. I sometimes wish that I worked in a Mad Men office. Have you seen the Le Corbusier exhibit at MoMA? It sounds pretty interesting. I just saw a Frank Gehry (sp?) display last week in Montreal, and how he used computer modelling to design a crazy house in Ohio.

At first glance it's a bit random, because there are so many references to so many different interests. But when you take it all in, it's clear that the guy was looking for a girl who smoked and was into art, and his generic message was specific enough to resonate with at least five of the women who read it, because that's how many replied.

ALGORITHMS

What about the algorithms that are supposed to help you find your soul mate? They're no doubt useful for helping online daters find their way into a pool of potentially compatible partners, and for that reason they can be useful. But even the designers who do the math that drives them acknowledge that they're far from perfect.

In 2012 a team of five psychology professors, led by Eli Finkel at Northwestern University, published a paper in *Psychological Science in the Public Interest* arguing that no algorithm can predict in advance whether two people will make a good couple. "No compelling evidence supports matching sites' claims that mathematical algorithms work," they wrote. The task the sites have set out for themselves—to pick out mates who are uniquely compatible—is, they conclude, "virtually impossible."[12]

Much of online dating, Finkel and company argued, is based on the faulty notion that the kind of information we can see in a profile is actually useful in determining whether that person would make a good partner. But because the kind of information that appears on a profile—occupation, income, religion, political views, favorite TV shows, etc.—is the only information we know about that person, we overvalue it. This can actually cause us to make very bad choices about whom we go on a date with.

"Encountering potential partners via online dating profiles reduces three-dimensional people to two-dimensional displays of information," the authors wrote, adding, "It can also cause people to make lazy, ill-advised decisions when selecting among the large array of potential partners." Sheena Iyengar, a Columbia University professor who specializes in research on choice, put it to me another way: "People are not products," she said bluntly. "But, essentially, when you say, 'I want a guy that's six foot tall and has blah, blah, blah characteristics,' you're treating a human being like one."

It's a good point, but at the same time, people doing online dating have no choice but to filter their prospects in some way, and once we accept that it's reasonable to select for, say, location and job, who's to say that it's superficial to select for a doctor who lives in your area? Even if you believe Iyengar's argument that sometimes online dating sites encourage people to treat one another like products, what choice do you have?

Helen Fisher, a biological anthropologist who advises Match .com, says the answer is to avoid reading too much into any given profile and to resist the temptation to start long online exchanges before a first date. As Fisher sees it, there's only one way to determine whether you have a future with a person: meeting them face-to-face. Nothing else can give you a sense of what a person is actually like, nor whether you two will spark.

"The brain is the best algorithm," Fisher argues. "There's not a dating service on this planet that can do what the human brain can do in terms of finding the right person."

This was probably the advice that resonated with me the most. I wouldn't know how to search for the things I love about my current girlfriend. It's not the kind of stuff you can really categorize.

When I've really been in love with someone, it's not because they looked a certain way or liked a certain TV show or a certain cuisine. It's more because when I watched a certain TV show or ate a certain cuisine with them, it was the most fun thing ever.

Why? I couldn't type out why.

That doesn't mean I'm skeptical of online dating; on the contrary, the research we've done has convinced me that millions of people have used it to find what they're looking for, from a one-night stand to marriage and a family. But our research also convinced me that too many people spend way too much time doing the online part of online dating, not the dating part. After years of observing people's behavior and consulting for Match.com, Fisher came away with a similar conclusion, which is why she advises online daters to keep their messaging to a minimum and to meet the person in real life as quickly as possible.

"This is one of the reasons that it's a misnomer that they call these things 'dating services,'" she says. "They *should* be called 'introducing services.' They enable you to go out and go and meet the person yourself."

Laurie Davis, author of *Love at First Click* and an online dating consultant, advises her clients to exchange a maximum of six messages before meeting off-line. This should provide enough information to let them know whether they'd have any possible interest in dating the person. Everything after that is usually just postponing the inevitable.

"Online dating is just a vehicle to meet more people," she says. "It's not the place to actually date."

For some people, mostly women, this advice wasn't convincing. As they see it, the Internet makes connections happen too fast, and their concerns about safety make them reluctant to go out and meet someone in person before they feel like they really know them. Many of the people who spoke to us in focus groups described texting or messaging a potential partner for weeks without actually going on a date. One woman in New York City named Kim showed us an exchange she'd had with a man on OkCupid that she'd ended because he asked her out for coffee after just a few messages within a twenty-minute span.

The two were involved in some funny instant messages, and Kim commented on how awkward meeting people online can be. The guy wrote back, "I would much rather connect with you in person than this online thing because just like you I think this is 'awkward.'"

This made Kim incredibly anxious.

"Unfortunately I don't drink coffee," she wrote. But then she wrote her real concern: "I actually don't know that you're not a serial killer."

The guy responded quickly. "I'm not sure you're not one either, but doesn't that make it more exciting. I'm willing to take a risk if you are. What about hot chocolate?"

Seems like this wouldn't be a huge deal. She's on the dating site to meet people and date them. They'd be in a public place drinking hot chocolate. He wasn't like, "How about we meet at that dumpster behind the Best Buy on Two Notch Road?"

But Kim was not having it. She ended it. "I don't know. The more messages you get, the more of a good feeling you have for that person. You don't want to go on a bad date. So if you have these messages going back and forth and you connect with each message, you like them more and the chances of it going well are higher."

No doubt there are many women who share Kim's perspective, and with all the creepy dudes out there who actually do harass women, I can't really fault them. As Helen Fisher sees it, though, all these messages aren't going to do much to assuage a person's deep concerns. Ultimately, meeting in person is the only way to know whether something is going to work.

SWIPING:

TINDER AND BEYOND

One of the tough parts of writing a book like this is you have no clue how the landscape will change once you're

done, but as of this writing, nothing seems to be rising faster than mobile dating apps like Tinder.

Contrary to the labor-intensive user experience of traditional online dating, mobile dating apps generally operate on a much simpler and quicker scale. Right now, Tinder is by far the industry leader and has spawned imitators. For our purposes, we'll use it as an example to describe the phenomenon in general.

Signing up for Tinder is almost instantaneous. You download the app and simply link in through your Facebook account. No questionnaires or algorithms. As soon as you sign in, Tinder uses your GPS location to find nearby users and starts showing you

a seemingly endless supply of pictures of potential partners. After you glance at each photo, you swipe the picture to the right if you're interested in the person or to the left if you're not. You can explore the profiles more and see some very basic information, but generally the user experience involves seeing someone's photo and swiping left or right pretty quickly depending on whether you are attracted to them. If you and another user are interested in each other, meaning you both swiped right on each other's faces, then the app informs you that you've found a match and you can begin messaging each other in private within the app to arrange a date or hookup or whatever. As of October 2014, the app has more than fifty million users and the company is valued anywhere from $750 million to $1 billion.

Tinder was conceived in 2011 by Sean Rad and Justin Mateen, two University of Southern California undergrads who set out to create an online dating experience that didn't feel like online dating. Modeling their interface on a deck of cards, Rad and Mateen wanted Tinder to seem like a game, one a user could play alone or with friends. It was low stakes and easy to use, and, if you played it well, you might hook up with someone in a matter of hours—the polar opposite of a tense, emotionally draining quest for a soul mate. "Nobody joins Tinder because they're looking for something," Rad told *Time*.[13] "They join because they want to have fun." And because his name is Sean Rad, he probably said that quote to *Time* and then tossed on a pair of cool shades, hopped on a skateboard, and blazed on outta there.

Like Facebook, Tinder's birthplace was college. But while Facebook began its rollout in the Ivy League, Tinder aimed for famous party schools like USC and UCLA.

Quick side note: In numerous interviews Mateen is identified as someone with a background in party planning, which is a ridiculous résumé item.

"Are you fit for the position?"

"Yes, I have a strong background in party planning. I promise you, *I can get this party started.*"

Mateen wanted to build buzz not through traditional advertising but by getting the app into the hands of "social influencers" who could spread Tinder by word of mouth. He personally tracked down and signed up the kind of people who didn't need to date online—models, sorority girls, fraternity presidents, and the like. Mateen and Tinder's then vice president of marketing, Whitney Wolfe, went door to door through the schools' Greek system, preaching the gospel of smartphone hookups. After Tinder's launch in September 2012—celebrated with a raging party at USC—the app took off and spread like wildfire across campuses. Within weeks, thousands of users had signed up, and 90 percent of them were between the ages of eighteen and twenty-four.

For a while Tinder was treated as the solution to a long-standing dilemma facing the online dating industry: How do we make a straight version of Grindr?

Grindr was a revolutionary app that took the male gay community by storm after its release in 2009, attracting more than one million daily users within a few years. A precursor to Tinder, it was the first major dating site that was primarily a mobile app that used GPS and a basic profile with a photo to match people.

Years before I heard of Tinder, I once sat with a gay friend in a sushi restaurant and was floored when he turned on his Grindr app and showed me a profile of a handsome guy. "It says he's fifteen feet away. Oh, shit. Look, he's right over there," he said, pointing to a guy sitting at the sushi bar.

It was mind-blowing, but companies struggled to replicate it for the straight world. The conventional wisdom was that straight women would never use a Grindr-type app, for reasons ranging from safety concerns to lack of such strong interest in casual sex with strangers. The Grindr team attempted it with an app called

Blendr, but it didn't catch on.

But Tinder added a key feature that Grindr—and Blendr, for that matter—didn't have: the mutual-interest requirement. This is the term I just made up to describe how, on Tinder, you can't engage with another user unless you both have swiped right, indicating interest in each other.

After our previous discussions of online dating, the appeal seems obvious. Take Arpan. No longer does he have to worry about writing a long message only to get dismissed based on his looks. The only people he can message are people who have already

indicated interest in him. On the reverse side, for women, a dude can't bother you unless you have swiped right on him. Women were no longer getting harassed by an infinite user base of bozos; they were engaging only with people they chose to engage. This change alone was enough of an improvement that, in October 2013, *New York* magazine proclaimed that Tinder had solved online dating for women.[14]

Also, the stress of weeding through profiles, à la our friend Derek, is gone too. You are just swiping on faces. It's like a game. This aspect of Tinder's user experience is huge.

Even the fact that signing up is so easy is a game changer. I remember signing up for a dummy OkCupid account, just to see what the site was like. It took forever. There were so many questions that I eventually just had an assistant answer them. It felt like a chore. Meanwhile, when researching Tinder, I was in the back of a cab and I quickly signed in through a Facebook account. Within seconds, I was swiping and enjoying the app with a friend. After each photo, my friend and I debated our thoughts on a particular person or checked to see if they had more pictures. Sometimes a user would come up with mutual friends, and that would spark a dialogue.

There was no denying it. There was something weirdly entertaining and gamelike about Tinder. When the app first started popping up, people in all our focus groups described signing up for amusement or as a joke and swiping profiles with friends in a group setting. They said using the app was actually fun and social, which was simply unheard of in all our conversations about other online dating sites.

At the same time, though, people's attitude toward Tinder was strange. When we first started asking people about it in late 2013, they wouldn't say they were on it looking for dates or even sex. They would say that they had signed up on a lark. They treated it like a party game. Anyone who was a serious user was basically using it as a hookup app for sex.

Here are a few exemplary quotes from a focus group we held in December 2013:

Hi, I'm Rena. I'm twenty-three and I signed up for Tinder, like, three months ago, just because I was drunk and with a friend.

Hi, I'm Jane. I'm twenty-four and I have a similar experience with Tinder where I was, like, at a party with friends and they were like, "This is the funnest game ever. Let's play this." And I downloaded it. And then, like, started seeing way too many people I knew. So I deleted it.

Those who did acknowledge that they'd actually used Tinder felt a little self-conscious about it. "I'm not gonna marry a guy from Tinder," one woman said. "Yeah, Tinder's very, like, hookup," added another.

What, we asked, would you do if you met someone you actually liked on Tinder? One woman said she'd be embarrassed to tell people she'd met someone on Tinder, whereas another site, like JDate, would have been fine.

But by late 2014 people's attitudes about Tinder were dramatically different, especially in the big cities where it first got popular. People we spoke with in New York and Los Angeles were using Tinder as *the* go-to dating app. It wasn't just a sex app. It wasn't a game. People were using it to meet people for relationships and dating because it was quick, fun, and easy. The change in perception was startling.

In October 2014 we asked people on our subreddit to tell us about their experiences with Tinder and other swipe apps. Sure, we got some stories about people using the site for drunken hookups, but we also got a lot like these:

I live in Atlanta, and when Dragon*Con came through I figured it would be the perfect opportunity for some hilarious stories. I started using it with my best friend and we'd send each other screenshots of our weird and scary messages and profiles we'd seen. Then I started matching with some legitimately cool dudes who I had shared interests with and had nice conversations with and I started taking it a lot more seriously . . .

I'm actually currently dating a guy I met off Tinder, we've been exclusive for about a month now? It's going well, I like him a lot and we're very happy. I deleted it after we agreed to be exclusive.

Based on the responses we got, it seems like many people who start on Tinder for laughs wind up finding something more meaningful than they expected. One man wrote:

The first time I had seriously used Tinder I ended up meeting [someone] who's now my girlfriend. I wasn't particularly looking for a serious commitment or anything, but I was just kind of going with it. It's weird because I always thought that I've done tinder wrong because it didn't end up in just a hookup and now I'm actually dating this girl. I haven't used the app since we started dating in the beginning of the summer.

Clearly, Tinder is working for people. Just two years after it was released, Tinder reported that it was processing two billion swipes and generating twelve million matches a day. And not just on college campuses. Today the average user is twenty-seven, and it's quickly becoming popular throughout the world.[15]

Near the end of 2014, Tinder claimed that the average user logged on eleven times per day and spent approximately seven minutes on each session, meaning they are there for more than 1.25 hours each day. That's an amazing amount of time to do anything, let alone move your fingers around a tiny screen.

There are also imitators. OkCupid developed a swipe-type app for its users. There is a popular start-up called Hinge that matches people Tinder style, but users have to have mutual friends on Facebook. Other new apps are surely on the way.

Swipe apps like Tinder definitely seem to be where online dating is headed. Weirdly, these apps have also come to signify a strange sense of wonder about what it means to be single today. In our interviews, people in relationships in their thirties or forties lamented the fact that they weren't able to experience the single life in the "age of Tinder." The app symbolizes the opportunity to meet/date/hook up with beautiful people whenever you want.

Is that the reality? In a sense, yes. The app is almost magical in the way you are so quickly exposed to exciting and beautiful possibilities for your romantic life. To think, just twenty years ago we were buying ads in a fucking newspaper!

One gentleman we interviewed told us that he literally could not get off the app, so overwhelmed was he by the enormous number of single women who were suddenly accessible. "I was literally addicted to it," he recounted. "I had to delete it." Another woman recalled being so hooked on Tinder that she was on her way to a date and swiping to see if there was another more attractive guy out there to meet up with in case her existing date was a bust.

But, like any dating trend, swipe apps have their pitfalls. The user base isn't exclusively attractive singles looking to have a good time; there is plenty of riffraff as well. Despite the mutual interest factor, you can find plenty of Tinder conversations on Straight White Boys Texting filled with matches who are spouting filth. Countless guys have also been lured to engage with women who were bad news or, worse yet, bots and/or prostitutes.

The biggest criticism of swipe apps is that, with their reliance on purely physical attraction, Tinder and the like represent increasing superficiality among online daters. ("Tinder: The Shallowest Dating App Ever?" asks the *Guardian*.[16])

But I think that's too cynical. Walking into a bar or party, a lot of times all you have to go by is people's faces, and that's what you use to decide if you are going to gather up the courage to talk to them. Isn't the swipe app just a HUGE party full of faces that we can swipe right to go talk to?

In the case of the girl I'm currently dating, I initially saw her face somewhere and approached her. I didn't have an in-depth profile to peruse or a fancy algorithm. I just had her face, and we started talking and it worked out. Is that experience so different from swiping on Tinder?

"I think Tinder is a great thing," says Helen Fisher, the anthropologist who studies dating. "All Tinder is doing is giving you someone to look at that's in the neighborhood. Then you let the human brain with his brilliant little algorithm tick, tick, tick off what you're looking for."

In this sense, Tinder actually isn't so different from what our grandparents did, nor is the way my friend used online dating to find someone Jewish who lived nearby. In a world of infinite possibilities, we've cut down our options to people we're attracted to in our neighborhood.

USING TECHNOLOGY TO GAIN ROMANTIC FREEDOM

For those who don't live in a world of infinite options, digital technology provides another benefit, and I hadn't thought about it until we interviewed people in one of the world's most unique dating cultures: Qatar.

The benefit is privacy. The secret worlds of the phone and the Internet provide single people a degree of freedom and choice in less open societies.

Needless to say, the singles scene in Qatar is not quite like what we observed anywhere else in the world. Those from religious and traditional families are literally prohibited from casual dating. Flirting in public places gets a young person in serious trouble, and it's especially dangerous for young women, who are expected to be chaste until marriage and risk bringing terrible shame to themselves and their parents if they are caught courting a man.

One online guide warns: "No public displays of affection: Kissing, hugging, and some places even holding hands . . . The result is jail time."[17]

That's a pretty grim prison story.

"Hey, man, what are you in for?"

"Doing five years for holding hands in the park."

"You?"

"Doing life . . . for smooches."

Since casual dating is prohibited, families—mainly the mothers—do the matchmaking in Qatar. Marriages are arranged, and for the women we interviewed, the incentives to tie the knot are oddly reminiscent of those expressed by the older American women we interviewed in the senior centers.

A twenty-seven-year-old named Amirah told us, "The main thing you need to understand about marriage here is that the parties to the contract are rarely the man and woman entering it. It's the families; it's the group.

"There's, like, a mating season," Amirah said, "and it's the mothers who do the initial screening. The mothers of boys go from one house to the other. They're looking for women who are suitable based on family background and education. They're looking for *naseeb*, their family's destiny for marriage.

"The other thing to know about marriage," Amirah continued, "is that it's attractive to young girls because they want to move out and get their freedom." Her friend Leila, a twenty-six-year-old lawyer who was also on the video chat, nodded in agreement. "When I first came back to Doha after I graduated from university, I went to visit [Amirah's] house," she began. "My mother called me and said, 'It's going to be nine P.M.; you should come home.' They'd always call me when I was out to find out where I was and ask when I was coming home. If I went shopping, they'd say, 'Stop. We have a maid who can do that!' If I was with a friend, they'd say, 'Come home!' They just didn't want me out."

After college, Leila couldn't tolerate this level of parental supervision. "I didn't want to be at home with my family all the time," she told us. "I wanted to have my freedom back. But women from traditional families can't live alone in Qatar. The only way you can leave your family's home is to get married or die."

I told Leila that this brought up another point: that *Get Married or Die Trying* would be a great name for her debut rap album.

Eventually Leila decided to get married. She told her mother that she was ready for a husband, and her family quickly found a suitable man. They spoke by phone and had a few visits with each other's families, though not any private time together. Leila was nervous. But she had the impression that "he really loved me." More important: "He was offering me a chance to start my own life."

Unfortunately, the new life he offered wasn't much of an improvement. The husband was basically as controlling as her parents. He would get upset when she went places without telling him. Leila was ready to be a modern, independent wife, but her husband wanted something more traditional. Neither Leila nor her husband was happy with the situation, and one day he came home and announced that he wanted a divorce. "The decision wasn't mine," Leila said. "And it wasn't easy. My parents kept things hanging—they wouldn't let me sign the divorce papers, because they had an idea that we might get back together. I had to move back in with them. I had a curfew again, around eleven P.M., depending on my dad's mood. I had to report where I was going. They called me all the time."

Leila was stuck in limbo. Her husband didn't want to be with her. Her parents wouldn't help her find another man because they didn't want her to get divorced. "So I actually waited for them to leave town and then I went to court and got divorced without them knowing," she explained. "They were furious, and they basically grounded me. I was on house arrest for months. Now the guy I was with is getting remarried, and my parents are willing to move on too."

Grounded? You realize I haven't been grounded by my parents since I had a bed frame that was shaped like a bright red race car. I couldn't imagine being under such strict supervision. I would do anything to get out of it—and so would the Qataris.

Qatari women's stories about feeling trapped at home and lacking basic adult freedoms sounded surprisingly similar to the stories we heard from the older American women we interviewed at the senior center in New York City. And, as for the Americans, for Qatari women marriage offered a way out. But the contemporary Qataris also have another option for getting a taste of freedom: digital technology.

With the rise of smartphones, social media, and the Internet, young Qataris are using technology to flout these repressive rules. For instance, socializing with the opposite sex in public is not allowed, so Qataris are using the Internet to organize small private parties in hotel rooms. One of the young women we met told us that hotels are a big part of Qatari culture, because that's where you find bars and restaurants, and these days it's not uncommon to receive a group message that tells people who know one another to meet in a certain room. Once they arrive at the hotel lobby, the cover provided by the females' burkas allows them to wander in anonymously and go wherever they need to go. By blending something old, the burka, and something new, the Internet, Qatari youth have created their own novel way to connect.

Qataris are not getting all the benefits of the Internet. Online dating sites have yet to take off. Instagram is starting to spread, but the culture frowns upon taking photos of all things personal, so instead people shoot and share interesting objects that they see in public life. "We've always been a photophobic society," one of the Qataris we interviewed told us. "People don't want any record of themselves in public. Especially when people are out in clubs or malls. Their families could get very upset." The record of such photos would be potentially scandalous.

Then came Snapchat. The app works on the promise that the image you send will disappear from users' phones after a few seconds. The app has allowed young Qatari singles to take risks in the privacy of their phone world that would be unthinkable otherwise.

"People send all kinds of photos, from explicit to casual," a young woman explained. "The technology is making people more ballsy. It gives people a way to connect." Occasionally things go wrong, of course. Sadly, "guys sometimes get photos of girls [through screengrabs] that would dishonor them and then use that to extract things from them," we learned. But overall, the young people we met argued, social media is giving people in Qatar and in the United Arab Emirates more new ways to meet and express themselves.

In the Emirates, and pretty much everywhere, social media and the Internet are introducing all kinds of new options into social and romantic life. And while it's exciting, sometimes even exhilarating, to have more choices, it's not necessarily making life easier.

CHAPTER 4

CHOICE AND OPTIONS

y parents had an arranged marriage. This always fascinated me. I am perpetually indecisive on even the most mundane decisions, and I couldn't imagine leaving such an important choice to other people. I asked my dad to describe his experience to me.

This was his process.

He told his parents he was ready to get married, so his family arranged meetings with three neighboring families. The first girl, he said, was a "little too tall," and the second girl was a "little too short." Then he met my mom. After he quickly deduced that she was the appropriate height (finally!), they talked for about thirty minutes. They decided it would work. A week later, they were married.

And they still are, thirty-five years later. Happily so—and probably more so than most older white people I know who had nonarranged marriages.

So that's how my dad decided on whom he was going to spend the rest of his life with. Meeting a few people, analyzing their height, and deciding on one after talking to her for thirty minutes.

It was like he went on that MTV dating show *Next* and married my mom.

Let's look at how I do things, maybe with a slightly less important decision. How about the time I had to pick where to eat dinner in Seattle when I was on tour in the spring of 2014?

First I texted four friends who travel and eat out a lot and whose judgment on food I really trust. While I waited for recommendations from them, I checked the website Eater for its "Heat Map," which includes new, tasty restaurants in the city. I also checked the "Eater 38," which is the site's list of the thirty-eight essential Seattle restaurants and standbys. Then I checked reviews on Yelp to see what the consensus was on there. I also checked an online guide to Seattle in *GQ* magazine. I narrowed down my search after consulting all these recommendations and then went on the restaurant websites to check out the menus.

At this point I filtered all these options down by tastiness, distance, and what my tum-tum told me it wanted to eat.

Finally, after much deliberation, I made my selection: Il Corvo. A delicious Italian place that sounded amazing. Fresh-made pasta. They only did three different types a day. I was very excited.

Unfortunately, it was closed. It only served lunch.

By now I had run out of time because I had a show to do, so I ended up making a peanut-butter-and-banana sandwich on the bus.[*]

This kind of rigor goes into a lot of my decision making. Whether it's where I'm eating, where I'm traveling, or, god forbid,

---

[*] **NOTE:** The next day I had Il Corvo for lunch and it was very delicious.

something I'm buying, I feel compelled to do a lot of research to make sure I'm getting *the best*.

At certain times, though, this "I need the best" mentality can be debilitating. I wish I could just eat somewhere that looks good and be happy with my choice. But I can't. The problem is that I know somewhere there is a perfect meal for me and I have to do however much research I can to find it.

That's the thing about the Internet: It doesn't simply help us find the best thing out there; it has helped to produce the idea that there *is* a best thing and, if we search hard enough, we can find it. And in turn there are a whole bunch of inferior things that we'd be foolish to choose.

Here's a quick list of things I can think of that I've spent at least five to ten minutes researching:

- Electric citrus juicer (Waiting on this one to arrive in the mail. Hope I didn't fuck it up. Don't want too much pulp in my juice!)
- Taxidermy (I started off looking for a deer or bear, but I ended up finding a beautiful penguin in Paris. His name is Winston.)
- Which prestigious TV drama to binge-watch next (*The Americans*, *House of Cards*, or *Orphan Black*? The answer: I watched all of them while telling my publisher I was writing this book.)
- Bag for my laptop
- Protective case for my laptop
- Internet-blocking program so I can stop using my laptop so much
- Museums (Gotta peep the exhibits online before I commit to driving all the way out there, right?)
- Coasters (If you dig deep, you can find some dope coasters with dinosaurs on them!)

- Vanilla ice cream (Had to step it up from Breyers, and there's a *lot* of debate in the ice cream fan community— there are fierce debates on those message boards.)

It's not just me, though. I may take things to extremes sometimes, but we live in a culture that tells us we want and deserve the best, and now we have the technology to get it. Think about the overwhelming popularity of websites that are dedicated to our pursuit of the best things available. Yelp for restaurants. TripAdvisor for travel. Rotten Tomatoes and Metacritic for movies.

A few decades ago, if I wanted to research vanilla ice cream, what would I have even done? Cold-approach chubby guys and then slowly steer the convo toward ice cream to get their take? No, thanks.

Nowadays the Internet is my chubby friend. It is the whole world's chubby friend.

THE "BEST" ROMANTIC PARTNER?

If this mentality has so pervaded our decision making, then it stands to reason that it is also affecting our search for a romantic partner, especially if it's going to be long-term. In a sense, it already has. Remember: We are no longer the generation of the "good enough" marriage. We are now looking for our soul mates. And even after we find our soul mates, if we start feeling unhappy, we get divorced.

If you are looking for your soul mate, now is the time to do it. Consider the rich social infrastructure of bars, nightclubs, and restaurants in cities. Add to that the massive online dating industry. Then throw in the fact that people now get married later in life than ever before and spend their twenties in "early adulthood," which is basically dedicated to exploring romantic options and having experiences that previous generations couldn't have imagined.

College, finding our careers, moving out on our own to different cities and parts of the world—in early adulthood we are constantly being introduced to new and exciting pools of romantic options.

Even the advances in the past few years are pretty absurd. You can stand in line at the grocery store and swipe sixty people's faces on Tinder while you wait to buy hamburger buns. That's twenty times more people than my dad met on his marriage journey. (Note: For those wondering, the *best* hamburger buns are Martin's Potato Rolls. Trust me!)

When you think about all this, you have to acknowledge something profound about the current situation: In the history of our species, no group has ever had as many romantic options as we have now.

So, in theory, this should be a great thing. More options is better, right?

Well. It's not that easy.

Barry Schwartz is a professor of psychology at Swarthmore College who has spent much of his career studying the annoying problems that come from having an abundance of options.

Schwartz's research, and a considerable amount of scholarship from other social scientists too, shows that when we have more options, we are actually less satisfied and sometimes even have a harder time making a choice at all.

When I thought back to that sad peanut-butter-and-banana sandwich I had in Seattle, this idea resonated with me.

Schwartz's way of thinking about choice grew popular when he published his book *The Paradox of Choice*. But for decades most people presumed the opposite: The more choices we had, the more likely we would be able to maximize our happiness.

In the 1950s the pioneering scholar Herbert Simon paved the way for people like Schwartz by showing that most of the time people are not all that interested in getting the best possible option. Generally, Simon argued, people and organizations lack the time, knowledge, and inclination to seek out "the best" and are surprisingly content with a suboptimal outcome. Maximizing is just too difficult, so we wind up being "satisficers" (a term that combines "satisfy" and "suffice"). We may fantasize about having the best of something, but usually we are happy to have something that's "good enough."

According to Simon, people can be maximizers and satisficers in different contexts. For example, when it comes to, let's say, tacos, I'm a maximizer. I'll do a rigorous amount of research to make sure I'm getting the best taco I can find, because for me there is a huge difference in the taco experience. A satisficer will just get tacos wherever they see a decent taco stand and call it a day. I hate getting tacos with these people. Enjoy your nasty tacos, losers.

If I'm picking gasoline for my car, though, I'm more of a satisficer. I drive into whatever gas station is close, load the cheapest shit I can to fill my tank, and get the fuck out of there. It sounds pretty mean to my car, but I really don't give a shit and notice no difference in performance for the quality of gas. Sorry, Prius.

Now, I understand that there is a certain kind of "car guy" out there who would find my choice of gasoline as horrifying as I find the choice of suboptimal tacos. To that I say: Stop caring so much about gasoline, you ding-dong! Spend that money on good tacos like a nice, normal person.

What Schwartz suggests, however, is that cultural, economic, and technological changes since the time that Simon wrote have changed the choice-making context. Because of smartphones and the Internet, our options are no longer limited to what's in the physical store where we are standing. We can choose from what's in *every* store, everywhere. We have far more opportunities to become maximizers than we would have had just a few decades ago. And that new context is changing who we are and how we live.

I noticed this in myself with Christmas ornaments. Why would I be anything but a satisficer with Christmas ornaments? It's pretty standard. The balls, the string of lights, etc. Well, do some Internet searching and you find some amazing ornaments. A *Back to the Future* DeLorean, little dinosaurs (!), a funny dude on a motorcycle. I ordered them all!

These types of ornaments wouldn't have even entered my mind before the Internet allowed me to see these other options. Now my standards for Christmas ornaments had gone up, and I wanted the best. Sadly, due to shipping delays, most of the ornaments I ordered arrived in late January, but my tree was extra dope in February.

Besides gasoline, it's damn near impossible for me to think of anything where I won't put in time to find the best. I'm a maximizer in nearly everything. Bottled water? Yup. You buy one of the bozo brands and you get bottled water that's just tap water in a bottle. Potato chips? Ruffles? No, thank you. Pass the Sweet Onion Kettle Chips. Candles? If you only knew how good the candles in my house smell.

It's so easy to find and get the best, so why not?

What happens to people who look for and find the best? Well, it's bad news again. Schwartz, along with two business school professors, did a study of college seniors preparing to enter the workforce.[1] For six months the researchers followed the seniors as they applied for and started new jobs. They then classified the students into maximizers (students who were looking for the best job) and satisficers (students who were looking for a job that met certain minimum requirements and was "good enough").

Here's what they found: On average, the maximizers put much more time and effort into their job search. They did more research, asked more friends for advice, and went on more interviews. In return, the maximizers in the study got better jobs. They received, on average, a 20 percent higher starting salary than the satisficers.

After they started their jobs, though, Schwartz and his colleagues asked the participants how satisfied they were. What they found was amazing. Even though the maximizers had better jobs than the satisficers, by every psychological measure they felt *worse* about them. Overall, maximizers had less job satisfaction and were less certain they'd selected the right job at all. The satisficers, by contrast, were generally more positive about their jobs, the search process, and their lives in general.

The satisficers had jobs that paid less money, but they somehow felt better about them.

Searching for a job when you're in college is hardly a typical situation, so I asked Schwartz if perhaps this study was just capturing something unique. It wasn't.

Schwartz is an encyclopedia of psychological research on choice problems. If asked to give a quote about him for the back of a book cover, I would say, "This motherfucker knows choice."

As he explained it, the maximizers in the job-search experiment were doing what maximizers generally do: Rather than compare actual jobs, with their various pros and cons, in their minds they wound up selecting the features of each particular job and creating a "fantasy job," an ideal that neither they nor, probably, anyone else would ever get.

Johnny Satisficer is sitting around at his dum-dum job, eating his disgusting subpar taco and thinking about hanging his generic Christmas ornaments later on. But he's totally happy about that.

Meanwhile, I've just found out the taco place I researched for hours is closed on Sundays, and even though this year I have my dope Christmas ornaments, I'm worried there's a better Christmas ornament out there that I don't know about yet and am spending my holidays with the Internet instead of my family.

THE PARADOX OF CHOICE IN RELATIONSHIPS

When applied to modern romance, the implications of these ideas on choice are slightly terrifying.

If we are the generation with the greatest set of options, what happens to our decision making? By Schwartz's logic, we are probably looking for "the best" and, in fact, we are looking for our soul mates too. Is this possible to find? "How many people do you need to see before you know you've found the best?" Schwartz asked. "The answer is every damn person there is. How else do you know it's the best? If you're looking for the best, this is a recipe for complete misery."

Complete misery! (Read in a scary Aziz whisper voice.)*

If you are in a big city or on an online dating site, you are flooded with options. Seeing all these options, like the people in the job example, are we now comparing our potential partners not to other potential partners but rather to an idealized person whom no one could measure up to?

And what if you're not looking for your soul mate yet but just want to date someone and commit to a girlfriend or boyfriend? How does our increase in options affect our ability to commit? To be honest, even picking lunch in Seattle was pretty tough.

If we, like the people in the job study, are creating a "fantasy" person full of all our desired qualities, doesn't the vast potential of the Internet and all our other romantic pools give us the illusion that this fantasy person does, in fact, exist? Why settle for anything less?

When we brought these ideas up in focus groups, people responded to these notions immediately. In the city with arguably the most options, New York City, people discussed how it was hard to settle down because every corner you turned revealed more potential opportunities.

I've felt it myself. For much of the past few years, I split my time between New York and L.A. When I first started dating my current girlfriend, when I was in New York, I'd see people everywhere and feel like, *Shit, should I ever take myself out of the single world? There's so many people!* Then I got back to L.A., where instead of walking in streets and subway stations full of potential options, I would be

---

* **NOTE:** If you listen to the audiobook version of this, I'm not going to say, "Read in a scary Aziz whisper voice," or this note, because I'm just going to do the actual voice, and I think it should be pretty terrifying.

alone in my Prius filled with shitty gasoline, listening to a dumb podcast. I couldn't wait to get home and hold my girlfriend.

But the surge of options is not limited to people in New York. As Schwartz told me, "Where did people meet alternatives thirty years ago? It was in the workplace. How many shots did you have? Two or three people, maybe, who you found attractive, who were the right age, or you meet somebody who your friend works with, and your friend fixes you up. So the set of romantic possibilities that you actually confront is going to be pretty small.

"And that, it seems to me, is like feeding in an environment where the food is relatively scarce. You find somebody who seems simpatico. And you do as much as you can to cultivate that person because there may be a long drought after that person. That's what it used to be like. But now," he said, "in principle, the world is available to you."

The world is available to us, but that may be the problem.

The Columbia professor Sheena Iyengar, whom we've met, was one of Barry Schwartz's coauthors on the job-hunting study, and she also knows a shit ton about choice. Through a series of experiments, Iyengar has demonstrated that an excess of options can lead to indecision and paralysis. In one of her most influential studies, she and another researcher set up a table at a luxury food store and offered shoppers samples of jams.[2] Sometimes the researchers offered six types of jam, but other times they offered twenty-four. When they offered twenty-four, people were more likely to stop in and have a taste. But, strangely, they were far less likely to actually *buy* any jam. People who stopped to taste the smaller number of jams were almost *ten times* more likely to buy jam than people who stopped to taste the larger number.

Don't you see what's happening to us? There's just too much jam out there. If you're on a date with a certain jam, you can't even focus, 'cause as soon as you go to the bathroom, three other jams have texted you. You go online, you see more jam there. You put in filters to find the perfect jam. There are iPhone apps that literally tell you if there is jam nearby that wants to get eaten at that particular moment!

LIMITED OPTIONS:

JOURNEYS TO WICHITA AND MONROE

Would forcing us to select from fewer options, as older generations did, actually make us happier? Should we all just follow my dad's example and find someone of an ideal height and lock it down? I decided to get out of New York City and explore some places with limited options. My two stops: Monroe, New York, and Wichita, Kansas.

Monroe is about sixty miles outside of New York City. It's home to approximately eight thousand people. It's a small community where most everyone knows one another. There's nothing but strip malls and second-tier grocery chains you never see elsewhere.

If you click on the "Attractions" tab on TripAdvisor's Monroe page, it brings up a message that says, "I'm sorry, you must have clicked here by mistake. No one could possibly be planning a trip to Monroe to see its 'Attractions.' I have a feeling about why you'd want to go to Monroe. Here, let me redirect you to a suicide-prevention site."

Basically, not much is going on.

Wichita is much, much bigger than Monroe. Its population is about 385,000. A quick Google search will show you many articles saying Wichita is one of the worst dating cities in the country. Granted, there isn't any scientific merit to these surveys, but the conditions used to gain this ranking make sense. There is a low proportion of single people and strikingly few venues where single people can gather, places like bars and coffee shops. The town is quite isolated and doesn't get much traffic from nearby towns.

One thing to note about people who live in places with limited options is that they get married young. Whereas in places like New York City and Los Angeles the average age at first marriage is now around thirty, in smaller towns and less populated states the typical age of first marriage for women is as low as twenty-three (Utah), twenty-four (Idaho and Wyoming), or twenty-five (a whole bunch of states, including Arkansas, Oklahoma, Alaska, and Kansas). Men in these states tend to marry just a year or two later than women.

Could the lack of options be forcing these people to commit earlier and get into serious relationships? Perhaps, but this doesn't always work out either. In recent decades the divorce rate in small towns and rural areas has skyrocketed, catching up to the levels commonly found in large cities.[3] So many of the people I met in Wichita told me about friends of theirs who'd married before the age of twenty-five and then divorced soon after. Heather, for instance, was only twenty-four, but she could already report that "a lot of my sorority pledge sisters got married and divorced within a year." Within a year. Damn.

Let's hope things don't end like that for me and the carefully researched electric juicer I just purchased.

Before our interviews I had romanticized the dating cities with fewer options and envisioned a happier, smaller community where people really got to know one another, and instead of hopping around trying to find the best party, they all just went to their one local spot and had a good time.

I imagined every guy had a girl next door. They grew up together. Got to know each other their whole lives and had a really deep bond. One day they just started boning and then they got married. I'm basing that on nothing, but it seems correct, right?

But talking with so many single people in Monroe and Wichita quickly demolished my fantasy that things were simpler and nicer in small towns. They generally hated their lack of options and the troubles that came with it.

Despite the difference in size, the problems of dating in Wichita and Monroe overlapped quite a bit. All our singles in both cities felt pressure to lock it down and definitely felt like outliers by being single in their late twenties. This stigma of being unmarried in your late twenties was never expressed in any of the focus groups in bigger cities.

A huge problem is that everyone already knows all of his or her options pretty well. Josh, twenty-two, said his main pool of dating options is generally limited to a set of folks that he and his friends have known since high school. "If I see a girl at a bar and I don't know her, within thirty seconds to a minute, I'll find out who that person is by just asking around," he explained. "Her life story. Who she's dated. You basically know everything about the person."

And from talking to these folks, it appears when you don't know someone already, usually the "everything" is not "Oh he/she's the best. Brilliant, hilarious, and without any baggage or complicated past to speak of. Strange you never met!" No, it's probably closer to "Oh, him? He steals tires and then sells them on eBay to buy corn chips."

In Wichita I met Miguel, who had moved from Chicago. He mourned the fact that he never met new people anymore. In Chicago he would meet all kinds of people: friends of friends, coworkers, friends of coworkers, and strangers whom he talked up in bars, in cafés, and even on public transit. In Wichita, though, Miguel said he mainly saw the few folks he worked with and spent his evenings with the same group of friends.

This cliquish mentality was reported in both Monroe and Wichita. One guy in Wichita described it like the gangs in *The Warriors*. People have their cliques and they rarely stray outside of them to meet new people. This leads to a lot of people dating their way through the same small groups, and after they've dated everyone, they're left in a bad spot. Finding new people isn't easy when no one new is coming to town.

Sometimes people think they've discovered a new person, only to discover that they share more connections than they realized. In both Monroe and Wichita we heard stories of people meeting someone they thought was a new person but then going on Facebook and seeing forty-eight mutual friends.

A girl named Heather told me that one time she met a great guy she'd never seen before and was really excited about the possibilities, only to discover that he'd once slept with a girl she totally despised. This soured the whole thing.

The girl? Actress Gwyneth Paltrow.

Not really, but can you imagine?

Soon afterward, a guy named Greg recounted a story of going out with a girl: On the date they started sharing the stories of how they'd lost their virginity. He soon figured out that the guy she'd lost her virginity to was a close friend and coworker of his.

That coworker? Football star O. J. Simpson.

Not really, but again, could you imagine? How weird would that be? To sleep with someone who lost her virginity to O. J. Simpson?! WEIRD!

"It's like a cesspool," said Michelle, a twenty-six-year-old from Monroe. "Everybody has slept with each other."

Also, when you're going out with people in such a limited pool of options, issues I'd never thought of came up.

One: When you go out on a date, you will run into everyone you know, so sometimes singles travel for a little privacy. "I went on a date last night, but it was in a totally different town," a twenty-one-year-old Monroe resident named Emily told us. "I would never go on a first date somewhere in my town because I know all the waiters. I know all the bartenders. I know everybody."

Two: You lose the initial discovery period of getting to know someone because you are so connected and familiar already. This can be an advantage and a disadvantage. The advantage is you get to prescreen everyone through friends of friends, but the downside is that you lose that fun of getting to know someone. In Monroe, Emily reported, "You already know their life story, so you don't even have to go on a first date. You have already prejudged them before you've even gone out."

And finally, if you do go out with someone and it goes badly, you have to deal with the fact that you're going to see that person all the time. Compare this with a place like Los Angeles, where Ryan, twenty-three, said that he could go out with someone and, if it went badly, be fairly confident he would never see them again. "It was almost like they were dead. Like, in a way, you murdered them in your mind," he said. Damn, Ryan, let's chill on the mind murders! But I understand his sentiment.

What about expanding the pool of options with the Internet and other social media? Were any of these singles using online dating? Smartphone swipe apps?

In Wichita people were shier about online dating. There was still a stigma, and with such a small pool there was a worry that people would see your profile and judge you.

Josh, from Monroe, decided to give Tinder a try: "I set [the range] for ten miles at first because I want to make this quick. Two people pop up, and I'm like, no [he swiped his finger to the left], no [he swiped again], and then . . . it was done. And I was like, *Damn, I thought there'd be more. Can I get those back?*"

Others had more luck. Margaret, one of the few Wichita singles who had tried online dating, said, "I think that the online dating thing, what I'm finding is that there's so much choice, I'm like, *Oh my god. All these guys could be great.*"

Another dater also tried Tinder. "I started in Wichita but ran out of people after just a week or so. I then went to Pennsylvania, near Penn State University, for a few days and decided to test it out there. I felt like I could swipe through people for years. This just showed me how limited options were in Kansas."

Of course, not everyone was disappointed by the lack of options in these small towns.

One gentleman in the Monroe group, Jimmy, age twenty-four, had a more positive attitude. Whenever someone expressed frustration with the lack of options in the dating scene, Jimmy would insist that you simply needed to invest time in people to really get to know them.

"If you're patient and you know what you like, you'll find what you like in another person. There's going to be things you don't like about them. They don't clip their toenails. They don't wash their socks."

I told Jimmy I felt like he could find someone with clean socks and trimmed toenails, and maybe the bar was set a bit too low.

"The point is there's always going to be something that bothers you, you know? But it's up to you," he said.

This positive attitude was echoed in Wichita as well. "I feel optimistic about Wichita," said Greg, twenty-six. "I know that there's people here that would surprise me. You have to put a little bit more effort into the relationship. But it's still there somewhere."

"I agree," said James, twenty-four. "There's still gold here. You just have to look hard enough."

It was a beautiful thing to hear. The attitude of these guys was to give people a chance. Instead of sampling a bunch of jams, they had learned how to focus on one jam and make sure they could appreciate it before they walked away.

The more I thought about that approach to dating, the more appealing it became. No matter how many options we have, the real challenge is figuring out how to evaluate them.

After my conversations in Monroe and Wichita, I thought about how popular online dating is in New York City and L.A., how almost everyone in all the focus groups there used the sites, and the stories like the woman who was Tindering on her way to a date to try to find a better date afterward.

Maybe we are turning into the people from the job study, trying to find a crazy, unattainable job.

Maybe we are trying to meet every single person in order to be sure we have the best.

Maybe we have it all wrong.

Maybe we need to have a little more faith in humanity, like our positive buds in Wichita and Monroe.

Look at my dad: He had an arranged marriage and he seems totally happy. I looked into it and this is not uncommon. People in arranged marriages start off lukewarm, but over time they really invest in each other and in general have more successful relationships. They are more invested in the deep commitment to the relationship, rather than being personally invested in finding a soul mate, which can tend to lead to the "Is there something better out there for me?" mentality.

ANALYZING OUR OPTIONS

Even before deciding to go on a date, our ways of analyzing our options are getting brutal. As a woman in L.A. told me about the flood of options she saw as an online dater, "It's fun, but it also opens up this door to be more and more and more picky and analytical. I was exchanging messages with a guy, and he mentioned that he listens to *Kevin & Bean* in the morning. And it was like, okay, you're done."

One radio-show choice had killed any chance of this relationship prospering. Somewhere that guy is sitting alone in his car listening to *Kevin & Bean*, staring at his last conversation with this woman and wondering, *Where did it all go wrong?*

Of course, these kinds of deal breakers end up making their way into the picture even if a contender does make it to a first date. "One of the problems with the first date is that you know very little about a person, so you overweight those few things that you do know," the anthropologist and dating guru Helen Fisher told me. "And suddenly you see they've got brown shoes, and you don't like brown shoes, so they're out. Or they don't like your haircut, so they're out. But if you were to get to know each other more, those particular characteristics might begin to recede in importance, as you also found they had a great sense of humor or they'd love to go fishing in the Caribbean with you."

OUR BORING-ASS DATES

How do we go about analyzing our options? On dates. And most of the time, boring-ass dates. You have coffee, drinks, a meal, go see a movie. We're all trying to find someone who excites us, someone who makes us feel like we've truly made a connection. Can anyone reach that high bar on the typical, boring dates we all go on?

One of the social scientists I consulted for this book is the Stanford sociologist Robb Willer. Willer said that he had several friends who had taken dates to a monster truck rally. If you aren't familiar with monster truck rallies, basically these giant-ass trucks, with names like Skull Crusher and The ReJEWvinator,* ride up huge dirt hills and do crazy jumps. Sometimes they fly over a bunch of smaller cars or even school buses. Even more nuts, sometimes those trucks assemble into a giant robot truck that literally eats cars. Not joking. It's called Truckzilla and it's worth looking into. Frankly, it sounds cool as shit, and I'm looking at tickets for the next one I can attend.

This is a monster truck that goes by the name Grave Digger. If you are a thug or gangster, please note that Grave Digger's graves are dug exclusively for trucks it is in competition with, and it does not dig graves to hide bodies from the authorities.

Anyway, for Willer's friends it started as a plan to do something campy and ironic, since they weren't big car and truck fans so much as curious about this interesting and kind of bizarre subculture. It turned out to be a great date event: fun, funny, exciting, and different. Instead of the usual boring résumé exchange, the couples were placed in an interesting environment and got to really get a sense of their own rapport. Two of the couples he mentioned were still together and happily dating. Sadly, another one of the couples was making out in a small car that was soon run over and crushed by a monster truck named King Krush. Very unfortunate.

In one of our subreddit threads we asked people to tell us about their best first dates, and it was amazing to see how many involved doing things that are easy and accessible but require just a bit more creativity than dinner and a movie.

One gentleman wrote:

> I took her to an alpaca farm after she said she thought they were the cutest thangsss. After sweet talking the farm owner, he let us walk into the barn where all the lil guys overcame their initial trepidation and then surrounded us in the most adorable way possible. After nuzzling with them for an hour, we went to Taco Bell. I burned myself horribly on an apple empanada, but it got her to laugh so I'll chalk that one up as a win. I was 18, the whole date cost about $7, and I got her to smile a bunch, so yeah, that was great.

---

* Okay, I made up ReJEWvinator, but it would be cool if there were a Jewish monster truck scene.

Here's another animal story:

His parents both work in media, and every year he goes to the Westminster Dog Show at Madison Square Garden and finds his way backstage through a combination of walking with a purpose and flashing media credentials his parents help with. Talk about impressing a first date! We then bought wine, which they served out of sippy cups, and made a drinking game out of the dog show. (Take a drink every time a dog jumps when it's not supposed to, and so on.)

Dating aside, I'm definitely playing a Westminster dog show drinking game ASAP. That sounds fun!

And here's one that involved the most typical activity imaginable, but with a simple wardrobe twist that transformed everything:

It was just dinner and drinks . . . I showed up to the restaurant and he was in a FULL beekeeper's suit, just sitting/chillin' at the table waiting for me.

It was THE total ice breaker. I laughed so hard (in an endearing way.) The staff seemed confused and some people at neighboring tables were laughing. One guy, about my age, asked if we were on a reality show. We talked about his bees and honey and the little honey business he's starting up. He even brought little honey samples for me to try! HAHA! (And I did, and it was delicious.) We had a great dinner and great conversation. He told me he was having a great time and asked if I wanted to go for a drink sometime, I said sure. He pulled out his phone and texted me at the table, "hey, are you free for a drink tonight?" I found that so sweet and silly, I texted him back and we totally went for drinks.

Now, granted, I'm not saying that we should all show up on dates wearing beekeeper suits. The dates that are not boring are not all super eccentric things. The common thread is that they weren't just résumé exchanges over a drink or dinner; they were situations in which people could experience interesting things together and learn what it was like to be with someone new.

THE EFFECTS OF NON-BORING-ASS DATES

There is social science that shows that more interesting dates like this can lead to more romantic success. In their famous 1974 study called "Some Evidence for Heightened Sexual Attraction Under Conditions of High Anxiety," Arthur Aron and Donald Dutton sent an attractive woman to the Capilano River in Vancouver, Canada.[4] The river runs through a deep canyon, across which were two bridges. One of the bridges—the control bridge—was very sturdy. It was constructed of heavy cedar, had high handrails, and ran only about ten feet above the water. The second bridge—the experimental bridge—was much, much scarier. It was made of wooden boards attached to wire cables and had a tendency to tilt and sway. The handrails were low, and if you fell, it was a two-hundred-foot drop onto rocks and shallow rapids.

Of the two bridges, only the second was, neurologically speaking, arousing. The researchers had the attractive woman approach men as they crossed each of the bridges. She then told the men she was doing a psychological study and asked if they'd take a brief survey. Afterward, she gave the men her phone number and told them to call if they had any additional questions about the experiment. The researchers predicted that men on the shaky bridge would be more likely to call, as they might mistake their arousal, actually caused by fear, for romantic arousal caused by attraction to the woman. Sure enough, more men on the shaky bridge made the call.

Must have been a bummer for those dudes, though:

> *"Hey, Sharon? It's Dave from the bridge study. I know this may sound weird, but I was wondering . . . would you like to grab a cup of coffee or something sometime?"*

"No, David. Sorry, this isn't Sharon. This is Martin. I'm a lab assistant. This was actually also part of the study. We wanted to see if you'd be more likely to call Sharon if you were on the more precarious bridge, and you were! This is great."

"Oh, okay . . . Do you know how to get in touch with Sharon?"

"No. I don't. This is the decoy number we gave all of you guys. Man, she is something, though, huh? [long pause] All right. Thanks again. Bye, David."

"Bye." [sad]

Aron published another study, titled "Couples' Shared Participation in Novel and Arousing Activities and Experienced Relationship Quality" (damn, dude, shorten the names of your studies!), where he took sixty couples who were doing okay and had them (a) participate in activities that were novel and exciting (e.g., skiing, hiking), (b) participate in activities that were pleasant/mundane (e.g., dinner, movie), or (c) participate in no activity (this was the control group).[5]

The couples that did the novel and exciting activities showed a significantly greater increase in relationship quality.

Now, many of you are probably thinking that this directly contradicts a study cited by Keanu Reeves's character at the end of the film *Speed*. "I've heard relationships based on intense experiences never work," he says. "Okay," replies Sandra Bullock's character, "we'll have to base it on sex, then."

I'm not sure where Keanu's character, Jack Traven, got his information, but if you trust that Aron and his colleagues aren't bullshitting us, it seems like participating in novel and exciting activities increases our attraction to people. Do the dates you usually go on line up more with the mundane/boring or the exciting/novel variety? If I look back on my dating life, I wonder how much better I (and the other person) would have fared if I had done something exciting rather than just get a stupid drink at a local bar.

So maybe for your next date think it through and plan it out perfectly.

Instead of dinner at a nice restaurant, go to dinner at a nice restaurant *but* hire some actors who can do solid German accents to show up and fake an eighties *Die Hard*–style terrorist takeover of the place to create the danger effect seen in the shaky-bridge study. Then, after you narrowly escape, go outside and see that the road you have to take is super hilly and very dangerous. That's when you say, "Maybe we should take my ride." You point her to your car— that's right, the monster truck Grave Digger. After that, you ride home, where you leap over dozens of cars and shoot fire from the sides of your tires.

Your date will be excited in no time.

MORE BORING-ASS DATES?

The quality of dates is one thing, but what about the quantity? When thinking about that question, I recalled a change I made in my own personal dating policy at one point. While I was single in New York, the city of options, I found myself and a lot of my friends just exploring as many options as we could. There were a lot of first dates but not as many third dates. We were consistently choosing to meet as many people as possible instead of investing in a relationship. The goal was seemingly to meet someone who instantly swept us off our feet, but it just didn't seem to be happening. I felt like I was never meeting people I *really*, *really* liked. Was everyone shitty? Or was I shitty? Maybe I was okay, but my dating strategy was shitty? Maybe I was kind of shitty and my dating strategy was kind of shitty too?

At a certain point I decided to change my dating strategy as a personal experiment. I would invest more in people and spend more time with one person. Rather than go on four different dates, what if I went on four dates with one person?

If I went out with a girl, and the date felt like it was a six, normally I wouldn't have gone on a second date. Instead, I would have been on my phone texting other options, trying to find that elusive first date that would be a nine or a ten. With this new mentality, I would go on a second date. What I found is that a first date that was a six was usually an eight on the second date. I knew the person better and we kept building a good rapport together. I discovered things about them that weren't initially apparent. We'd develop more inside jokes and just generally get along better, because we were familiar.

Just casually dating many people had rarely led to this kind of discovery. In the past I had probably been eliminating folks who could have possibly provided fruitful relationships, short- or long-term, if I'd just given them more of a chance. Unlike my enlightened friend in Monroe, I just hadn't had enough faith in people.

Now I felt much better. Instead of trying to date so many different people and getting stressed out with texting games and the like, I was really getting to know a few people and having a better time for it.

After doing the research for this book and spending time reading papers with long-ass titles like "Couples' Shared Participation in Novel and Arousing Activities and Experienced Relationship Quality," I realized the results of my personal experiment were quite predictable.

Initially, we are attracted to people by their physical appearance and traits we can quickly recognize. But the things that really make us fall for someone are their deeper, more unique qualities, and usually those only come out during sustained interactions.

In a fascinating study published in the *Journal of Personality and Social Psychology*, University of Texas psychologists Paul Eastwick and Lucy Hunt show that in most dating contexts, a person's "mate value" matters less than their "unique value."[6]

The authors explain that they define "mate value" as the average first impression of how attractive someone is, based largely on things like looks, charisma, and professional success, and "unique value" as the extent to which someone rates a specific person above or below that average first impression. For instance, they explain the unique value of a man they call Neil like this: "Even if Neil is a 6 on average, certain women may vary in their impressions of him. Amanda fails to be charmed by his obscure literary references and thinks he is a 3. Yet Eileen thinks he is a 9; she finds his allusions captivating." In most cases, people's unique traits and values are difficult to recognize, let alone appreciate, in an initial encounter. There are just too many things going through our minds to fully take in what makes that other person special and interesting. People's deeper and more distinctive traits emerge gradually through shared experiences and intimate encounters, the kinds we sometimes have when we give relationships a chance to develop but not when we serially first date.

No wonder that, as Eastwick and Hunt report, "Most people do not initiate romantic relationships immediately after forming first impressions of each other" but instead do it gradually, when an unexpected or perhaps long-awaited spark transforms a friendship or acquaintance into something sexual and serious. According to one recent study, only 6 percent of adolescents in romantic relationships say that they got together soon after meeting.[7] The number is surely much higher among adults, especially now that online dating is so prevalent, but even people who meet through Tinder or OkCupid are much more likely to turn a random first date into a meaningful relationship if they follow the advice of our Monroe friend Jimmy: There's something uniquely valuable in everyone, and we'll be much happier and better off if we invest the time and energy it takes to find it.

But seriously, if the person doesn't clip their toenails or wear clean socks, look elsewhere.

There are plenty of options.

CHAPTER 5

INTERNATIONAL INVESTIGATIONS OF LOVE

hen I decided to write this book, one of the things I really wanted to explore was how the different issues in modern romance manifested themselves in other countries. My interest in this started one night when I was doing stand-up in a small club in New York. I was talking about texting and I asked for a volunteer who'd met someone recently and had been texting back and forth with them. I read the back-and-forth messages of one gentleman and made jokes about how we were all dealing with some version of this nonsense.

I quickly noticed that one woman seemed very puzzled. I asked her why she looked so bewildered, and she explained that this was something that just didn't happen in France, where she was from. This kind of back-and-forth simply didn't exist, she claimed.

I asked her, "Okay, well, what would a guy in France text you, if you met him at a bar?"

She said, "He would write . . . 'Fancy a fuck?'"

And I said, "Whoa. What would you write back?"

She said, "I would write yes or no depending on whether I fancied one or not."

I was stunned—that kind of makes so much more sense, right?

Internationally, there's a huge variety of dating cultures that have their own quirks and dilemmas. Our interviews in Doha were interesting and made me excited about the possibilities of researching dating in other cultures. Obviously, we couldn't study all of them, so Eric and I had to be very selective about where we went. After a lot of debate, the places we landed on were Paris, Tokyo, and Buenos Aires.

The reason for Paris is obvious. It's the city of love, blah, blah, blah. Also, relationships in Paris are similar to what we'd read about in other European countries, where dating as we know it in America is not really part of the culture. People hang out in groups of friends, and if they want to start a relationship with someone, they just do it. They are also a bit more casual about sex and have a different attitude toward infidelity, as we will see in the next chapter.

Tokyo was the next place I suggested. This was done less in the interest of the book and more in the interest of me enjoying some delicious ramen. However, after discussing the idea with Eric, we realized Tokyo was a great place to go because Japan is going through a crisis of sorts. Marriage and birthrates are in a huge decline, many young people are showing a lack of interest in romance, and also, again, I love ramen. It was clear Tokyo was a great choice, both for the book—and our tummies.*

While Japan is experiencing a decline in sexual interest, we also wanted to see the other extreme, so we went to explore the romantically aggressive culture of Buenos Aires. There's a good reason that Buenos Aires is often called the world's best city for dating.[1] PDA is rampant. People are dancing in sweaty clubs until eight or nine in the morning. Sex is everywhere you look.

So there's our itinerary. While we couldn't go everywhere,

---

* Aziz Ansari, "I Ate a Lot of Fucking Delicious Food in Tokyo," 2014, unpublished.

these places all provided a uniquely interesting take on modern romance around the world. Okay, let's go. First stop, Tokyo!

TOKYO:

THE LAND OF HERBIVORES AND TENGAS

My initial thought was that Tokyo would have a highly active dating scene. It is a booming metropolis, throbbing with life and energy, arguably even more so than New York. You have everything—the tastiest restaurants, the coolest stores, and the weirdest stuff that you can't find anywhere else in the world. An entire video arcade filled with nothing but photo booths? Yep. A vending machine that grows and sells fresh heads of lettuce? Yep. A restaurant with a dinner show where bikini-clad dancers ride in on huge robots and tanks? What else do you think goes down at the Robot Restaurant in Shinjuku?

THE ROBOT RESTAURANT IN TOKYO. SERIOUSLY. This is a real place. What the hell is happening in this picture? It appears that three Asian women are dancing on three giant Asian women *robots*. Too meta? Those people in the photo sure do seem entertained.

Plus, I'd heard rumors of "love hotels"—which are what they sound like: hotels specifically built for hooking up. But, of course, this being Japan, they sometimes have really amazing decor—there's even a *Jurassic Park*–themed one. Seriously, this exists. I am not joking.

NOTE: There were no photos available online so this is an artist rendition commissioned by me for the book. I hope the rooms are this cool and you get picked up from the airport in a tricked-out *JP* Ford Explorer from the nineties.

At night the neon signs turn the city into an adult adventure land: The streets, bars, and clubs are raucous and busy. Something fun and interesting is lurking in every nook and cranny. You can wander onto the third floor of an office building and find an amazing high-end cocktail bar behind one door, a record store behind another, and past the hallway a bizarre nightclub filled with Japanese men wearing Bill Clinton masks giving back rubs to dogs.

Walk through many of the big neighborhoods often enough,

and you are bound to stumble upon a little hidden corner with sex stores and the aforementioned love hotels—which are actually nice, clean hotels that rent by the hour and are used by couples to pop in and do their thing. Upon first glance, the city closest to Tokyo in terms of dating infrastructure would seem to be New York.

I also assumed the tech-obsessed Japanese were probably on the next level of dating websites and apps. These people invented emojis, for god's sake! They were texting and they thought, *Yeah, this is great, but it'd be* really *dope to be able to send a small image of a koala bear too.** Who knew what their texting back-and-forth would look like? I couldn't wait to do our interviews and see what kind of stuff was going on.

It all seemed ideal for the perfect dating city, but I could not have been more off. All my assumptions were wrong. Start doing even the slightest research into Japan and love, and you'll quickly find sensational articles describing a full-blown crisis. According to demographers, journalists, and even the Japanese government, it's a hot potato.

Sorry, I needed another word for "crisis," and when I entered the word "crisis" into Thesaurus.com, it suggested "hot potato" as a synonym. I could not write this book without letting you know that Thesaurus.com lists "hot potato" as a synonym for "crisis."

"Hey, did you hear about what's happening with Israel and Palestine? It's becoming a real hot potato."

Anyway, back to Japan. You read these articles and they are just filled with panicky language: "No one's fucking!" "No one's getting married and having kids!" "Young people aren't interested in boning anymore!!"

Those aren't direct quotes, but that's pretty much what you read.

It sounded alarmist to me. Young people are just *not interested*

---

* If the Japanese dude who decides what emojis go on the iPhone is reading this, can I make a plea for a turbanless brown-guy emoji? Would be very useful for me. No offense to the turban-dude emoji or any real-life dudes who wear turbans, who are surely grateful for that emoji's existence.

in sex?! How could that be possible? Let's bust out some scary-ass statistics.

- In 2013 a whopping 45 percent of women aged sixteen to twenty-four "were not interested in or despised sexual contact," and more than a quarter of men felt the same way.[2] I've always wanted to describe a statistic as "whopping," and I think we can concur, this is indeed whopping. Seriously, read those numbers one more time. *Despised* sexual contact.

- The number of men and women between eighteen and thirty-four who are not involved in any romantic relationship with the opposite sex has risen since 1987, from 49 percent to 61 percent for men and from 39 percent to 49 percent for women.[3]

- A whopping one third of Japanese people under thirty have never dated,[4] and in a survey of those between thirty-five and thirty-nine, more than a quarter reported that they'd never had sex.[5] (Okay, that was the last "whopping" I'll use.)

- Almost half of Japanese men and one third of women in their early thirties were still single as of 2005.[6]

- In 2012, 41.3 percent of married couples had not had sex in the past month, the highest percentage since the figures became available in 2004. There was a steady rise over the previous ten years, from 31.9 percent in 2004.[7]

- Japan's birthrate ranks 222nd out of 224 countries.[8] A report compiled with the government's cooperation two years ago warned that by 2060 the number of Japanese will have fallen from 127 million to about 87 million, of whom almost 40 percent will be sixty-five or older.[9]

This last stat is particularly alarming. The Japanese are legitimately worried about running out of Japanese people. No more ramen?? No more sushi?? No more high-end Japanese whiskeys??! You see how this is really a hot potato.

The situation has reached a point where even the government has seen the need to step in. Since 2010 the Japanese state has paid parents a monthly allowance of between $100 and $150 per child, to take some of the financial burden out of child raising. But before you can have a kid, you need to find someone to love and marry, right? Japanese prime minister Shinzo Abe allocated $25 million in the 2014 fiscal budget for programs designed to get people to pair off and have babies, including government-funded dating services. An official survey conducted in 2010 showed that 66 percent of all prefecture governments and 33 percent of city/ward/town/village governments were implementing some form of marriage support. Even more do so today.[10]

We asked the Japanese American sociologist Kumiko Endo, who studies the new "marriage support" programs that the Japanese government has established, to give us some examples. In Niigata Prefecture, she said, "marriage support events include tours (e.g., bus tour to nearby shrine), cultural events (e.g., cooking classes), sports events, and seminars (coaching sessions for men while fishing)." Saga Prefecture has set up a Department of Connection that fixes up singles who want to meet new people, and both Shizuoka and Akita prefectures now provide Internet communication services for singles, whom they inform about various parties and events for singles, some of which are supported by the government. Finally, Fukui Prefecture recently launched an online dating site called the Fukui Marriage-Hunting Café, and couples who meet on the site and marry receive cash and gifts.

The government is sending Japanese couples wedding presents? What on earth is happening there?

Learning about this crisis—and remembering how much I was fiending for authentic ramen and all the other delights of Tokyo—it was clear I needed to hit the ground myself to find out what was happening.

Contemplating the sexual crisis in Japan while wearing a kimono in Kyoto...

THE HISTORY AND CURRENT
STATE OF MARRIAGE IN TOKYO

Before getting into the current situation in Japan, it's important to understand that Japan has also seen a large shift in how adults view and pursue the institution of marriage. My sociologist friend Kumiko explained to me that up until World War II, arranged marriages were more common than any other form of matrimony. Even in the 1960s approximately 70 percent of all marriages were set up by families. In the 1970s the workplace became a prime site for finding a mate. Large companies would organize social gatherings, and cultural norms dictated that most women would quit their posts after they married and started a family.[11]

Today, however, that system is a relic. Arranged marriages are uncommon (down to 6.2 percent as of 2005).[12] Like the United States, Japan has adopted a more individualistic culture based on personal choice and happiness. The Japanese economy has been sluggish since the 1990s, and the modern workplace has become a site for stressful competition. It's no longer acting as a de facto singles bar for professionals.

So, if the old system is now broken, what has replaced it?

HERBIVORE MEN

After arriving in Tokyo, I knew I had a limited amount of time to do what I needed to get done: visit the five best ramen shops in the city. After eating my fill of ramen, it was time to get down to business: visiting that robot restaurant, because, man, who could pass up an opportunity like that? Then duty called: I also had to visit that Bill Clinton mask/dog back-rub place. It was awesome. Then a quick nap, and finally I started doing some research for this book.

First we organized some focus groups to discuss dating in Tokyo. Dozens of young adults in their midtwenties and early thirties spoke to us (or, in most cases, spoke to Kumiko, who translated their Japanese).

Going in, one of the notions I was most curious about was the "herbivore man." This is a term that has become ubiquitous in Japan over the past few years to describe Japanese men who are very shy and passive and show no interest in sex and romantic relationships. Surveys suggest that about 60 percent of male singles in their twenties and thirties in Japan identify themselves as herbivores.[13]

In the first group we held, one of the first to arrive was Akira. A good-looking young Japanese dude in a really sharp suit, Akira, thirty, looked like he was probably doing well for himself. He seemed like a successful, confident young man. This guy wasn't an herbivore, right?

We did interviews and focus groups with singles on four continents, and in most of them we broke the ice by asking people to tell us how many people they'd asked out or flirted with on their smartphones in the past few weeks. When we asked Akira that question, he just shrugged. Pretty much all the guys shrugged.

Akira said he was working now and too busy to have a girlfriend. Several others we interviewed echoed this sentiment. "I just got a job in construction and there aren't many girls my age, so there's nowhere for me to meet them," said Daisaku, twenty-one.

His friend Hiro nodded. "I'm busy with work and it's not very urgent. I have to deal with work first, and that takes up my weekdays. I play video games when I go home. On the weekends I hang out with Daisaku and we go out drinking."

"Can't you meet women when you're out drinking?" we asked. "No." Hiro blushed. "It's *charai* [kinda sleazy, in a playboy way] to try to pick up a woman you don't know. But also, if a girl said yes to me, I wouldn't want to go out with her. I don't like girls who would want to be with a guy openly like that. Looking, smiling, winking. I want a girl who's *seiso* [pure]."

"Pure?" Eric asked. "Like, a virgin?"

They laughed uncomfortably. "Not exactly," Daisaku said. "But it has to be someone with the right background, with the right family. If it was someone I just met somewhere, I'd be too embarrassed to tell my parents. They'd be disappointed."

"How did your parents meet?"

"At work," Daisaku said.

"An arranged marriage," Hiro offered.

"This situation seems really difficult," Eric said. "You want a girlfriend, and the women we meet want boyfriends, but no one knows how to make it happen. Do you feel like it's a problem?"

"I don't really think anything about it," Hiro replied matter-of-factly. "It's not a problem and it's not *not* a problem. It is what it is. Because everyone's like that here. I don't even think about it because it's the norm."

Akira said that he would only ask a woman out if it was clear without any doubt that she was interested. When asked why, he said, "She could reject me," and every other guy in the room literally groaned in support. It was clear that the fear of rejection was huge, and much more so than I'd seen among men in America.

I asked the women about the herbivore men and whether they wished guys would take more initiative. It was a resounding yes. These women yearned for the men in Japan to step up and just ask them out. From their perspective, the men's extreme need for assurance and comfort from the women was irritating. Their frustration was palpable. You could see that they were indeed becoming what the press called "the carnivorous woman." Some of these women described how they would now take the role more commonly played by Western men and approach Japanese men and ask for phone numbers. *Wow, how* charai *of them*, I thought, remembering the word I had learned three minutes earlier.

However, they said it wasn't always easy. They described how even if they did meet a guy and engage with him, it was like an even more nightmarish version of the American guy who just keeps texting and doesn't ask a girl out. The texts would keep going and going.

"He will just be so shy and he just needs to feel *soooo* comfortable with you," one woman said. "Unless men are really confident that the woman likes them back, they can't make the move," another lamented. As one man described it, "They're waiting for the woman to be totally embracing of them before they make any kind of move." The fear of rejection even manifests itself in the phone world.

I asked for an example of a back-and-forth text. A woman told me about one guy who had texted with her. The way she described it was that he was never really flirtatious. It would be very direct, impersonal things about movies he'd seen or his pets. One night he texted her and said, "I have this big head of cabbage. How should I cook this?"

I asked if this was maybe a very, very lame, roundabout dinner-date invitation—to ask her to come over for cabbage. "No, he was really asking me how to cook cabbage," she moaned.

The same guy e-mailed her a few days later with this gem, and again, this is not a joke: "I recently got my futon wet and put it outside to dry, but it got caught in the rain, so now it's wet again."

Wow. Quite a suspenseful tale.

What begat the rise of the herbivore man? There seems to be an almost perfect stew of social and economic ingredients that has cultivated this stereotype. Speaking of stew, while in Tokyo, I went to an *izakaya* called Kanemasu that had an amazing short-rib dish, one of the most succulent—okay, sorry, getting off track again.

Social scientists argue that the herbivore man emerged with the decline of the Japanese economy. In Japanese culture, as in many cultures, men's confidence and sense of self is tied to their professional success. Everyone we talked to in Tokyo seemed to recall the booming eighties as a different era for romance, with salarymen, flush with cash, who could confidently approach a pretty woman and ask for her number without fear. This too is probably an exaggeration, but a telling one. With career jobs now gone, it's not only harder for men to meet a partner but also harder for them to support her financially. So it makes sense that insecurity might leave men feeling more scared of rejection.

Many single men also now live at home with their parents well into their twenties and thirties. The women in the focus groups felt that this situation only worsened a mothering complex already prevalent in Japanese culture. A man who lives at home can expect his mother to cook, clean, and do his laundry for him. The theory goes that guys are so used to being taken care of, they lose their manly instincts.

On top of that, men in Japan are probably not as comfortable around women in general because they didn't grow up spending as much time with them. Much of the educational system in Japan is single sex, and there's also sex segregation in co-ed schools. Physically, socially, and to some extent psychologically, boys and girls grow up on separate tracks until at least high school and often until college. Many people don't date until their twenties. Nearly 50 percent of the single guys in Japan don't even have friends of the opposite sex.[14]

When you combine the economic decline, men's infantilization by their mothers, their fear of rejection, and the lack of contact with the opposite sex throughout their lives, the herbivore man starts making a lot of sense.

Now, I don't want to paint the picture that every Japanese guy is a super shy dude who has no interest in sex. There definitely seems to be a lot of that, but there are also plenty of Japanese men who are nonherbivores, who have dating lives that resemble those of the typical omnivorous American man. In our focus groups we met Koji, a young bartender, who seemed to be the most omnivorous of the bunch.

The thing is Koji wasn't some super stud or anything. Compared with the other guys, he was a little shorter. He wasn't dressed in a super sharp suit like Akira and the other professionals. He wore a gray vest and a brown fedora. What he had was a casualness and forthrightness to him that, though fairly normal by American standards, really stood out in Japan. Those in the focus groups who knew Koji spoke of his seemingly mythical love life in hushed tones and were in awe of his confidence. Again, Koji was not some Asian Ryan Gosling figure; he just seemed to be comfortable with himself and not particularly shy. Like most fedora wearers, he had a lot of inexplicable confidence.

He and another friend of his wanted to make sure we knew there were some Japanese men who weren't herbivores and that maybe the media was blowing this out of proportion.

"Can I just speak for real? If I don't have a girlfriend, I can go find someone to have sex with. I think those guys who say they're not having sex for a long time? I think they're bullshitting. They just don't talk about it," he said.

"If you're single in New York, you get on your phone and text people late at night and try to meet up with someone. There's a whole culture of a 'booty call.' What's the process here?" I asked.

"My friends and I do the same thing. I call all of them and no one will pick up."

"Well, the same thing happens in New York sometimes too," I said.

At the same time Japanese men are undergoing a transformation, a new kind of Japanese woman is emerging as well. Historically, educated women would get office jobs after university, meet men there, and then leave the job to become wives and mothers. Now women are pushing back, and more educated women want to work. They learn skills, like speaking English. They travel the world. They pursue careers of their own. These professional women don't want to conform to the old norm of being the submissive woman who abandons her own career ambitions to be a housewife. However, being educated, speaking English, and having a good job seem to intimidate some men, with some women even describing their success as a "turnoff" for their would-be suitors. "Men here, they have high pride," one woman told me. "They don't want a successful woman who makes a pretty good salary. The minute they find out I'm bilingual, they're like, *Oh no . . .* "

By the end of our focus groups, it was pretty clear that Japanese men and women are on different trajectories. Women are still far from equal, but they are beginning to establish themselves in the Japanese economy and they are gaining all sorts of rights and privileges in the culture as well.

Men are struggling to hold on to their status. Whether in the workplace or in the family, they've fallen from the heights of previous generations and are having trouble figuring out what to do next.

Some are clearly so confused that they have taken to wearing fedoras.

A difficult period indeed.

A RICE COOKER AS A PROFILE PIC: WELCOME TO ONLINE DATING IN JAPAN

Given the state of Japanese dating culture, you would think online dating would be a perfect solution. Sending a message to a potential mate on a website is much less intimidating than asking someone for their number in a bar, right? What better way to mitigate your fear of rejection? The Japanese are also notorious early adopters. If one-third of U.S. marriages are now formed by people meeting online, you'd guess that even more Japanese marriages begin digitally. But although the rise of online dating could be very helpful in Japan, alas, it is not to be. The concerns about being perceived as *charai* (sleazy playboy type) extend into the social media world as well, and some of the necessary facets of online dating are frowned upon in Japan.

Consider profile pictures. Dating online requires self-promotion. A dating profile is a kind of advertisement, a way of marketing yourself to prospective partners. But this attitude doesn't really fit well with Japanese culture.

In Japan, posting any pictures of yourself, especially selfie-style photos, comes off as really douchey. Kana, an attractive, single twenty-nine-year-old, remarked: "All the foreign people who use selfies on their profile pic? The Japanese feel like that's so narcissistic." In her experience, pictures on dating sites would generally include more than two people. Sometimes the person wouldn't be in the photo at all.

I asked what they would post instead.

"A lot of Japanese use their cats," she said.

"They're not in the photo with the cat?" I asked.

"Nope. Just the cat. Or their rice cooker."

Let's do this, ladies . . .

"I once saw a guy posted a funny street sign," volunteered Rinko, thirty-three. "I felt like I could tell a lot about the guy from looking at it."

This kind of made sense to me. If you post a photo of something interesting, maybe it gives some sense of your personality? I showed a photo of a bowl of ramen I had taken earlier in the day and asked what she thought of that as a profile picture.

She just shook her head.

OH, I GUESS I CAN'T HOLD A CANDLE TO THAT STREET SIGN DUDE, HUH?

MACHIKON AND GOKON

So online dating is not taking off. What else? There is a traditional group date called a *gokon*, where a guy invites a few guy friends and a girl invites a few girlfriends, and the group goes out for dinner and drinks. But even at these gatherings women report that most guys are too shy to ask for their numbers. For an exchange to happen, the host would have to announce, "Okay, everyone, let's all exchange numbers." I actually participated in a *gokon* in Tokyo once as part of a travel piece for *GQ* magazine. Unfortunately, the women they selected did not speak English and I was armed only with the Japanese phrase for "Do you like pizza?" By the end of the evening, filled with delicious yakitori (grilled meats) and beer, most of the women thought I had a story arc as "Indian Chandler" on *Friends*, and I could confirm that two of them did indeed enjoy pizza.

For those men we met who said that they were too busy with work at the moment, *gokon* seemed like the most comfortable option for them to explore meeting women. But this presents challenges for men who don't have any female friends to organize a *gokon* with.

A newer trend for meeting people is *machikon*. In *machikon* men and women pay to participate in a huge, roving party filled with hundreds and hundreds of singles who wander through a neighborhood's bars and restaurants. At some *machikon* most people go solo; at others partygoers begin the event by sharing a meal with the one or two friends who come with them, as well as with a few strangers of the opposite sex; after that the organizers move people around, musical chairs style, and participants wind up mingling with lots of other singles. What's amazing about these events is that both the private sector and the Japanese government are now subsidizing the establishments that host them. According to Kumiko Endo, the sociologist who showed us around Tokyo and studies *machikon* for her dissertation, bar and restaurant owners get twenty-five to thirty-five dollars per seat that they give to the parties.

In all the research I've done on dating, I haven't heard of another place where the state is throwing money into the singles scene, effectively buying a few drinks for every young person willing to go on the prowl. Thus far the public investment in these events is modest, but it's a signal of how seriously the government views the marriage drought and of how much it will take to reinvigorate the matchmaking market.

THE RELATIONSHIP REPLACEMENT INDUSTRY: EGGS, PROSTITUTES, AND SOAPLAND

For a lot of the herbivore-esque guys we spoke to, it still seems like it would take quite a lot to overcome the hurdle of shyness to properly engage in these group dating activities. There were also women who weren't willing to settle for the restrictions that come with traditional marriages and families. Like women in the United States and Europe and an ever-growing number of other places, they want to have rewarding work lives and careers too. The problem in Tokyo is that people who aren't interested in or capable of entering a traditional romantic relationship don't have the alternative of an active casual dating culture like you may find in New York.

Lucky for them, Japan has not only a huge sex industry but also what some have dubbed a "relationship replacement" industry that provides everything from "cuddling cafés" (where clients pay for things like pats on the head, eye contact, and ear cleaning with a Q-tip) to full-on sex robots that are built to last for years.[15] I never thought I would say this, but of those two things, having sex with a robot seems like the more reasonable option.

The most popular kind of establishment in the relationship replacement industry is the hostess club, which is basically the latest variation of a long-standing Japanese business tradition where men go to a nice bar-type atmosphere and pay women to provide intimate personal service in a romantic but not explicitly sexual way. The women are like modern-day geishas: They light the men's cigarettes, serve them drinks, and listen attentively to their conversation, doing more or less what an ideal Japanese wife or girlfriend would do.[16] Lots of men stop by these clubs after work, either alone or in groups. To be clear, though, this doesn't lead to any sexual contact. No nudity or sex happens at hostess clubs. It's basically like prostitution, but they just hang out with you. I was very confused.

Al, a young expat originally from Baltimore, tried to explain the motivations. "It's like, *I'm lonely, I'm scared of people*," he said. "*I need to vent or just have a drink with someone who will listen to me and not judge me.* They're paying for the security. They're paying not to be rejected."

Women also go to host clubs, which provide the same service: outgoing men who converse and have drinks with them. Again, this does not lead to sex; it's purely for companionship. These women are basically paying to hang out with nonherbivore men for a while.

But what about sex? Prostitution of the penis-into-vagina sort is illegal in Japan, and while there is a black market, the Japanese have also developed some creative legal alternatives. One that is quite popular and came up several times in our focus groups was Soapland, where a guy lies on a waterproof mattress and a woman covers them both in soapy water and slides all over him. You can pay extra for additional services like oral sex or a hand job. Soapland, which is just a ridiculous word, does not carry a huge stigma. (On a side note, I would give pretty much anything to have been in the room where the guy said, "I've got it! We'll call it . . . Soapland!")

Some men told us if they went out in groups of friends, it wouldn't be absurd for one dude to be like, "Okay, I'll catch you guys later. I'm going to hit Soapland real quick." Again, it seems that, beyond the sexual pleasure, Soapland is providing a safe outlet for rejection-free romantic exploits. Why go to a nightclub to try to find casual sex and risk rejection when you can go to Soapland and be 100 percent sure a woman will place you on a waterproof mattress, cover you in lubricant, and then slide up and down your oiled-up body?

And of course there are straight-up illegal prostitutes. When we pushed this topic, we were surprised at how prostitution seemed much more common and accepted than in the United States. One participant in a focus group was a teaching assistant at a local university, and he told us that his college students often talked to him about their trips to visit prostitutes. It didn't seem to be a big deal to him. The students might as well have said that they went to get ice cream after class.

Now, admittedly, there are no perfect data on how often men go to prostitutes in different countries. But the best statistics we could find showed that roughly 37 percent of Japanese men have paid for sex at least once, compared with 16 percent of French men, 14 percent of American men, and 7 to 9 percent of British men.[17]

For those men in Tokyo who aren't into Soapland and brothels, there are sex shops everywhere, and they cater to every fetish imaginable, from French maids to girls in school uniforms to anime characters.

There's also a booming market in sex toys, which are sold with no stigma attached. One of the most popular recent inventions is the Tenga. What's a Tenga? If you go on the company's website, you'll see what might be the greatest slogan of any corporation ever: "The future of masturbation . . . is NOW."

The company specializes in masturbation devices like the egg, a single-use silicone egg that men fill with lubricant and masturbate inside. When you're done, you seal it up and throw it away.

Fun fact: One of the directors of the Tenga Corporation, Masanobu Sato, holds the world record for the longest time spent masturbating: nine hours and fifty-eight minutes. That means he could have watched all three *Lord of the Rings* films in a row while masturbating, and as the credits of *The Return of the King* finished rolling, he'd still have had *forty-one* minutes of masturbating to do.

This also made me realize: The only thing sadder than holding the record for longest masturbation is realizing you lost it to someone else.

"Sorry, man, he just jerked off for a few minutes longer. Better luck next year."

None of the news articles that described the lack of interest in sex in Japan really delved into this whole world of strange sexual alternatives, and when you learn about it, it does kind of explain the alleged "lack of interest" in sex. The herbivore sector is interested in sexual pleasure but just not interested in achieving it through traditional routes. In their eyes, it seems, if you're so mortified at the thought of rejection by a woman, why not just jerk off in an egg and call it a day?

At this point you are probably wondering: What was my top meal in Tokyo? Well, it's tough to say. I really enjoyed Sushisho Masa, a high-end sushi restaurant. However, I also really enjoyed the tasty tempura I had from the working-class vendors in Tsukiji Market. And of course there was the ramen.

To be honest, the food scene in Tokyo was way easier to understand than the singles scene. It's hard to figure out why sex and relationships have changed so dramatically, so quickly, and why so many people have turned inward—staying home alone, playing video games, or hanging out in cat cafés—rather than reaching out for one another.

On my last night in Tokyo, I decided to keep an open mind and buy a Tenga. Every stage of it was a bummer. I went into a convenience store and had to say, "Do you guys have Tengas?" The lady gave me a sad look and pointed me in the right direction. As I paid, I smiled and said, "Research for a book project!" It didn't seem to convince her that I was cool. Instead, she's probably convinced I'm doing some very bizarre book called *Masturbating Across the Globe: One Man's Journey to Find Himself*.

When I got back to my hotel room, I opened the thing up and

gave it a go. I was kind of excited to see if it really was masturbation taken to the next level. Masturbation at the current level feels pretty good, so maybe this wouldn't be bad? Again, no. The experience of using an egg-shaped masturbation device was both odd and uncomfortable. The thing you put your thing into was cold and weird. It felt like I was masturbating with a thick, cold condom on, and I didn't understand the appeal.

But in a symbolic sense the Tenga seemed to be an alternative to casual dating and sex. It was a way to avoid putting yourself out there and having an actual experience with another person. Say what you will about casual sex and the substance and quality of that experience, but the more casual encounters I had in my own periods of singledom helped me grow as a person and brought me to a place to be ready to have a serious relationship. It also made me realize the true value of that sort of connection and better understand the advantages and disadvantages of a serious relationship. Dating has its downsides, but it can be a lot of fun. Even when it isn't, when you're meeting other people there are always experiences that you remember and learn from.

No matter what happens, you get a lot more out of it than you do from blowing your load into a cold silicone egg.

BUENOS AIRES:

THE LAND OF *CHONGOS* AND *HISTÉRICO*

After our trip to Japan, I got interested in seeing what happens in a dating culture where men are more omnivorous. Eric and I searched around for the world's particularly aggressive dating scenes and decided a good place to go was Argentina. If Tokyo is the capital of the "herbivore man," then Buenos Aires must surely be the capital of the "rib eye–eating maniac."

Whether or not they deserve it, Argentine men have a global reputation for their hot-blooded, romantic passion, which often bleeds over into something pathological and scary. In 2014 a survey conducted by a nonprofit organization called Stop Street Harassment revealed that more than 60 percent of women in Buenos Aires had experienced intimidation from men who catcalled them.[18] To a lot of men in Buenos Aires, women's concern came as a surprise. When asked about the survey, Buenos Aires's mayor, Mauricio Macri, dismissed it as inaccurate and proceeded to explain why women couldn't possibly have a problem with being shouted at by strangers.

"All women like to be told compliments," he said. "Those who say they're offended are lying. Even though you'll say something rude, like 'What a cute ass you have' . . . it's all good. There is nothing more beautiful than the beauty of women, right? It's almost the reason that men breathe."

To be clear, this is *the mayor*. Upon reading this quote, I investigated, and I can confirm that at the time of this interview he was *not* wearing one of those helmets that holds beers and has straws that go in your mouth.

As you can imagine, these statements didn't go over well. Hundreds of women—including the mayor's own daughter—condemned Macri's remarks, forcing him to publicly apologize.

Among men in Buenos Aires, however, Macri's opinion probably isn't uncommon. In Argentina, where Eric and Shelly, a sociology graduate student, spent a month doing interviews and leading focus groups, hitting on women with abandon is deeply ingrained in the city's cultural traditions. Men are *expected* to be pursuers in what Argentines casually refer to as "the hunt," and the primary arena for such pursuits is the street.

In Buenos Aires the streets are filled with sexual energy: There is sensual tango dancing, *chamuyo* (flirtatious chitchat) and various sexual quips are heard left and right, and people make out publicly in parks, restaurants, and on buses.

In Japan a woman would be surprised to be directly approached, but in Buenos Aires the women we interviewed said that being the object of unsolicited male attention was a daily occurrence, and many men were reluctant to take no for an answer. "Guys here, they don't care if you turn them down or deny them," one woman told us. "They just keep talking to you."

Talking is the least of it. Many of the women we interviewed told us that Argentine men can be uninhibited in their pursuit of sex. In one memorable focus group, a woman named Tamara reported that men she'd just met had kissed her, touched her leg, and tried to slip their hands up her skirt despite her clear lack of interest in them, and that when she told them to stop, they responded as if frustrated and asked, "Why?" As she told the story, every other woman in the group nodded to show their familiarity with this situation. "That's normal," one explained.

"When I go out and I get approached by a guy, no matter if I say I'm in a relationship and if I'm not interested, they still keep on going," said another. "They'll say, 'Is your boyfriend here right now? Do you live with your boyfriend?' It's, like, totally acceptable. As much as you say, 'no, no, no,' they get closer and closer into your face."

Rob, a twenty-eight-year-old expat from New York, tried to explain this behavior to us during a focus group. He said the attitudes in Argentina were much different from the "no means no" culture of the United States. "Here, if [women] say no, they're interested. If they're really not interested, they just don't say anything to you. They just completely ignore you." So now Rob only keeps clear if women literally turn their back to him. On his reading of courtship in Buenos Aires, "no" is usually just a prelude to "yes."

You can see how much trouble this could generate. In our focus groups both men and women said it was common for a propositioned woman to play hard to get and then, only after the man had made a sufficient number of attempts, finally agree to a date. Many woman attributed this farce to a need to keep up appearances. If they responded too quickly, they might appear cheap.

"I have a friend who told me last week that she said no a few times to a guy she actually liked before saying yes just to play hard to get," one woman explained. "It was just to make sure that he wanted something serious and to not be taken for an easy girl." Sexually, too, women described a fear of appearing too eager. "We women know that if we have sex on the first date, then it's over," said another.

Argentine women have plenty of ways of signaling their interest to suitors, but as in the United States, men tend to initiate contact. Women sometimes approach men, but most of those we spoke with said they thought men found aggressive women a turnoff. "I think they love the chase," said Sara. "Whenever you're forward, it's like, *Whoa—why is she after me?*"

The use of technology in Buenos Aires mirrors the street culture. There's a level of aggression that Americans just don't hit. Emilio, a twenty-eight-year-old from the United States, told us that he'd taken to friending hot friends of friends on Facebook just to ask them out. Eduardo, thirty-one, said he messaged about thirty women a week in hope of making something click. He'd hit them up on Facebook, Instagram, anywhere he could find them.

Despite all this, very few young people we spoke with actually used online dating sites like OkCupid, in part because online dating still carried a stigma of desperation. But, more important, it simply wasn't necessary. As Eduardo put it, "If you're an Argentine woman, you don't need online dating to hook up with other people because men will be after you all your life."

Texting, however, was huge. When we asked the single people in our focus groups in Buenos Aires how many partners they were currently texting, few had less than three. It wasn't uncommon for people to be in multiple relationships of various levels of seriousness. One expat from the United States, a twenty-seven-year-old named Ajay, compared the dating scene in Buenos Aires to an *asado*—a barbecue.

"You get all these different cuts of meat cooking at once," he said. "You've got your sausage, which cooks fast. You've got your big steak, which is your best cut, which takes some time, right? You got to talk to all these girls at once just like you take care of all the meat at once."

After he made this analogy, I presented Ajay with a trophy that said "Most Sexist Food Analogy of All Time: Meat and BBQ Division."

When it comes down to the business of actually getting into a relationship, Argentines have a reputation for being *histérico*. The idea of *histérico* (*histérica* for women) came up frequently in our discussions. It's one of those culturally specific words that's kind of hard to define to someone who isn't from that culture, but I understood it to mean that someone acts one way toward you initially and then completely reverses course. A woman who says, "no, no, no" and then, finally, "yes" is said to be *histérica*, as is a man who flirts madly, then suddenly disappears for weeks without contacting you again.

"When they are trying to pick you up, they really act like men," said Sara. "They will talk to you and talk to you . . . until you hook up with them. And then they will act like girls. If you're not interested in them, they will become obsessed with you. If you are interested in them, they will disappear. It's like . . . it's like math. It's an equation."

One common approach we heard about involved a man pursuing a woman by repeatedly professing his love for her and proving it in a distinctively Argentine manner: inviting her to meet his parents for a Sunday barbecue. "He'll say, 'I love you, you are the love of my life, I want to marry you, I want to have kids,'" said a twenty-seven-year-old Argentine woman named Sofia. "But then he never calls. In Spain they tell you, 'I love you,' because they really mean it. It's not just a word. Here they don't mean it." Another woman told us about a popular Argentine phrase that means, "Lie to me because I like it." It's all part of the chase.

Even people in notionally committed relationships said they liked to keep a past lover or potential partner waiting in the wings, ready to swoop in if their current relationship fell through. Several people we spoke with had a backup plan in case their current relationship didn't work out. Isabell, twenty-eight, reported flirting with several men over text, even when she was in a relationship. She called it *hacerte la linda*, which translates roughly as "to make yourself pretty" and refers to a kind of flirting. "Just because you're on a diet, it doesn't mean you cannot check out the menu," she said. "I mean, just as long as you don't pick up that particular plate."

What's up with these people and the food analogies?!

"Even when I had a boyfriend, if I went to a bar or something and I met a guy, I would give him my phone number just in case," said Marilyn, twenty-five. "Like, I wouldn't cheat, you know?"

"But you kept your options open," interjected another woman.

"Yeah," said Marilyn. "Because you never know, right?"

Casual sex was, predictably, everywhere. In Argentina women in relationships often have a *chongo*, which literally means "strong man" or "muscleman," but is also a catchall term for a casual sexual partner, one that can refer to a friend with benefits, a regular hookup, or someone whom you're seeing on the side while in a serious relationship. Used in a sentence: "Nah, we're not serious. He's my *chongo*."

One married woman at a focus group told us that during her previous relationship she'd had a *chongo* whom she saw regularly for several years. "It was just skin," she explained, to make sure we understood that she wasn't cheating on her relationship, only meeting a sexual need. "I didn't even know his parents' names."

I hope I'm never in a casual relationship with someone in Argentina and catch feelings. Imagine how much it would suck to hear, "What? Relationship?! Are you serious? This is just for skin. Come on, I thought I was very clear: You're my *chongo*, nothing more."

Amazingly, the widespread interest in casual sex has shaped the buildings and neighborhoods of Buenos Aires as well as the culture. The city is teeming with *telos*, love hotels with no detectable stigma, where rooms are available by the hour. *Telos*, which exist at all price ranges and are available in the roughest as well as the most high-end neighborhoods, are designed for maximum privacy. The people we interviewed described a variety of techniques that ensure user discretion: In one *telo* guests drive into the parking lot, ask for a room, and then park in a spot numbered so that their open car doors are adjacent to the door to their room. In another there's a small chamber between the front door and the room where hotel staff can deliver room-service items without seeing the patrons.

That said, at some hotels maintaining privacy during peak hours is impossible. In Buenos Aires most young single people live with their parents in relatively small apartments, as do children, of course. What that means is that nearly everyone who wants to have sex winds up using a *telo* on occasion, and late nights can be especially busy. Eduardo, the thirty-one-year-old who messages thirty women per week, told us that occasionally he's had to sit in a waiting room when he arrives at three or four o'clock in the morning, along with everyone else who's come in from bars and clubs. One expat who lived next door to a *telo* said that she'd noticed a lot of traffic during lunch hours, when, her host mother speculated, "bosses like to screw their secretaries."

If, on the one hand, the whole *telo* and casual-sex scene sounds fun and liberated, on the other hand, for at least half the population Buenos Aires can be pretty tough. In our focus groups people reported that they'd often see young women crying hysterically in public places, like park benches and bus stops. When Eric asked why it was so common, the response was always the same: men.

The dating culture in Buenos Aires is extremely exciting and sensual, full of flirtation, pursuit, and casual sex. There is also an undeniably darker side, though, with unwanted aggression, manipulation, and infidelity. Everyone suffers the pain of love in Buenos Aires, but I couldn't help but conclude that things were a lot rougher for women than they were for *chongos*.

CHAPTER 6

OLD ISSUES, NEW FORMS:

SEXTING, CHEATING, SNOOPING, AND BREAKING UP

T he advent of smartphones and the Internet means that our romantic lives now inhabit two worlds: the real world and our phone world. In the phone world we have an unprecedented, highly private forum for communication that forces us to deal with age-old issues like jealousy, infidelity, and sexual intimacy in new formats that we're still trying to figure out.

SEXTING

Of all the changes in modern romance brought on by the phone world, the most radical has come in the form of sexting: the sharing of explicit sexual images through digital media.

Conceptually, sexting is a timeless phenomenon. Nude photos, erotic letters, and the like have been documented throughout civilization. While something like the Anthony Weiner scandal seems unique to our time, there are precursors, such as the salacious love letters written by U.S. president Warren G. Harding to his neighbor's wife, in which he nicknamed his penis Jerry and her vagina Mrs. Pouterson.

I wish I had been there when the historian analyzing the letters had the eureka moment: "Hey, wait a second. Whenever he says 'Mrs. Pouterson,' I think he means . . . his neighbor's wife's vagina??"

Most strange to me is that, whereas "Mrs. Pouterson" is a horrible nickname for a vagina, "Warren G. Harding" is actually a great nickname for a penis.

When it comes to photographs and video, our ability to capture ourselves has evolved with the technologies. Consumer film cameras were great for capturing high-quality images, but they had their disadvantages. Unless you had your own darkroom, you had to drop off the film to get developed, so your privacy would be compromised.

Between the 1970s and the mid-1990s, Polaroids and low-cost video cameras allowed people to produce sexual content on their own and keep it private, but sometimes a kid would open up a box labeled "DON'T OPEN" and get scarred for life.

Digital media, the Internet, and—most important—the rise of smartphones, changed all that. Today almost everybody has a remarkably high-quality camera and video recorder within arm's reach at every waking moment. In addition to having a high-tech way to capture the imagery, you also have a seemingly private place to store the images for yourself and your partner, but, like the box that says "DON'T OPEN," sometimes it falls into the wrong hands.

The key difference, though, is the ease of use and distribution. In the past, we can safely assume, most men weren't mailing Polaroids of their penises to girls they met at bars. It would have been creepy and also a bit of a hassle. However, when a high-res camera is literally a few inches from your penis at all times—and you can instantly share the glorious photo—it's a game changer.

We don't have any numbers on the rates at which sexual images were shared prior to the smartphone era, but the numbers now are staggering. Sexting, especially among young people, isn't quite yet the norm, but it's quickly getting there.

Here are some of the best stats on sexting that we could find:

- Half of eighteen- to twenty-four-year-olds have received sexts.
- One third of older teens have sent a sext.
- Sexting is increasing among all age groups—except fifty-five and older.
- You're more likely to sext if you own a smartphone.
- People who own iPhones are twice as likely to sext as people who use Androids.
- The most popular time to sext is Tuesday between 10:00 A.M. and noon. Yes, we looked this up twice. Strange!
- People who are married or in committed relationships are just as likely to have sent sexts as their unattached peers.[1]

Why do people sext? The main reasons we discovered are to share intimacy with a partner, to build sexual attraction, to appease a partner, and, in some cases, to maintain intimacy over long distances.

The technology journalist Jenna Wortham did a piece on sexting where the subjects each forwarded Wortham a sext they'd sent and then let her interview them about it. "What I discovered," Wortham wrote, "is that sexting—like anything else done on our phones—was mostly just meant to be fun, for fun, grown folks doing what grown folks do."[2]

People she interviewed had all kinds of good reasons for sexting, and their comments, seen together, actually make it seem like a healthy and compelling way to sustain a modern erotic relationship.

One twenty-seven-year-old editor sexted her hookup because it gave her a feeling of power. "It's kind of a control thing," she explained. "I wanted to make him want me." D, a thirty-year-old artist, said she sexted with her fiancé to spice things up.

"We have already seen each other's bodies a lot, and we will be seeing them a whole lot more," she said. "So sometimes eroticism can come from what is unseen, or presenting something in a different way."

M, a brand marketer, sent her boyfriend a picture of her breasts to help him cope with a case of nerves before a presentation at work.

This is my favorite. I just love the idea of the guy opening up his phone, seeing the boobs, and thinking, "Ahhhh. Okay, you got this, Phil! Let's nail this PowerPoint presentation."

On our subreddit one woman gave a whole slew of reasons for why she'd sent sexts in the past: "Because it feels good to know someone wants you from far away. because it's something to think about. because it boosts confidence. because i'd never done it before. because i liked them. because i'd just broken up with someone . . ."

For some the privacy and distance provided by the phone world allowed them to be more honest about their sexuality. "I started because I'm a very sexual person and sexting was an easier way for me to discuss intimate things with my partners," said one female user on our subreddit. "I found it hard to ask for what I wanted or needed in the bedroom in person so this way was easier for me to discuss my needs and fantasies. Now it's become something I enjoy, like a form of foreplay. I like to send something sexy to my mate before we're going to see each other." Another woman wrote: "A guy I hooked up with a few years ago used to ask me for pics all the time. Finally, because I felt like I might lose him (. . . it was not a healthy hook-up relationship), I got into it. I LOVED it. I just felt super sexy taking them, and I still feel good looking at them now. Plus, one day, my boobs will be down around my waist and it will be nice to remember."

Many of our subreddit users said sexting provided a forum to maintain intimacy over long distances.

One woman wrote:

I'm a girl who lives in the U.S. and my boyfriend lives in Wales. I would say we sext at least once a week. When it's a long distance relationship like that, and we have to go 2-3 months without seeing one another, I think it's almost a necessity. I want to keep him interested and excited. Since we had only been together a short time before he went to Wales, we hadn't really discussed our likes/dislikes in the bedroom. But through sexting we were able to express that and get it all out in the open. So the next time we see each other we will already know the others' desires. If you asked me a year ago, I would've felt "dirty" if I was sexting, but now I'm totally for it in a relationship.

Another user explained:

I think in general it would be much harder to maintain an exclusive long distance relationship without the technology in general. Just being able to communicate on gchat or via text during the day and actually see each others faces while we talk every night is a pretty necessary part to maintaining our intimacy and our relationship. The sexting is just a nice way to spice things up without actually being present.

The conclusion was clear: Without sexting, these relationships would be much harder to maintain and might not even last. Sexting provided an effective way of coping with a well-established and often heartbreaking dilemma: how to love someone when they are very far away.

The same technology that affords us the luxury and privacy to share these intimate moments is also, sadly, what allows us to betray our partner's trust on a massive scale.

The main reason people give for why they don't sext is that they're afraid of being exposed. One woman reported, "I've never sexted and I don't think I ever will. The thought of it seems hot and exciting, but the possible consequences are terrifying. If the relationship goes south and he's still in possession of the pictures, then who knows where they'd end up. It just looks like an avoidable, unnecessary situation."

We did hear some nightmare stories that would confirm this view of sexting. One woman who was initially reluctant to sext tells us what happened when she gave in:

> *My boyfriend wanted to, I was uncomfortable with the idea but he begged and dropped the "if you love me you will" line. Said some stuff back and forth. I wasn't really sure what to say. He asked for a picture of me fingering myself. I obliged, then started getting texts from random numbers calling me things like "nasty slut." Turns out he was at a party, passing his phone around and showing people what I sent. Utterly humiliating. That was years ago, and I haven't sent another sext since.*

Sending a photo to someone who could turn around and be pure human garbage, like the person above, is a widespread fear. And, although in theory everyone could be exposed this way, in reality the risks affect women in a very different way from men.

In 2014 private nude photos of various female celebrities leaked onto the Internet after hackers posted them on the 4chan website.[*] The images were clearly meant for these women's partners and were never to be shared. While the hackers who stole the photos were condemned, the women who had their photos stolen were scolded too, for being reckless. "Don't want your nude photos leaked? Don't take any!" went a typical response. Taking naked photos of yourself with your iPhone, the argument went, was indulgent, vain, and immature. The implication was that regular, sexually healthy people do not sext, despite the abundance of evidence to the contrary. Of course, not everyone agreed with this narrative, but it was still a popular argument.

The fear of this kind of condemnation was another reason people gave for not sexting, but many of the younger women we heard from believe that the prevalence of sexting is already changing the perceptions of these risks. One twenty-four-year-old told us that she sees something empowering in her sexting and has decided that, if her nudes were leaked, she wouldn't be judged for it.

The warnings about sexting (mainly directed toward women) center around the worst-case scenario—your nudes being posted publicly, like on a revenge porn site. This is presented as something that will follow you for the rest of your life and haunt your career and future relationships. I don't think that will happen to me, but if it does, I like to think the viewers will draw the obvious conclusion— that I am a sexually confident woman who made a video for someone she cared about. If someone I knew saw the images and judged me negatively for making them, I feel confident that the problem is with them, not with me . . . So when I sext with my boyfriend, the main goal is to get us off. But it's also my little way of reassuring

---

[*] There was, like, one dude around in some photos, but the shots of him were not really the headline-grabbing images that spread around. Those were overwhelmingly images of women.

myself that I decide what to do with my body, and I get to decide which risky behaviors are worth taking.

This view is becoming quite common among young people, particularly teens. For the generation that grew up in a smartphone culture, sexting has become a common step in the journey toward becoming sexually active. Along with a first kiss, now, at some point, there is often a first sext.

When the journalist Hanna Rosin examined a high school in central Virginia where rampant sexting and promiscuous image sharing sparked a police investigation, a surprising number of the kids she met expressed confidence that the situation was no big deal.[3]

When an officer questioned some girls about their concerns about the photos being disseminated online, he was shocked when one insisted, "This is my life and my body and I can do whatever I want with it," while another said, "I don't see any problem with it. I'm proud of my body." Some girls, he discovered, had taken naked photos of themselves specifically for sharing on Instagram. The idea that this should be treated with shame or that it would come back to haunt them seemed absurd.

Regardless of how you or any officer sees the risks and rewards of sexting, it's becoming more and more of a common practice. And, as we've seen with other aspects of modern romance, what seems insane to one generation often ends up being the norm of the next.

CHEATING

Of course, sending naked photos is not the only sexually charged behavior that smartphones enable or make easier. Consider infidelity. In the past, men and women who were cheating could flirt only in person or over a landline. People would have codes: "I'll let the phone ring twice, then hang up. That'll be your signal to go to the window, and there you'll see a zip line.

Take the zip line down to the tree house and I'll meet you there at 10:30 P.M."

Now you can be in bed with your spouse and ask, "Hey, honey, what are you looking at on your phone?" She could reply, "Oh, just reading this op-ed in the *Times*," when she's actually sending your neighbor a photo of her Mrs. Pouterson.

Have all the increased romantic options and the technology to access them led to more people straying? I remember reading the Anthony Weiner Facebook messages. Seeing the way he was just messaging random women all over the country and watching the messages quickly escalate from innocuous to very sexual was unbelievable.

This is a transcript of a chat session he had with one of these women, a lady named Lisa from Las Vegas.[4] Weiner and Lisa, sorry to bring this back, guys, but it is fascinating:

──── **August 13, 2010** ────

L
> i am trying to find the wonderful anthony wiener who i feel in love with for yelling at those damn repubs the other day! and u are funny as hell on the daily show! your friend requests are full..you must friend me! you are awesome!

> thank you lisa. glad you have my back. you keeping an eye on that wackadoodle [Sharron] Angle for us?

AW

L
> how insane is she? who needs social security, medicare or education? if this wacko wins my state i swear i will have to move! she may be dumber than plain! and that is tough to find!

L like this cute new pics of you! when r you coming to vegas to help me beat up the right wing crazies?

this is my "pull my finger" shot. glad you like. i'm ready for a vegas trip. truth telling during the day. got a night plan for us? **AW**

L haha..that was a very loaded questions! i've got all kinds of night plans for us! when are you coming?

dunno. make me an offer i can't refuse. **AW**

L to get us in the mood. first we watch back to back episodes of the daily show and colbert report ... then, to really spice things up we go deface all of my neighbor's sharon angle yard signs ... then when we are really hot we go to the bookstore and cover all of the glen beck books with copies of "the audacity of hope!" ... i do this about once a week (you can tell i am a very exciting girl!) ... or if this i not your thing, we can just get drunk and have mad, passionate sex!

For me, the most offensive part was that he used the word "wackadoodle."

Also, did you catch that sly, almost subliminal, blink-and-you-might-miss-it allusion to sex? It was when she said they could have mad, passionate sex!

That last message basically signaled a shift in their Facebook chat and opened the floodgates for all sorts of sexual messages and infamous penis photos.

What fascinates me most, though, is that this is something that simply could not have happened thirty years ago. Sure, he might have still wanted to sexually stray from his relationship, but the privacy of Facebook, the ease of access to potential people to cheat with, and the ability to flirt with caution via the medium of chat—that perfect storm for temptation is undeniably a new development.

Given the sensitivity of the subject and the potential judgment that would occur in an in-person focus group, we used the privacy of the Internet to gain insight into people's real-world experiences with cheating and social media.

I posed these questions in our subreddit: Has anyone started an affair or cheated on someone through social media? If social media didn't exist, would something like this have happened anyway?

One gentleman said that he started a relationship through a social media site. It initially began as harmless chatting but, like the Weiner chat, over time it escalated. Though not as aggressive as the Weiner chat, it started getting flirty and the two began sharing their innermost feelings and problems.

> *It certainly wouldn't have happened without social media, as my wife had successfully cut me off from most of the non-family women in my life. I don't necessarily see it as a completely bad thing either—without my talking to the other woman (and the sort of honesty that relative internet anonymity provides), I wouldn't have realized just how fucked up my relationship was with my then-wife, and the numerous things that I always thought were normal, and were really her doing her best to control every aspect of my life, and generally make me unable to leave her.*

Another user said that he started an affair that he simply wouldn't have had the gumption to start without Facebook.

They worked together and were casual acquaintances. One day he looked her up on Facebook and sent her a message asking, "Would you like to get a drink sometime?" Soon after that the affair began.

"If Facebook didn't exist, I doubt I would have gathered the courage to ask her directly. It made the initial step that much easier," he said.

The advantages of technology that facilitate regular dating (such as the ease of access and the absence of the pressure found in an in-person interaction) also transfer over to cheating. This includes the ease of escalation, which, when engaging in something as scandalous as cheating, is quite valuable. With messages you can slowly test the waters of potentially starting an affair. Once you find out the other person is on the same page, it can ramp up very fast. Or you can easily backpedal without quite the same level of embarrassment you'd experience if it had happened in person.

Here's an example:

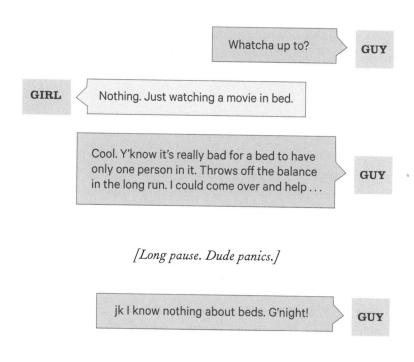

> Whatcha up to? **GUY**

GIRL > Nothing. Just watching a movie in bed.

> Cool. Y'know it's really bad for a bed to have only one person in it. Throws off the balance in the long run. I could come over and help . . . **GUY**

[Long pause. Dude panics.]

> jk I know nothing about beds. G'night! **GUY**

The other person may think you are a creep, but either of you can just act like it was a misreading of the message. In the Weiner situation, phrases like "got a night plan for us?" and "make me an offer i can't refuse" allowed him to safely test the waters and see if Lisa was really interested in something sexual.

Also, the privacy of our phones means we have a new place to foster and grow clandestine relationships. In the past, people who wanted to engage or flirt with someone outside their relationship would have to sneak away to a remote bar or restaurant to reduce the risk of being spotted by friends or loved ones. Today, with proper precautions, our phones provide a private refuge that can house intimacy that no one else is privy to.

In one focus group a gentleman told us he once started innocently texting with a married coworker and it eventually turned into a full-on clandestine relationship. Normally they had no reason to chat beyond the office. One day the guy sent a jokey text when he saw something that reminded him of something he and the woman had laughed about at work. She responded and a fun, witty banter took hold.

These instances increased in frequency, and soon the two were also spending time together after work. Eventually both parties caught feelings, and it developed into a secret relationship, with the married woman constantly sending texts to this other guy in secret. The texts were getting so frequent that the guy had to change the woman's contact info in his phone so as to not arouse the suspicion of others, who might wonder why this married lady was texting him so much. Instead of getting texts from Susan, it looked like he was getting texts from a male friend named David.

If I ever was texting frequently with someone and wanted to make an alias, I think I'd go with "Scottie Pippen." Then any friends who were peeking at my screen could be left wondering why I was texting with the former Chicago Bulls star on the reg.

I only hope Scottie Pippen's wife never has an affair where she uses the same strategy and the guy texts while Scottie is in the room and he can see her screen. Scottie Pippen would likely believe it was an impostor Scottie Pippen from another dimension, sent to steal his wife and kill him. The psychological damage inflicted on poor Scottie Pippen would be far worse than discovering a simple affair.

Back to our real situation: Eventually both parties decided it was best to end the affair. But again, would this kind of thing have taken off if these people hadn't had the privacy of text messages to introduce a romantic element into their relationship?

She was married and I respected that. I wouldn't have made a voice call to say little jokey things to her. It would have been weird. Since it was just texting, it seemed pretty innocuous. But as it went on, we both couldn't help but realize, there was a spark between us. When you're both on your phones, you have this safe zone that no one else can break into. It was this private little world where we could talk about all the stress and confusion and love that the whole dilemma was creating. If it weren't for text messages, I'm not sure anything would have started between us.

Some people we heard from, however, felt that ultimately technology doesn't turn us into philanderers. If you're gonna cheat, you're gonna cheat, they said. Social media or no social media, in the end it's two people together in the flesh.

"I don't think that someone who is otherwise a faithful partner in a relationship is going to suddenly start cheating because someone sends them a winky face in an IM," said one user on the subreddit, in the thread's most popular post. "I'd say it makes it easier to cheat, but doesn't make it harder to be faithful."

But even if it doesn't lead to full-on cheating, social media presents new problems and temptations, even for the faithful. Besides offering privacy, social media also presents us with a forum where other potential partners are constantly on display. One gentleman recalled how, when he got into a new relationship, social media such as Instagram provided an outlet to view all the options out there.

I love my girlfriend, but when we were first getting serious, I would go on Instagram and see all these hot girls. And its like, 'Whoa

should I be dating these girls? Or just settle down and be in a re-
lationship?' It felt like the opposite of 'out of sight, out of mind.'
They were in sight and IN my mind.

The privacy of the Internet and phone world has also led to the rise of settings where people can be adulterous without any judgments. The most well-known example is Ashley Madison, a terrifyingly popular online dating website that is designed specifically to help people have affairs. The company's motto is "Life is Short. Have an Affair."

The company enrolls its full-paying members in the "Affair Guarantee Program," which offers a full refund if they don't find someone within their first three months on the site. The site's home page offers users a click-through icon that lets them "Search and Chat with Married People in Your Area," as well as a blog and Twitter feed featuring advice such as "How to Get and Keep a Fuck Buddy" and news items such as "Men Not Bothered by the Idea of Wives' Infidelity."

Apparently it's growing quickly, from 8.5 million members in 2011 to a self-reported 11 million members in 2014.[5]

Now, I know that people have been cheating on each other for as long as they've made promises to be monogamous and that, to date, there's no hard evidence that the Internet is making people more likely to commit infidelity. That said, it's impossible to imagine something like Ashley Madison getting this popular this fast in a world without digital media. Whether or not we're cheating more often, it's certainly easier to do.

BREAKING UP IN THE PHONE WORLD

Another thing that's become easier because of modern technology is breakups. Not long ago breaking up with someone required an emotionally wrenching face-to-face conversation or, at the least, a phone call in which the person who wanted to end things had to own up to their feelings and, usually, explain themselves too. Generally the breakup conversation also required being thoughtful about the other person's feelings and vulnerability, and doing everything possible to say things that would boost the morale of the person being jilted.

This is why our culture developed lines like "It's not you, it's me" and "I'm just not ready to be in a relationship now" and "I'm sorry, I just want to focus on my dragon art."

Of course, no one liked these conversations. But we all saw them as obligatory, because they were the decent human thing to do for another person.

Today a growing number of people, and a majority of younger adults, are more likely to break up with someone by text, instant message, or social media than in person or by phone. According to a 2014 survey of 2,712 eighteen- to thirty-year-olds who'd had a relationship end during the previous year, 56 percent said they had broken up using digital media, with texting being the most popular method (25 percent), followed closely by social media (20 percent), and then e-mail (11 percent), which people used because it let them "fully explain their reasons."

By contrast, only 18 percent had broken up through a face-to-face interaction, and a mere 15 percent had split up with a call.[6] A startling 0.0014 percent had broken up by hiring a blimp that said, "Tammy I think we need to see other people." (Note: I think this was just one dude named Phil from Indiana.)

The most common reason people gave for breaking up via text or social media was that it is "less awkward," which makes sense given that young adults do just about all other communication through their phones too.

Oddly, 73 percent of those young adults—the very same ones who said they had broken up with other people via text or social media—said they would be upset if someone broke up with them that way.

To be clear, the study above didn't specify how serious these relationships were, so it didn't account for how the length or intensity of the relationship affected the preferred breakup method. Obviously there's a huge difference between breaking up with someone after three weeks and after three years. In fact, the anthropologist Ilana Gershon has found many young people in casual relationships would actually prefer to be dumped by these less traditional methods.[7]

On the subreddit we asked people how they felt about the new ways of breaking up. A lot of people who responded acknowledged that they'd broken up with their partners via text or social media to avoid stress and conflict. One woman explained: "I didn't have to look at his face or hear his voice, so I could be completely honest with him. He was a sweet guy but I wanted to move on."

What's interesting here—but also kind of scary—is that she's saying texting allowed her to be more honest, because she didn't feel compelled to sugarcoat the reasons she was ending things. Maybe texting means we'll stop giving those nonsensical "It's not you, it's me" messages and become more direct instead.

At the same time, most stories seemed to paint a picture of someone who was using modern messaging to avoid confrontation rather than further honesty. This included many people who broke up in this fashion in relationships that were far beyond the casual point. Several users shared stories like this:

It was a normal day. I was supposed to meet the guy I had been seeing for two years for brunch. I drove to the place and he wasn't there. I called him an excessive amount of times to no answer. I went home. I got on Facebook and there he was on Facebook chat. He says, "Hey, I've been thinking about us and I keep going back and forth on whether or not I want to be with you :/" And that was it.

I was overall surprised and couldn't believe that was the way he decided to end it, even know [sic] I had seen him the day before and was supposed to see him that day as well. I did make him call me to clarify the situation after this, which made it worse of course. Haven't spoken to him since for obvious reasons.

It was brutal to read. After two years the relationship was ended with a ":/," not even a fully fleshed-out emoji. There were many more stories like this, with passive-aggressive nonbreakups that actually ended things way more obnoxiously, and painfully, than a face-to-face conversation.

Ending things by changing their status on social media without telling their partner is another way people break up these days. One woman told us: "In college my boyfriend broke up with me by changing his Facebook status to single. We got back together six years later, and then he broke up with me over text message. I should probably stop dating him." If you start dating him again and he says he needs to stop by the "blimp place," maybe brace yourself to read bad news in the sky.

This one is astounding because of the depth of the relationship that preceded the breakup text:

Back in June of 2012 when I was 43, my boyfriend broke up w/ me via a text message after being together for 8 years! I practically raised his daughter, and had been totally committed to him [and] everything that came w/him. I was really offended and hurt as I felt that I at least deserved to be broken up with in person or at least on the phone!

Apparently the wound didn't run too deep, though, because look what happened next:

After 10 months of no contact, his uncle passed away [and] I called him [and] left a message w/my condolences. We finally talked after that [and] eventually got back together. I still love him completely [and] have forgiven him for how things went down. And you best believe I gave him hell for the text! :-)

No offense, but at this point let's take a moment to be thankful we are neither of the people in that relationship.

When I discussed this topic with people from my generation,

they were shocked to learn that so many people were breaking up in this fashion. The younger generation has taken another idea that seemed bizarre and made it into a norm. Is it that surprising, though? If you subscribe to Sherry Turkle's argument that the prevalence of text-based communications is leading to a decline in face-to-face conversations and the skills to conduct them, the shift makes total sense.

EXES LIVE ON IN THE PHONE WORLD

For those getting out of relationships, especially for the jilted, social media also presents an easy outlet to reconnect with past loves. We heard many stories of former flames who reconnected over flirty Gchat or Facebook messages and wound up cheating on their new partners.

But even if it didn't lead to cheating, having to see their former love's presence on social media was tough for the jilted. "It makes it harder to let go," one person told us. "Even if you are one of those unicorns that can leave a relationship with friendly feelings and a clean break, your self-control is tested when all you have to do is click a button to see how they are living their lives without you."

The temptation to continue to creep on your ex over the Internet is nearly universal. One study found that 88 percent of those who continued to have access to their ex's Facebook page said they sometimes monitored their ex's activities, while 70 percent of people who had disconnected from an ex admitted to trying to spy on the ex's page by other means, such as through a friend's account.

Many people we talked to advocated a complete "unfriending" on all accounts, but others thought those kinds of social media plays created drama in and of themselves. Even if you do unfriend or unfollow, though, it's hard to avoid your exes. As one person told us: "It gets complicated the longer you had a relationship with them. Can you block them on Facebook? Sure. But you have the same friends, or at least befriended her friends on Facebook. You're going to see them doing the same stuff via pictures that your friends post."

Some people have gotten pretty creative about how to solve the problem of the social media ex. One nineteen-year-old girl from Toronto named Cassandra Photoshopped pictures of Beyoncé over her ex-boyfriend's face and put them up on Tumblr.

"If imagining yourself at your happiest with Beyoncé doesn't help, I don't know what will," she told BuzzFeed.[8]

I personally have thought about this strategy and decided that other celebrities might be good as well.

Ladies, trouble getting over your man? Why not Photoshop in *The Transporter* himself, Jason Statham?

Fellas, does it make you sad to have those vacation photos of you and your lady in Hawaii? What if instead you were in Hawaii with the funnest dude ever: Dwayne "The Rock" Johnson?

Ladies, are you sad when you look back on that romantic dinner with your ex who left you for your best friend? What if that wasn't a romantic dinner but a stimulating conversation with Supreme Court Justice Sonia Sotomayor?

Even if neither you nor your partner is being tempted to use social media to facilitate cheating—since we all know how easy it is—there is another trend that is seeping into modern relationships: snooping.

SNOOPING

If social media makes it easier to cheat, there's no question that it makes it a lot easier to get caught. Every interaction with someone online creates part of a digital paper trail.

This digital paper trail and the knowledge that our partners have this secret world in their phones can lead to what we will refer to as "snooping."

Here's a tip: As you read this section, when the word "snooping" comes up, read it in your head with a quiet, sneaky, Aziz whisper voice. It'll make the section more fun. Try it now. Snooping . . . See?

Both in our in-person focus groups and on the subreddit, many people discussed how secretly viewing their partner's texts, e-mails, and social media led to their finding incriminating evidence that made them angry and sometimes even ended the relationship.

"I broke up with a girl because of a text I had seen on her phone," someone recounted. "We were in bed and she got up to go to use the bathroom. After a few moments I heard her phone vibrate on the bed. It was a text. On the lock screen was a text from her ex-boyfriend that said something along the lines of 'Are you coming over again tonight?'"

"My ex and I both got into a bad pattern of checking each others phones and it lead [sic] to a lot of trust break downs," said one gentleman on Reddit. "Most of the time there was nothing at all to hide, but before the last fight I found out she had been lying to me about going to a Bible Study and instead going to spend time with a guy she met at that Bible Study."

And no, it wasn't her new best friend, Jesus Christ.

So there you have it, readers, if your boyfriend or girlfriend says they are out at Bible study—they are more likely out boning someone *from* Bible study.

Even in instances where someone snooped and didn't find evidence of cheating, the act of going through your partner's phone can create its own problems. In seeking to make sure that your partner is being faithful, you may inadvertently breach his or her trust.

In our interviews people on the other end of snooping had varying feelings about being snooped on. Some didn't care, because they had nothing to hide anyway. Many subscribed to the theory that if you leave your accounts logged on, it's fair game. But others believed that looking at your partner's screen is a violation of trust or that it reveals underlying jealousy issues. Some even said it was grounds to end a relationship.

One thing that stuck with me, though, was that whether or not your partner is actually cheating, these suspicions and the snooping that follows can boil into full-blown paranoia that drives you mad.

Snooping . . . (Are you still doing the voice? Just checking!)

One gentleman in a large focus group held in New York described how he caught his girlfriend cheating when her Gmail account was left open. He saw an open exchange between her and an old boyfriend and felt compelled to check it based on his previous suspicions. This led to the crowd of roughly 150 people generally agreeing when I asked, "So if someone forgets to log out, your attitude is *If the shit's open, I'm reading it?*"

She was in fact cheating but agreed to end it with the old boyfriend. They worked through the issue, but it led to a dangerous downward spiral where he kept checking her e-mails, Gchats, and texts. The girl would change passwords, but he would crack them. Sometimes he found something suspicious, like deleted chats, and other times he didn't. Eventually he found an e-mail that made it clear that the relationship with the old ex-boyfriend was not going to end as she had promised. They then broke up.

What was interesting was that even though the snooping ultimately helped him catch his cheating girlfriend, after that experience he felt in future relationships he would never snoop again. He felt that snooping only led to suspicion and paranoia that could break the fundamental trust needed to maintain a relationship.

His sentiment made sense to me after I took in all the stories in our interviews. So many people we interviewed told us that the slightest glimpse into their partner's private phone or social media could spark an uncontrollable need to snoop and read more. One flash of an incoming text or e-mail from a stranger of the opposite sex or NBA all-star Scottie Pippen is all it takes to raise questions. People generally recognize that most of the time there's nothing to worry about. Even so, it's hard not to follow the trail once you find it.

In most relationships, the barriers to our private digital world break down without our realizing it. As a relationship progresses, a couple winds up sharing passwords out of convenience.

"Hey, honey, what's the password on your laptop? I want to listen to that awesome Pitbull song on Spotify!"

"My password is 'Pitbull'!" she replies.

"Wow, that's crazy!"

Next thing you know, you're listening to Pitbull's hit album *Planet Pit*. Then a Gchat message comes up from a guy named Armando.Perez@gmail.com. You think to yourself, *Holy shit. Armando Perez . . . That's Pitbull's real name! Why is he messaging my girlfriend?*

Is your girlfriend having an affair with Pitbull? Do you read the Gchat message to make sure she's not? Do you possibly violate your partner's trust just momentarily to put your fears at ease? It's a conundrum you didn't plan on facing, but now you have to.

Snooping or accidentally getting a glimpse into your partner's private messages isn't the only way to descend into madness. Simply reading the messages posted publicly on a partner's social media is often enough.

A woman in one of our focus groups described getting suspicious when another woman was being very active on her boyfriend's Facebook wall.

"This girl was just constantly writing on his wall," she said. "It was just like, *Ugh, you know he has a girlfriend.*"

She became agitated and decided to check his text messages, upon which she confirmed he was cheating.

Men and women also described partners getting upset when someone of the opposite sex was "liking" a lot of Instagram pictures or even seeing certain types of photos.

One gentleman we interviewed described how his girlfriend would get very jealous if she saw Instagram photos of him with other girls or other female users liking or commenting on too many of his photos.

"One time I made the mistake of liking a photo of this friend of mine in a bikini. All hell broke loose," he said.

These are not necessarily new problems. Is a girlfriend getting upset that you liked an Instagram photo of a cute girl wearing a bikini any different from a girlfriend getting upset because you ogled a cute girl at the beach?

All the mundane misunderstandings and fights that we've always gotten into in our relationships get reinvented in weird and interesting ways in the digital world.

One gentleman, Sean, told us a tale that involved him getting suspicious of cheating due to a glimpse of his girlfriend's social media at a very stressful moment:

> *My girlfriend was in a ski accident. I was in the ambulance with her and she gave me her phone to call her parents.*
>
> *Afterwards, I looked down and I noticed that she downloaded Snapchat. I didn't really know what Snapchat was. And all that I had heard about it was that it was an app specifically for sending nude pics.*
>
> *So I checked, and there were like eight Snapchats from this one guy whose name I didn't recognize.*
>
> *And I was furious. But I didn't say anything. Because she was in a back brace. Which seemed like bad timing.*
>
> *And months later, we threw a party, and I met this dude. And he was gay, which was extremely reassuring.*

I experienced a version of this myself once, when my girlfriend got upset with me due to Instagram activity. I was taking off for a flight to New Zealand for a cousin's wedding. Before boarding, I called her. I got her voice mail. I texted her a message saying, "Hey! Taking off soon. Just wanted to talk before the flight took off. Gimme a ring." She wrote back, "I called you four hours ago."

I could tell she was upset because she also included the emoji of the Indian guy with a gun beside his head.

I called her back and eventually she answered. I explained that I was busy packing and getting ready for my trip and that I knew I would have time to talk when I got to the airport. She said, "Oh, so you were busy packing? Well, I saw on your friend's Instagram he posted a photo of you hanging out by the pool taking Polaroids, so I feel like if you have time to play with a Polaroid camera, you'd have time to call or text me back."

I simply said I was sorry and it wouldn't happen again.

A week later, though, it was Valentine's Day. I pulled out all the stops. It was our first Valentine's together. I sent her her favorite flowers at work, along with Fuzzball (a stuffed animal from the Disney Michael Jackson show *Captain EO*, to remind her of our trip to Disney World) and some chocolates that were the same type she had loved on a trip we took to Mexico together.

When she came to meet me at home after work, I made her close her eyes and walked her into a room where I had on one of her favorite Stevie Wonder records. When she opened her eyes, she saw glasses of her favorite wine for the both of us. Then it was time for the gift exchange.

I went first.

I said, "Hey, so you remember a week ago you were upset that I didn't call you back before my trip, and you were mad because I was playing with the Polaroid camera. Well, the reason I was doing that is I bought you this nice vintage Polaroid camera and I was just making sure it worked before I gave it to you, so . . . here's your gift."

She felt HORRIBLE.

It was the greatest Valentine's Day gift I've ever received.

HOW PREVALENT IS CHEATING?

Fear and suspicion of cheating aren't always unjustified. According to nationally representative survey data, in the United States 20 to 40 percent of heterosexual married men and 25 percent of heterosexual married women will have at least one extramarital affair during their lifetime, and 2 to 4 percent of all married people are willing to tell survey researchers that they've had an affair in the past year.

In nonmarried but "committed" couples there is a 70 percent

incidence of cheating. In addition, 60 percent of men and 53 percent of women confess that they've engaged in "mate poaching"[9] (trying to seduce a person out of a committed relationship). This is not to be confused with rhino poaching, where someone tries to seduce a rhinoceros into a cross-species romantic tryst. Or egg poaching, where someone tries to seduce a delicious egg into their belly without overcooking it.

Let's take the "best case" cheating scenario. Your partner of ten or more years has had a one-night stand with someone they will never see again, they regret it, it didn't mean anything, and they would never do it again.

According to Match.com's nationally representative survey, 80 percent of men and 76 percent of women would prefer that their partner "confess their mistake . . . and suffer the consequences," rather than just "take their secret to the grave."

I asked a lot of people in the focus groups how they'd feel about their partner having a one-night stand with someone else. Their discomfort seemed to be less about their partner hooking up with someone else—in practical terms, it wouldn't change much about the relationship—and more about knowing that their partner had been unfaithful.

"In theory I'd be okay with it," said Melissa, twenty-six. "But actually knowing it happened? I don't think I could handle that."

As we all saw in the hit film *Indecent Proposal*, just because Woody Harrelson *thinks* he'll be cool with something doesn't mean he will be when it actually happens.

Others were not at all accepting of the hypothetical situation. For many it would be an immediate relationship ender. One woman we met recalled a night when she told friends, a couple with a new baby, about an extramarital relationship that she'd had.

The wife turned to her husband and said, "If you ever cheat on me, I am divorcing you and taking the baby," then got up and went to bed. And he said, "Sounds good to me. Sayonara, lady!"

Okay, the latter part of that exchange didn't happen, but there definitely were those who had zero tolerance for infidelity, and also marriages that have ended with someone angrily leaving a room and shouting, "Sayonara, lady!"

FRANCE:

MONOGAMY AND MISTRESSES

In the United States there's an optimistic expectation that most people will remain faithful to their partner, but actual data show great numbers of people will not. As we've seen, when it comes to sex and relationships, what we believe in theory does not line up with what we do in practice.

When the *New York Times* opinion writer Pamela Druckerman conducted interviews for *Lust in Translation*, her book on infidelity around the world, cheaters in the United States seemed to try to distance themselves from their act. "A lot of people I interviewed started off by telling me, 'I'm not the kind of person who would have an affair,'" she explained. "And I'd always think, *Of course, you are exactly the kind of person who would have an affair, because there isn't one kind.*"

According to a recent survey of attitudes about extramarital affairs in forty different nations, 84 percent of people in the United States said infidelity was "morally unacceptable."[10] Another poll, from Gallup, found that infidelity is more universally disapproved of than polygamy, animal cloning, and suicide.[11]

So if there were two guys at a bar, one cheating on his wife and another with a cloned pig named Bootsie, it would be the cheater, not Bootsie the pig, getting more disapproving looks.

When you compare this level of disapproval with the data on the actual prevalence of cheating, it paints a strange picture. Do we really believe that all these masses of people who engage in affairs are immoral monsters? That's quite a lot of monsters. It seems that we often reluctantly accept the act of cheating in our own lives while still condemning the practice at large.

Not all cultures condemn infidelity so fiercely.

The country that has by far the highest tolerance for extramarital affairs is—no surprise here—France, where only 47 percent of people surveyed found such activity morally unacceptable. That's good, because France is the country with the highest rates of infidelity: 55 percent for men and 32 percent for women, according to the latest data.[12]

The second-most-tolerant nation is Germany, with 60 percent

PERCENTAGES OF PEOPLE WHO SAY EXTRAMARITAL AFFAIRS ARE "MORALLY UNACCEPTABLE"

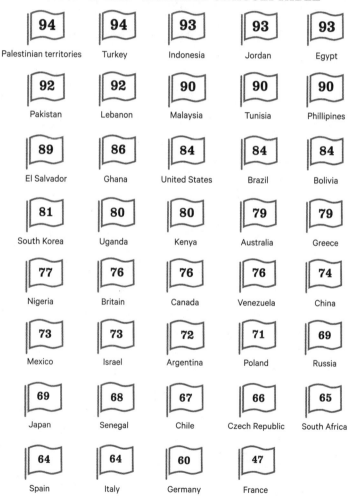

94	94	93	93	93
Palestinian territories	Turkey	Indonesia	Jordan	Egypt

92	92	90	90	90
Pakistan	Lebanon	Malaysia	Tunisia	Phillipines

89	86	84	84	84
El Salvador	Ghana	United States	Brazil	Bolivia

81	80	80	79	79
South Korea	Uganda	Kenya	Australia	Greece

77	76	76	76	74
Nigeria	Britain	Canada	Venezuela	China

73	73	72	71	69
Mexico	Israel	Argentina	Poland	Russia

69	68	67	66	65
Japan	Senegal	Chile	Czech Republic	South Africa

64	64	60	47
Spain	Italy	Germany	France

considering extramarital affairs morally unacceptable. Several other European nations, including Spain and Italy, are in that range.

In contrast, the countries that rank close to the United States are mainly in Latin America and Africa, places like Ghana, Bolivia, and Brazil. Those where disapproval rates are highest, in the ninetieth percentile, are mainly traditional Islamic nations in the Middle East.

Seizing an opportunity to eat amazing food in Paris, I decided to travel to France and try to learn about their romantic culture.

Now, granted, everyone knows France is famously tolerant of infidelity. But there's a difference between reading a number from a survey of attitudes and talking to real people about their experiences with something as messy as having affairs. We went to France not to verify that people cheat and feel differently about it from how we do but to find out how their more open attitudes about monogamy affect their relationships, their families, and their lives. We didn't romanticize the way they do things there, but we wondered what, if anything, people in more conservative places could learn from the more lenient French approach.

During our interviews and focus groups, most of the French people I met said it's natural, if not inevitable, to seek sexual novelty and excitement. They'd still get angry about cheating, but not in the same way we do in the States. They don't judge the transgression so harshly.

"In France, you can be a good guy and still have affairs," a young Parisian named Lukas told us.

"I don't think you can be faithful all your life," said Irene, twenty-three. "It's unreasonable to think you wouldn't be attracted to someone else. If I was married and we had kids, I wouldn't give that all up if he slept with someone else."

"You know pretty much everyone has strayed, so there's more understanding when it happens," said George, a twenty-five-year-old who'd lived in France and in Austria. "In the subconscious of French people is an idea that everyone cheats, even though in fact not everyone does."

In France most people have come to expect that their political leaders will have affairs, at minimum, and often an entire second family too. When François Mitterrand was president, his mistress Anne Pingeot, and their daughter, Mazarine Pingeot, would often visit him at the Élysée Palace, despite the fact that he had a wife and children. At Mitterrand's funeral in 1996, his second family sat alongside his first family.

Politicians aren't the only ones who do this kind of thing. The focus group participants shared tales of other arrangements French couples have that would be hard to fathom in the United States. One woman told us that her uncle used to quietly take the bones from his wife's meat dishes to feed the dog of his mistress, and eventually her aunt, annoyed by the charade, simply started bagging the bones for her husband's mistress herself.

When I interviewed the dog about this situation, he told me, "It's weird, but hey, I'm not complaining. *Double the bones, man!*"

Another woman told us that in her family an older relative would vacation with both his wife and his mistress, together, taking separate rooms but otherwise doing a surprising amount of stuff together.

The mistress thing was very widespread. The most jarring fact I learned was that on Valentine's Day the flower shops advertise with the slogan "Don't forget your mistress!"

As I left the final focus group, I ran into that dog on the sidewalk. He said:

I don't know, man. I get it in a sense. Their expectations of romantic fidelity are more realistic, but the mistress shit?

Seems like men are taking advantage of the women's goodwill and they are resigned to this demeaning situation.

It's a bummer, minus that whole double bones thing, ya know?

I admire the French for embracing honesty and their sexual nature, but there must be a middle ground between unrealistic monogamous expectations and full-on second families.

Hey, you don't happen to have a plastic bag on you, do ya? Why? No reason . . .

CHAPTER 7

SETTLING DOWN

I've never been a "relationship guy." My first serious relationship happened when I was around twenty-three and lasted three years. It began when I was living in New York, but at the three-year mark I had to move to Los Angeles. I was twenty-five. The girl was ready to move with me to L.A., but it just seemed too much for me to live with another person at that age and especially to have her move cross-country. We eventually ended things after a year and change of trying to do the long-distance thing.

I enjoyed being in that relationship, but I was also very happy being mostly single between the ages of twenty-six and thirty-one. Earlier we discussed how having lots of options makes it difficult to settle on the right person. That's a real problem, but there's also an upside: With all these options, being single can be a shitload of fun!

I also had a lifestyle that was pretty bad for maintaining a serious relationship anyway. I was constantly shuffling between New York and L.A. for work and was unsure where my future career would take me.

I had a great time in the casual dating scene, but at a certain point I got tired of the work that went into maintaining a fun single life. Like others we interviewed in the book, the single world had worn me out.

At one point I was the hopeful romantic who would stay out till 4:00 A.M. every morning, worried that if I went home, I'd miss that magical, amazing woman who showed up at the bar at 3:35 A.M. After many late nights and brutal mornings, though, I realized that most amazing, magical women don't walk into a bar at 3:35 A.M. They're usually in bed by that hour. Usually the men and women who are going out this hard are less the "amazing/magical" sort and more the "nightmare/train wreck" variety.

As I hit thirty, I started to despise the bar scene. I had experienced every single version of those nights. I knew all the possible outcomes, and I knew the probabilities of those outcomes. When you hit that point, you realize how fruitless trying to find love by barhopping can be; you have enough data to know that statistically the smartest thing for you to do when you walk into a bar is go to the bathroom, jerk off, and leave.

I also started losing single friends. One day I stood alone at a barbecue at my house and saw nothing but couples around me. It seemed like I was the only single dude in the mix. Everyone else was splitting their racks of ribs into halves and sharing. Meanwhile, I had to eat a whole rack by myself like some kind of lonely fatso. I felt like it was time for a change. It was time to settle down a bit.

I decided I wanted to at least try having a relationship. It'd been so long. I started thinking about the advantages. I'd have someone whom I really cared about, who also cared about me. No more texting-back-and-forth nonsense. We wouldn't flake on each other. I'd always have someone to see a movie with, or go to a new restaurant with, or, as I would describe my dream at the time, "stay home, cook food, and do nothing" with.

It was fun being single, but I had reached what I will describe as a "point of exhaustion." I had experienced this personally, but when I did interviews for the book, I realized it is quite universal.

At a certain point the cost of the work needed to maintain a fun single lifestyle outweighs the benefits. The nights when you have amazing casual sex start getting outweighed by the times you wander home alone wasted and wake up hungover with a half-eaten burrito sitting on your chest.

The endless string of first dates where you just say the same shit over and over again in the same places starts getting tiresome. The casual scene was fun, but in between the fun, a lot of times there was emptiness.

Settling down offers the chance to fill that void with the dependable, deeper, intimate love of a committed relationship.

Now I had to find the right person. When I was out, I tried to keep an eye out for someone who could be relationship material. At first I had no luck, but then I had lunch with a friend who put it in perspective.

"I want to settle down, but I don't ever meet anyone I really like," I said.

"Well, where are you meeting these girls?" he asked.

"Bars and clubs," I replied.

"So you're going to horrible places and meeting horrible people and you're complaining about it? Live your life like a decent person. Go to the grocery store, buy your own food, take care of yourself. If you live a responsible life, you'll run into responsible people," he said.

It made sense. I was staying out like a lunatic and complaining that I only met lunatics. I realized if I was going to try to find someone to settle down with, I had to change the way I was going about my search. Instead of bars and clubs, I'd do things that I'd want a theoretical girlfriend to be into. I went to more museums, more food events, more low-key/interesting bars at earlier times, and things got better.

I made more of an effort to date friends of friends and began accepting setups, in the hope of meeting better people who were filtered through my existing social framework. I also decided to really get to know the girls I was dating. As I noted in chapter 4, instead of trying to lock down so many first dates, I tried to go on more fifth or sixth dates.

A few months later I ran into an amazing woman whom I had met years earlier. I had liked her then, but she had been in a relationship at the time. She was beautiful, funny, and a chef!!! If you've counted all the food references in this book, you realize what a great thing this is for me. We started dating. Pretty soon we were staying home, cooking food, and doing nothing all the time. It was great.

After a few weeks it started getting serious and I was faced with the decision of whether to truly settle down. Did I *really* want a girlfriend? Did I *really* want to give up the single life?

I thought for sure that I wanted a relationship, but when this amazing woman found her way to me, I was still scared. Settling down seemed like a frightening proposition.

I've explained how this is the era of the most romantic options and how, when you get in a relationship, you are closing the door on all of them.

Being single is a lot of work, but so are relationships. There were the inconveniences of my touring schedule and the giant hurdle of long distance (I was going back to L.A. and she lived in New York).

Eventually I decided to dive in.

Today we live together in L.A. and cook food and do nothing on a regular basis. She's amazing and I'm very happy in my relationship, but making the decision to dive in was tough. And it's tough for many singles out there.

FEAR OF SETTLING DOWN, FEAR OF SETTLING

When the opportunity to settle down presents itself, the glamour of the single life and all the potential options loom over our heads. The continuing fear many singles expressed in our interviews was that by getting into a serious relationship, they weren't settling down but settling.

In today's romantic climate, many people are plagued by what we will call "the upgrade problem." Singles constantly wonder whether there is a better match, an upgrade.

This was especially prevalent in larger cities. In walking cities like Chicago and Boston, people described how it was hard to settle down because every time they turned a corner, they saw more attractive and hypothetically interesting people.

As one woman told us, "For guys and girls equally . . . there's just so many people. And there's someone around the corner or uptown or downtown who you might like just a fraction better than the person who's across from you right now."

Even without being in a walking city, we all see way more faces in the digital world. And in a strange way, all the faces we see in the world or even on social media feel like real options that we are closing the door on when we settle down. Have you ever aimlessly browsed around on Instagram? It can be like going down a rabbit hole: clicking on friends, friends of friends, people who've liked those friends' photos. You see photos of all these beautiful people. You take a look at a few photos of someone's feed and you can begin to get a sense of who they are. You start to wonder, *Wow, what if this person and I connected?*

In a world where you sit around all day in your pajamas and swipe right on the faces of your dreams, the options problem rears its ugly head, making settling down seem so damn limiting. Yes, you have someone great, but are you sure they're the greatest?

But even for those who overcome this hurdle and commit to settling down, more challenges lie ahead.

PASSIONATE LOVE AND COMPANIONATE LOVE

Common wisdom says that in every relationship there are two phases. There's the beginning, where you fall in love and everything is new and magical. Then, after a certain point, maybe a few years, things get less exciting and more routine. There's still love, but it's just not like the magic you had in the beginning. As Woody Allen says in *Annie Hall*, "Love fades."

"Not in my relationship! Everything is great. We peaked and then that peak turned into a plateau and now we've been peaking ever since!"

Okay, why are you even reading this book about relationships? So you can see what mistakes sad, lonely people are making to cause them to have so much shittier lives than you? You know, why don't you just put this book down and go have sex with your partner you're so into, you asshole?

But wait, hold on a second—science says you are possibly lying. Yeah, I'm talking brain scans and shit. BRAIN SCANS.

Researchers have actually identified two distinct kinds of love: passionate love and companionate love.

In the first stage of a relationship you have passionate love. This is where you and your partner are just going ape shit for each other. Every smile makes your heart flutter. Every night is more magical than the last.

During this phase your brain gets especially active and starts releasing all kinds of pleasurable, stimulating neurotransmitters. Your brain floods your neural synapses with dopamine, the same neurotransmitter that gets released when you do cocaine.

"Carol, I can't describe how you make me feel. Wait, no, I can—you make my mind release pleasure-inducing neurotransmitters and you've flooded my mind with dopamine. If the experience of snorting cocaine and getting so high out of my mind that I want to climb a telephone pole with my bare hands just to see if I can do it were a person, it would be you."

Like all drugs, though, this high wears off. Scientists estimate that this phase usually lasts about twelve to eighteen months. At a certain point the brain rebalances itself. It stops pumping out adrenaline and dopamine and you start feeling like you did before you fell in love. The passion you first felt starts to fade. Your brain is like, *ALL RIGHT!! We get it, we get it. She's great, blah, blah, blah.*

What happens then? Well, in good relationships, as passionate love fades, a second kind of love arises to take its place: companionate love.

Companionate love is neurologically different from passionate love. Passionate love always spikes early, then fades away, while companionate love is less intense but grows over time. And, whereas passionate love lights up the brain's pleasure centers, companionate love is associated with the regions having to do with long-term bonding and relationships. Anthropologist Helen Fisher, the author of *Anatomy of Love* and one of the most cited scholars in the study of sex and attraction, was part of a research team that gathered and took brain scans of then-middle-aged people who'd been married an average of twenty-one years while they looked at a photograph of their spouse, and compared them with brain scans of younger people looking at their new partners. What they discovered, she writes, is that: "Among the older lovers, brain regions associated with anxiety were no longer active; instead, there was activity in the areas associated with calmness."[1] Neurologically it's similar to the kind of love you feel for an old friend or a family member.

So love goes from feeling like I'm doing cocaine to feeling how I feel about my uncle? I don't want to make companionate love sound like a bummer. It is love, just less intense and more stable. There is still passion, but it's balanced with trust, stability, and an understanding of each other's flaws. If passionate love is the coke of love, companionate love is like having a glass of wine or smoking a few hits of some mild weed. That makes it sound a little better than the uncle thing, right? We all like booze and weed more than we like our relatives, right? Great.

It also makes sense that passionate love shouldn't last. If we could all have lifelong passionate love, the world would collapse. We'd stay in our apartments lovingly staring at our partners while the streets filled with large animals and homeless children eating out of the garbage.

This transition from passionate love to companionate love can be tricky. In his book *The Happiness Hypothesis*, NYU social psychologist Jonathan Haidt identifies two danger points in every romantic relationship.

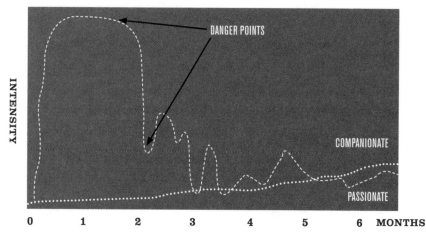

One is at the apex of the passionate love phase. We've all seen this in action. People get all excited and dive in headfirst. A new couple, weeks or months into a relationship, high off passionate love, go bonkers and move in and get married way too quickly.

This is like when you do a bunch of cocaine and decide you have a great life plan that you're ready to put into action.

"I figured it out, bro! I gotta melt old VCRs and mold the melted plastic to make action figures. I'll sell those and then I'll use the profit to fund my business that sells reversible clothes! I'll call them 'Inside Out Pajamas.' Think about it! One side is regular street clothes, then at night you turn 'em inside out and BOOM, PAJAMAS! Hey, is my nose bleeding?"

Sometimes these couples are able to transition from the passionate stage to companionate love. Other times, though, they transition into a crazy, toxic relationship and they get divorced and wonder what the hell they were thinking.

"Shit, so apparently the pajama side gets real dirty and gross during the day. Maybe you wear the pajama side the night before you wear the clothes side? Ah, fuck, what am I doing?! Stupid! Stupid! Fuck. I probably shouldn't have hacked into my parents' bank account and cleaned out their retirement fund. I'm going to need *way* more cocaine to figure this out . . ."

The second danger point is when passionate love starts wearing off. This is when you start coming down off of that initial high and you start worrying about whether this is really the right person. A couple weeks ago you were giddy and obsessed. All the new quirks and facts you learned about your lover felt like wonderful little surprises, like coming home and finding a chocolate on your pillow. Now you're like, *Okay, I get it. You like sewing historically accurate Civil War uniforms!!*

Your texts used to be so loving:

> It's hard to focus on anything at work, cause all that's in my head is you.

Now your texts are like:

> Let's just meet at Whole Foods

or:

> That dog that you made us buy shit in my shoe again.

You conclude there's something wrong with the person or the relationship since it isn't as exciting as before. So you break up, without ever giving companionate love a chance to bloom.

But Haidt argues that when you hit this stage, you should just be patient. With luck, if you allow yourself to invest more in the other person, you will find a beautiful life companion.

I had a rather weird firsthand experience with this. When I first started dating my girlfriend, a few months in, I went to a friend's wedding in Big Sur. I went alone, because my friend did me a huge solid and declined to give me a plus one. Which, of course, is the best. You get to sit by yourself and be a third wheel. Plus you get to constantly squeeze your head in between the heads of various couples and cutely go, "Whatchu guys talkin' 'bout?" It's GREAT!

The vows in this wedding were powerful. They were saying the most remarkable, loving things about each other. Things like "You are a prism that takes the light of life and turns it into a rainbow" or "You are a lotion that moisturizes my heart. Without you, my soul has eczema." It was the noncheesy, heartfelt version of stuff like that.

After the wedding four different couples broke up, supposedly because they didn't feel like they had the love that was expressed in those vows.

Did they call it off too early, at their danger point? I don't know, but I too felt scared hearing that stuff. Did I have what those people had? At that point, no. But for some reason I felt deep down that I should keep investing in my relationship and that eventually that level of love would show itself. And, so far, it has.

DO YOU NEED TO GET MARRIED?

In relationships, there's commitment and COMMITMENT, the kind that involves a license, usually some kind of religious blessing, and a ceremony in which every one of your

close friends and relatives watches you and your partner promise to stay together until one of you dies.

What happens to people's graphs of love once they get past the initial phases of love and power through their danger points?

This graph, which we got from Jonathan Haidt, measures the intensity of love over the course of a marriage.

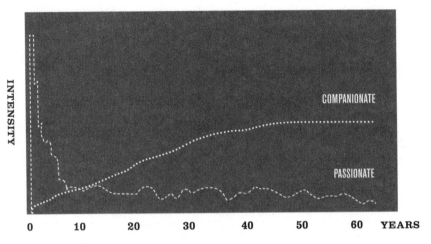

In the beginning, when you first get married, you get a shot of passionate love. This boost lasts about two years. Then the passion fades and you have various ups and downs. You go through the experiences of living together and raising a family. When the kids finally flee the coop—at about the twenty-five-year mark in the second chart—you and your mate get a rush of loving intensity. You can bask in the romance and maybe even rekindle some of the passion that brought you together in the first place. Then, soon after that, you're dead.

Whenever I'm at a wedding watching a beautiful couple exchange vows under a tree or at a mountain or a rainbow or whatever, I start thinking about this graph.

The brutal truth is that no matter how much they love each other, how beautiful the ceremony, how poetic and loving the vows, once they finish their wedding, you know their love is going to get less passionate and their life is going to get more complicated, and not in the most fun ways.

The romantic part of the relationship has peaked.

After the rings, the priest should just say, "Enjoy it, bing-bongs. Due to our brain's tendency toward hedonic adaptation, you won't feel quite this giddy in a few years. All right, where's the pigs in a blanket? I'm outta here."

So why get married at all?

In recent decades, and in most developed nations, marriage rates have dropped precipitously, leading some to wonder whether it is a dying institution. Philip Cohen, one of the leading demographers of the family, has documented the steep and widespread decline in global marriage rates since the 1970s. According to his calculations, 89 percent of the global population lives in a country with a falling marriage rate, and those who live in Europe and Japan are experiencing something more like a plummet.[2]

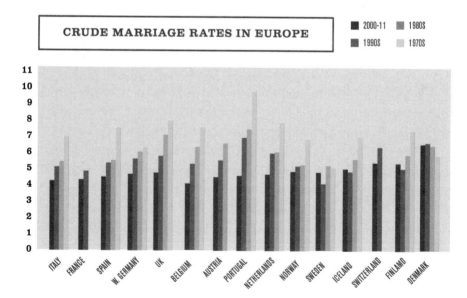

In the United States marriage rates are now at historic lows. In 1970, for instance, there were about seventy-four marriages for every thousand unmarried women in the population. By 2012 that had fallen to thirty-one per thousand single women—a drop of almost 60 percent. Americans are also joining the international trend of marrying later. In 1960, 68 percent of all people in their twenties were married, compared with just 26 percent in 2008.[3]

For the first time in history, the typical American now spends more years single than married.

What are people doing instead of getting married?

As Eric wrote in his book *Going Solo*, we are living in a time of incredible experimentation with different ways of settling down. Long-term cohabitation with a romantic partner is on the rise, especially in Europe. Living alone has skyrocketed almost everywhere, and in many major cities—from Paris to Tokyo, Washington, D.C., to Berlin—nearly half of all households have just one resident.

But marriage is not an altogether undesirable institution. After all, reams of social-science research show that successful marriages can make people live longer and be happier and healthier than single people. (Admittedly, a great many marriages aren't successful, and those who divorce or become widows or widowers may not get all these benefits.)

Good marriages also bring people more financial security, and these days one of the things that sociologists worry about is that better-off people are marrying more—and more successfully—than poor people, which increases inequality overall. In the United States, sociologist Andrew Cherlin writes, "marriage has become a status symbol—a highly regarded marker of a successful personal life."[4]

When I saw this graph (p. 219), I had a thought. Might it make more sense to forgo marriage and, instead, set out to experience a lifetime's worth of, say, one- to two-year, intensely passionate relationships? Wouldn't that be better than toiling through the doldrums of decades of waiting for your rise in companionate love?

Then your graph would look like this, right?

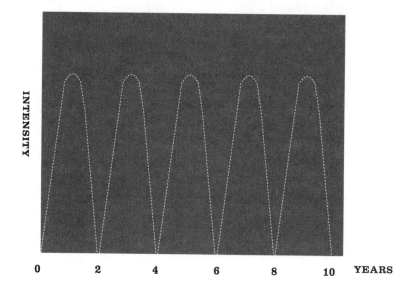

INTENSITY

| 0 | 2 | 4 | 6 | 8 | 10 | YEARS |

I contacted Jonathan Haidt, the psychologist who drew the passionate/companionate love graphs, and asked what he thought about the hypothetical graph. Here was his response:

There are two ways of thinking of satisfaction. One is the passionate/companionate love hedonic view, that the best life would be the one with the most passion in it. The other is a narrative view, that the best life is about building a story.

If you think the best life would be one with the most passion in it, then yes, that strategy would be much better than getting married. Falling in love is the most intense and wonderful experience—the second-most intense, after certain drugs, which are more intense for a few hours. Short of that, falling in love is the most wonderful thing.

But I didn't get much work done when I was falling in love with my wife. And then we had kids, we finally had children, and that was totally involving—and it would be weird to be such a romantically involved couple when you're raising kids. And now that that insanity has passed, I can return to writing books, which I really love doing. And I have a life partner who I think about all day long. And that's not tragic. That's not even disappointing. I have a life partner. We work together really well. We've built a fantastic life together. We're both really, really happy.

If you take a narrative view, there are different things to accomplish at different stages of life. Dating and having these passionate flings are perfect when you're younger, but some of the greatest joys of life come from nurturing and from what's called "generativity." People have strong strivings to build something, to do something, to leave something behind. And of course having children is one way of doing that. My own experience having children was that I discovered there were rooms in my heart that I didn't even know were there. And if I had committed to a life of repeated sexual flings, I never would have opened those doors.

If you think the whole point of life is to gaze into your lover's eyes all day until you die—well, then, I wouldn't want your life.

Was he quoting James Van Der Beek in *Varsity Blues* at the end there? Odd choice. Other than that, though, Haidt's analysis made a lot of sense to me. Passionate love is a drug that makes you feel amazing. A plan to just repeat that feeling over and over sounds nice in theory but in practice would be kind of dumb. Ecstasy makes you feel amazing too. But if I told you that my life plan was to make enough money to just do ecstasy all the time for twenty years, you'd think I was a lunatic.

Also, it's nice to imagine that graph being nothing but a series of high peaks with little valleys below, but as anyone who's been single for an extended period knows, the graph would probably be much weirder:

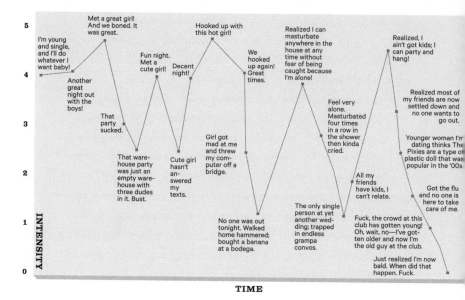

MONOGAMY, MONOGAMISH

There are many great things about being in a committed relationship. You have a bond full of love, trust, and stability. It's beautiful. But the excitement and novelty of a totally unexpected romantic encounter? That part of your life is dead.

For many people we interviewed, this creates a conflict that isn't easily resolved. No matter what their dating situation, people are torn between the benefits of a faithful, monogamous relationship and the novelty and excitement of single life.

Some people, including many prominent evolutionary psychologists and biological anthropologists, say that men and women aren't even wired to be monogamous.

I spoke at length about this with the biological anthropologist Helen Fisher. Fisher contends that our cave-dwelling ancestors, compelled to spread their genetic material, had many sexual partners simultaneously, and after thousands of years of promiscuity, human brains are still wired to mate with multiple people.

The current norms of faithfulness and sexual exclusivity are actually relatively new even in modern times. According to the marriage historian Stephanie Coontz, in the eighteenth century American men were quite open about their extramarital escapades. She found letters in which husbands described their mistresses to their wives' brothers and recounted how they contracted sexually transmitted diseases from prostitutes. I wasn't able to find one of those letters, but I imagine it was something like this:

My Dearest Charles,

I hope this letter finds you in the halest and heartiest of conditions. I'm sure it will, as your constitution, as I recall, was always most impressive for its resilience and fortitude.

What do you make of this so-called "Revolution"? I fear that, win or lose, we shall be feeling its reverberations for decades to come.

In other news, in addition to your sister, I am fucking Tina, this woman I met at the bar last week. I also caught syphilis from a prostitute I met in Boston.

Fondly, your brother-in-law,
Henry

Men, Coontz explains, believed sexual adventure was their birthright, and women basically accepted this as a facet of the relationship. "For thousands of years it was expected of men they would have affairs and flings," Coontz told the *New York Times*. "That would be unthinkable today."[5]

So what changed?

I spoke with the journalist and sex columnist Dan Savage, who has written at length about the age-old conflict between being faithful and having sexual adventure outside of a committed relationship. Savage contends that the women's movement during the twentieth century fundamentally changed our approach to the problem. Women, he explains, rightly contested the presumption that men could fool around while they had no outside sexual options. But the decisive shift came when, rather than extending to women the leeway men had always enjoyed to have extramarital sexual escapades, society took the opposite approach.

Men could have said, "Okay, let's both mess around." But instead men got preemptively jealous of their wives messing around and said, "What? No, I don't want you boning other dudes! Let's just both not mess around." This, Savage says, is when the monogamous expectation was placed on men and women, and it's an expectation that neither sex is wired to meet.

"You're told in the culture that if you want to fuck somebody else you need to do the right thing and end this relationship before you fuck somebody else or you're a bad guy or you're a bad girl," he said. "I think that that's bullshit. There's higher loyalty. There's a greater good. A relationship is more than just not touching anybody else with your penis ever again."

I put myself to the test with a thought experiment. Let's say my girlfriend was in Miami for a bachelorette party, and she ran into R&B superstar/actor Tyrese Gibson (*Fast and the Furious* franchise, *Baby Boy*). And for some reason they hit it off, and she ended up hooking up with Tyrese. It was a one-night thing. She wasn't in love with Tyrese. She wasn't trying to be with Tyrese. She wasn't trying to get invited to dinner at GibsiHana, the custom restaurant Tyrese had built in his backyard to mimic a Benihana Japanese steak house.*

If that were the case, I think I would be okay with it—if I didn't know about it.

I posited this hypothetical situation to my girlfriend and reversed the roles, with it being me who took another partner. She

---

* This is real! Please Google it.

didn't feel the same way. She saw no reason for us to stray from our monogamy and felt that doing so would be a violation of the trust in our relationship. She said if I got drunk and something like that did happen, she would be understanding, but it would be a big deal and she'd want to know about it. However, she also said there was a big difference between me being really drunk and making a mistake and actively pursuing a sexual tryst outside our relationship, hitting bars and texting women to have a quick fling.

Also, probably best if I had this whole conversation at home in private, as opposed to a bar, where I definitely got looks from people who seemed to be curious as to why I was discussing my girlfriend hypothetically cheating on me with Tyrese.

Savage believes that cheating is tempting for just about every-one and that for some people it's simply too hard to resist. Rather than succumbing to urges we all have, cheating behind our partner's back, getting caught, and destroying the relationship, Savage thinks we'd be better off acknowledging that we have these desires and de-ciding how to deal with them—as a couple.

"If you have children together, if you have a history together, if you have property together, if you melded two extended families together, all of that has to weigh more than one blow job you got on a business trip," he said.

Savage isn't opposed to monogamy. He recognizes its advan-tages for those who can sustain it and produce successful relation-ships. The problem, he says, is that today far too many people are making commitments that they cannot realistically honor.

The idea of trying to maintain a committed relationship while also satisfying our urges for sexual novelty has led to a lot of exper-imentation over the years with "open relationship"-type arrange-ments. Couples have tried everything from open marriages to being "swingers" to maintaining "don't ask, don't tell" policies.

Just how many people have experimented with these arrange-ments? The latest survey data show that 26 percent of American men and 18 percent of American women report having engaged in "an open sexual relationship." Surprisingly, young adults between the ages of twenty-one and thirty are the least likely to have tried this, at only 19 percent, whereas it is most prevalent among those in their forties, at 26 percent. And seniors? Twenty-two percent of them have tried an open sexual relationship. Damn!

"Open relationships? Is that where you fuck other people? Yeah, we do that sometimes."*

Savage coined the term "monogamish" to describe his own open relationship with his partner. The gist of it is that the couple is deeply committed to each other, but there is room for outside sexual activity.

"Monogamish" is not a one-size-fits-all concept. Each couple works out their own terms and agrees beforehand to what sexual activity outside the relationship will be tolerated. Some demand complete honesty from their partner, while others may prefer a "don't ask, don't tell" policy. Some restrict how close the outside person must be—at least a friend of a friend, at least a friend of

---

* **NOTE:** To cover myself legally, I need to again let you know that this is a couple who posed for a stock photograph, and I have no idea if they are together or if they indeed have an open relationship and "fuck other people." They are not real people. Well, they're real. They're not, like, clones or something. Whatever. You get what I mean. For real, though, they're cyborgs.*

* **NOTE 2:** I just heard back from my lawyer that to be 100 percent legally in the clear, I need to be explicit that these are not cyborgs and that they are just people who posed for a stock photo image. Sorry for any confusion.

a friend of a friend, a stranger neither of you will ever see again, someone who lives in a different state, or it can *only* be Michigan State University provost June Pierce Youatt. (All right, the last one not as much.)

In our interviews and on our subreddit, we met several couples who had set up arrangements in the vein of what Savage discussed. Some of the people were incredibly enthusiastic about their experiences. On the subreddit one woman wrote:

> *I've been in open relationships for the last ten years now, and have been with my husband for 8 years. I chose to be in one when I realized that every boyfriend I ever had cheated on me, and I cheated on every one of them. I finally decided that maybe I need variety, and that I was attracted to sexually adventurous men.*
>
> *Being in an open relationship is such a relief—no more lies, no more horrible break ups, no more guilt. My husband and I have rules we follow, like he can only see someone else once a week, and if I don't like the girl he picks I can make him stop seeing her.*
>
> *The best part is, we can be honest about how we feel without judgement. No more hiding crushes or sexual tension. We are madly in love, and have a daughter together. I know it's not for everyone but it works for us.*

Other couples used these kinds of arrangements to facilitate long-distance relationships. One woman, who had been seeing her musician boyfriend for a few months, told me about the agreement they made when he went away on tour. She understood that he was on the road for months at a time, and in the interest of maintaining the relationship, she would let him have some leeway while on tour—up to a point. They created "tour rules" that he had to follow. "No sex, just blow jobs. That's as far as it could go," she said.

And she didn't want her boyfriend maintaining contact with anyone this stuff happened with. "I don't want to be in bed and look over and seeing him texting some girl from Cincinnati," she explained. "And while he's away, I have the same privileges."

We also met a woman from Brooklyn who had just starting dating someone who made it clear that he wanted to occasionally hook up with other people. They entered into an agreement where they could have sex with others, but only under the following conditions: The person had to be at least two degrees outside their friend group (a friend of a friend), it was "don't ask, don't tell," and if they were out hooking up with someone else, they had to make a good excuse that didn't let on that they were out messing around. It was an "out of sight, out of mind" type of arrangement, and it was working.

In her case, however, having an open arrangement was not exactly ideal. When we asked why she and her partner did it, she explained that it wasn't because she wanted more variety and sexual adventure in her own life. It was more of a protective mechanism, so that she didn't risk her boyfriend straying from the relationship because of his interest in sleeping with other people. "I feel like he'll probably cheat anyway," she said, "and at least this way I'm controlling it."

We met other people who had entered open relationships in which the two partners were not equally enthusiastic about the arrangement. A gentleman on the subreddit told us that he had agreed to an open relationship with a woman who wanted one because he didn't want to lose her altogether. But, as he explains, that just turned out to be a long, painful way to get hurt:

I was so into her that I decided that being with her in an open relationship was better than nothing. Because I wasn't really interested in anyone else it was mostly me being with her, and her being with a few other guys until she found someone she liked more than me. It was a weird situation. I'd call her up and be like, "Hey wanna go see a movie or grab dinner?" and she'd be like, "Oh. Awkward. I'm actually with Schmitty Yagermanjensen tonight." Or she wouldn't answer at all, which was even worse, because then I had to guess what she was doing . . . Being a placeholder sucks, and that's pretty much how it was for me.

Another woman wrote that entering into an open relationship was "the worst decision I'd ever made."

"When the going got tough, I was the one who got screwed over. Under the guise of 'we all love each other and care about each other, primary and secondary come first,' he slept with a third woman that I wasn't comfortable with yet, and basically told me to f--- off. We don't talk anymore," she said.

Sometimes both parties are equally into creating an open arrangement—at least in theory. In practice, though, they soon discover that sleeping with other people can be a messy affair.

We met Raina, a woman who tried to strike such an agreement with her new husband. They moved to Hong Kong after getting married and agreed to allow outside sexual partners with a "don't ask, don't tell" policy. They both were enthusiastic about entering an open relationship, but at a certain moment Raina found things had gone far beyond her expectations:

I thought I was being realistic. So I once had a conversation, and said I'm not gonna divorce you if there's an indiscretion or two, but you have to be like the CIA about it. I don't want to know about it. I don't want to sniff it. You've got to be that level, so that it's invisible.

But we had the secondary policy that if I ever wanted to know, that he had to tell the truth.

And so, we were on vacation for my birthday in Kyoto, and I asked.

He said, "I don't think I want to tell you this on your birthday."

And I thought, "Okay, so now I know that he's doing something."

And I said, "Well, why don't you just tell me how many people?"

And then he said, "Give me a second."

He needed to calculate it.

He came back with the following number.

And I want you to notice that at this point we're 13 months into our marriage.

26.

26 individuals.

I was expecting one, maybe two.

I did not expect 26.

Well . . . happy birthday, Raina!

The relationship ended soon after.

I told Savage that my fear in trying to have an open relationship with someone is that it would become a dangerously slippery slope. Maybe it wouldn't venture into Raina territory, but I could still see things easily getting out of hand. Anytime I hear about couples experimenting like this, they eventually break up.

Savage didn't accept that explanation.

"When a nonmonogamous relationship fails, everyone blames the nonmonogamy; when a closed relationship fails, no one ever blames the closed relationship," he said.

Savage also explained that the nonmonogamous relationships that did work were built on a strong foundation.

"From my observations of many, many years and my personal experience, the relationships that are successfully monogamish or that have an allowance of an understanding were monogamous for years," Savage told me. He also said both participants need to really want an open relationship and neither party can be wishy-washy. If it's clearly a one-sided desire, it isn't going to work.

The model ultimately seems built to address the fact that passionate love cannot last long-term, and that the foundation of a strong relationship is not perpetual excitement and intensity but a deep, hard-earned emotional bond that intensifies over time. In other words, companionate love.

Savage's argument for more honesty about our desires is compelling. But for most people, in the United States at least, integrating outside sexual activity into a relationship is difficult to imagine. When I'd bring it up in casual conversations or in focus groups, there was massive skepticism. Some people were afraid that even bringing up such notions to their partner could lead to trouble in a relationship.

"If I brought up something like that to my wife," one man said, "it would be a game changer in the relationship. If she wasn't into it, I couldn't take it back and say, 'Oh no, I was just kidding, I don't think about having sex with other people. That doesn't appeal to me at all.' Instead, the seeds of doubt would be planted, and I'd be screwed. It would open up a shit can of issues. And they would never go away."

Others understood the rationale behind wanting an open relationship in theory, but they doubted that they could pull it off. "For me personally, I couldn't be cool with it," one woman at a focus group told us. "I want to be, but I couldn't roll with it."

Many women we met said if their boyfriend asked if they were willing to have a more open relationship, they'd start to doubt how serious he was. "At that point, why even be with someone?" one woman asked, with apparent disdain for the monogamish idea. "If you don't want to be committed, just go jerk off." (To be clear, she was talking to her hypothetical partner. She wasn't telling me to leave the interview and go masturbate.)

Experts, even those who agree with Savage in theory, have also voiced concern about how realistic these arrangements are in practice. "I can certainly see the appeal of suggesting we try and make this an open, mutual, gender-equal arrangement," said Coontz, the marriage historian. "I'm a little dubious how much that is going to work."

Barry Schwartz, our authority on choice and decision making, also worried about the idea of trying to make choices and explore other options on the side. "When I was your age, open marriages became the vogue," he told me. "All these high-powered, intellectual types were convinced they could have loving relationships with their partners and also sleep with other people. They were above the petty morality of their parents. Every single one of them ended up unmarried within a year of starting. So, at least back then, it couldn't survive. Monogamy could not survive promiscuity."

Maybe the person who puts this whole issue in perspective

best is rapper Pitbull. In perhaps my favorite discovery in all of the research I've done for this book or life in general, I found an interview where he discussed how he has an open relationship with his girlfriend. Pitbull lives by the words *Ojos que no ven, corazón que no siente*, or "What the eyes don't see, the heart doesn't feel."

"People are stuck on what's normal, what's right, what's wrong," Pitbull said. "Maybe what's right to you is wrong to me . . . What counts at the end of the day is everybody being happy."[6]

I wish you knew how psyched I am to end this chapter on a deep, insightful thought from Pitbull.

WHEN I STARTED THIS BOOK,

I had a lot of burning questions about modern romance. The shenanigans we all have experienced often left me confused, frustrated, and angry. Trying to find love (or even something casual) in a romantic climate filled with endless scheduling texts and hurdles like Tanya's "silencing" of 2012 can be a stressful experience.

Then, even after finding a great, healthy relationship with a loving partner, a whole new set of questions arose. I worried about settling down. Should I close all the exciting doors of today's single world? If things start to feel routine and less exciting, is sexting going to make our romantic life any better? If I suspect that my partner has something going on the side, what are the ethics of looking at her Facebook or phone messages to find out? And if passionate love fades eventually, should I be seeking a long-term, monogamous relationship anyway?

I wrote this book because I wanted to better understand all the conundrums that come up in modern romance. So, after teaming up with an eminent sociologist, interviewing hundreds of people, consulting the world's foremost experts on romance and relationships, conducting fieldwork in five countries, and reading a mountain of studies and books and news articles and academic papers, what exactly have I learned?

A lot, actually.

Here's what I took away from this entire experience:

Finding someone today is probably more complicated and stressful than it was for previous generations—but you're also more likely to end up with someone you are really excited about.

Our search for the right person—and even our idea of what "the right person" actually means—has changed radically in a very, very short amount of time.

If I had been a young person a few generations ago, I would have gotten married pretty young. Most likely, I would have wound up marrying some girl who lived in my neighborhood in my hometown of Bennettsville, South Carolina, around the time I was twenty-three. She would have been even younger, which means she would have been going straight from her father's arms into mine, with no time to develop or pursue her own interests.

Let's say her family owned the local Hardee's franchise.*

Her parents would meet me early on and decide I was a decent

---

* For those not from the South, Hardee's is a fast-food chain that specializes in breakfast biscuits. They do other shit, but I mainly remember being into them for the biscuits. Particularly the chicken biscuit.

guy with a decent job who wasn't going to murder anyone. We'd set off on a brief period of dating and then get married.

I'd run the Hardee's and probably be pretty good at it. Maybe I'd catch wind of a guy who was running a huge "biscuit extortion" scam to smuggle biscuits across the border to Georgia. The scam would work like this: The guy and his partner would steal biscuits from our store and then sell the stolen biscuits at a lower cost on the biscuit black market. After getting suspicious of his frequent trips to Georgia, I would hide in the bed of a Ford F-150, under a bunch of biscuits, and when they reached their destination, I'd dramatically pop up and go, "GIMME BACK MY BISCUITS."

The family would be proud.

Ideally, my wife and I would grow together and have a happy relationship. But maybe, as we grew, we'd become different people and realize the relationship wasn't working. Maybe my wife would resent her homemaker role and have desires and goals beyond those afforded to women of the era. Maybe I'd be a dissatisfied grump who eventually joined Alfredo in a retirement home where we schemed for doughnuts on the reg.

But I don't live in that era. When I hit twenty-three, I wasn't thinking about marriage at all. Instead I got the chance to experience "emerging adulthood" and grow as a person. I met people from all over the world in this part of my life. I wasn't limited to just the folks I knew in my neighborhood in Bennettsville. So as I grew older, I figured out my career, I dated people in New York and Los Angeles, and eventually I started dating a beautiful chef from Texas whom I met through friends of friends in New York.

We would have never met in previous generations, because I would have been married to the Hardee's girl and she would have probably been settled down in Texas with some guy she met in her neighborhood, maybe a hot-sauce king named Dusty.* And

---

* I went to school with a kid in South Carolina named Dusty Dutch. For real. How amazing is that name? Had to include this fact. Finally glad this info is out in the world.

who knows if we would have even hit it off if we did meet? I became a very different person between the ages of twenty-three and thirty-one.

The situation I have now is probably a better deal for me than the one I would have had a few generations ago. If you are a woman, forget about it. With all the cultural advancements, middle-class and professional women of this era have gained the freedom to have their own lives and careers without the need for marriage. Having a husband and kids isn't a prerequisite to having a well-rounded, fulfilling adult life anymore. To be clear, I'm not saying that filling that traditional housewife role over being a professional is a bad thing to do today, and I know that the decisions women make about work are complicated. Also, I'm not saying that women who do choose careers hate their kids, etc. Am I clear here? I'M NOT SHITTING ON ANYONE'S LIFE CHOICE (unless the choice is to smoke crack and treat your kids like the Mo'Nique character treats Precious in the movie *Precious*). But what's important is that more women than ever are able to make that choice for themselves.

Even if women do make the choice to pursue their careers, the research shows that they still do way more of their share of the domestic work than men (step it up, dudes), but overall they are closer to being equitable partners than they were a few generations ago. They don't have to settle down at twenty with some bozo who their parents think will be a good match because he has a good job or whatever.

The "good-enough marriage" is definitely not good enough for today's singles. We're not content to marry someone who happens to live down the street and gets along okay with our parents.

Sure, there were lots of people in previous generations who met someone in the neighborhood and grew to have a deep, loving soul mate–level bond. But there are many others who didn't. And the current generation won't take that risk. We want a soul mate. And we are willing to look very far, for a very long time, to find one.

A soul mate isn't just someone we love. As for our grandparents, there are probably lots of people out there whom we could settle down with and, in the fullness of time, grow to love. But we want more than love. We want a lifelong wingman/wingwoman who completes us and can handle the truth, to mix metaphors from three different Tom Cruise movies.

Historically, we're at a unique moment. No one has ever been presented with more options in romance and expected to make a decision where the expectations are so astronomically high. And with all these choices, how can anyone possibly be sure that they've made the right one?

Get over it: You can't! So you just have to power through and have hope that as you grow and mature, you'll eventually learn to navigate this new romantic world and find someone who does feel right for you.

Technology hasn't just changed how we find romance; it's also put a new spin on the timeless challenges we face once we're in a relationship.

One of the strange things that happens in modern romance is that once you start dating someone, your physical lives aren't the only things that get entangled; your phone worlds also merge. Today couples have a shared space that they can use for something intimate like sexting. Sometimes this shared phone world is a source of excitement and novelty, but other times the phone world becomes a new source of jealousy. We wind up snooping rather than trusting our special person.

And the fears that make us snoop are valid, because, let's face it—people cheat. In fact, people make mistakes in relationships all the time. On this issue the United States might be able to learn something from France. I'm not very comfortable with a French woman being forced to live with her husband having a long-term mistress, but I do like that the French are willing to realistically acknowledge the essential fallibility of human nature and the fact that people, despite their best intentions and their love for their partners, do stray. Like Dan Savage (and, to an extent, Pitbull) says, a relationship is bigger than the idea of sexual exclusivity.

Treat potential partners like actual people, not bubbles on a screen.

With online dating and smartphones, we can message people all over the world. We can interact with potential mates on a scale that simply wasn't conceivable for previous generations. But this shift to digital communication has a powerful side effect. When you look at your phone and see a text from a potential partner, you don't always see another person—you often see a little bubble with text in it. And it's easy to forget that this bubble is actually a person.

As we see more and more people online, it can get difficult to remember that behind every text message, OkCupid profile, and Tinder picture there's an actual living, breathing, complex person, just like you.

But it's so, so important to remember this.

For one thing, when you forget you're talking to a real person, you might start saying the kinds of things in a text message that no person in their right mind would ever say to a real-life person in a million years.

If you were in a bar, would you ever go up to a guy or girl and repeat the word "hey" ten times in a row without getting a response? Would you ever go up to a woman you met two minutes ago and beg her to show you one of her boobs? Even if you are just looking for a casual hookup, do you really think this will work? And if so, do you *really* want to bone someone who responds to this?

Yet people send these kinds of text messages all the time. I can only conclude that it's because it's so easy to forget that you're talking to another human being and not a bubble. And the content of these bubbles can really shape how you, the person, are judged.

We have two selves: a real-world self and a phone self, and the nonsense our phone selves do can make our real-world selves look like idiots. Our real-world selves and our phone selves go hand in hand. Act like a dummy with your phone self and send some thoughtless message full of spelling errors, and the real-world self will pay the price. The person on the other end sees no difference between your two selves. They never think, *Oh, I'm sure he's much more intelligent and thoughtful in person. This is just his "lazy phone persona."*

If you text something innocuous like "Wsup" to someone you just met and want to go out with, it may not seem particularly dumb. But when you think back on all our interviews and remember how much of that garbage is in everyone's phones, you realize it makes you seem like a pretty boring, generic person.

Don't just write a stupid "Wsup" message. Try to say something thoughtful or funny and invite this person to do a nice, interesting thing. Make it personal. Mention that thing you were joking about, like seeing a dog driving a hovercraft—I mean, wow, how lucky were you two to see that together? I wish I could've been there. Who knows, this could be the person you spend the rest of your life with! I have many friends who start something with the intention of its being casual, but there is a spark and it ends up being serious. It even happened to me.

Your most casual encounter could lead to something bigger, so treat those interactions with that level of respect. Even if it doesn't blossom, treating the messages with that level of respect will surely make the person on the other end more receptive as well. There is *no* downside to it.

And if you really want to go nuts, maybe a thoughtful phone conversation wouldn't be the worst thing in the world?

On another note, I also learned that everyone plays games with texting, like waiting longer than the other person to text, sending replies of equal length, always trying to get the last word, and the like. Even if you say you "don't play games," *that* is a type of game—it is the "I don't play games" game.

Everyone hates these games and no one wants to play them.

For the most part, people just want to be honest and say how they feel, and they definitely want others to be honest and open with them. But here's the thing: Unfortunately those games are actually kind of effective. No matter how much people want things to be different, I don't think we can defeat the insecurities and tendencies built into our internal psychology.

But let's all realize we are in the same boat dealing with the same shit. So if you aren't into someone, before just ignoring them, try to be mindful of how frustrating it is to be on the other side of that and maybe try crafting them an honest message or, at the least, lie and say: "Hey, sorry, working on my debut rap album, *Fantabulous*, so gonna be in the studio nonstop and need to focus, not dating at the moment. I'm very flattered though and you are a great person, all the best."

In books like this it's easy to get negative about technology and its impact. This shift in communication can be very annoying, and hearing older generations bemoan it, you can easily romanticize the past. But I was at a wedding recently where I saw that there is a beautiful side to things as well.

During the toasts, a bridesmaid shared some early e-mails that the bride had sent her years ago when she was first pursuing the groom, who was painfully oblivious to her advances. The initial e-mails showed her being sad that the guy didn't love her back and worried that she should give up. Her friend even said that she should "hang it up" because she was becoming "that girl." But she kept on, and months later there was an e-mail saying that she was madly in love.

Hearing those e-mails was remarkable, and it made me realize that digital technology gives all of us the chance to have this very unique record of our romantic relationships.

On our one-year anniversary my girlfriend gave me a huge book that compiled the entire history of our text messages from the first year of our relationship. It was hilarious to look back on all the things we said. For certain messages she wrote out what was going on in her mind, and it was amazing.

Since I've done this to hundreds of people, I will finally do it to myself. Let's look at *my* exchanges. To set the scene, I got her number at a barbecue in Brooklyn and we talked about getting ramen later that week.

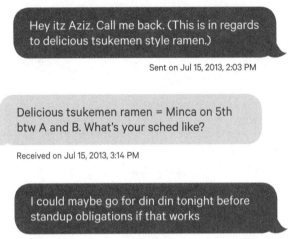

> Hey itz Aziz. Call me back. (This is in regards to delicious tsukemen style ramen.)
>
> Sent on Jul 15, 2013, 2:03 PM

> Delicious tsukemen ramen = Minca on 5th btw A and B. What's your sched like?
>
> Received on Jul 15, 2013, 3:14 PM

> I could maybe go for din din tonight before standup obligations if that works
>
> Sent on Jul 15, 2013, 5:13 PM

Okay, so the first message was sent by me after I called and sent the text in lieu of a voice mail. My girlfriend didn't call me back, though; she texted. In the book she gave me, she reveals that at the time, she didn't realize that I'd asked her to call. After realizing her mistake, she freaked out and was worried that by texting instead of calling she would come off looking too nervous or scared.

> I can't tonight, having a going away dinner for one of the milk bar gals. I could do tomorrow or Wednesday. Also- never seen you do stand up, DEF want to get down on that. Curious- on a scale of 1-10, how funny are you?
>
> Received on Jul 15, 2013, 5:20 PM

> Hey— let's do Minca tonight at 815 and we'll go to Comedy Cellar after and I'll drop in. Cool? My skill on a scale of 1-10 . . . Hmmm let's just say I'm kinda like the hokey pokey cookie of standup comedy.

Sent on Jul 16, 2013, 10:13 AM

> Sweet!—The Hokey Pokey is definitely Milk Bar's funniest cookie. See you at Minca.

Received on Jul 16, 2013, 11:09 AM

I didn't respond to her next message until the next day at 10:13 A.M. I definitely intentionally waited so as not to come off as overeager. And I specifically remember running a draft by a friend and rewriting it several times before sending it off. (The hokey pokey cookie is a reference to a cookie that her restaurant made, one that she knew I loved.)

Today I know for a fact that my waiting did indeed cause some uneasiness. She told me that she felt I must have somehow been offended by the "how funny are you?" comment. But the same night she was waiting, she got word that I'd asked a friend of hers if she was in fact single, so she knew all was well.

Still, the waiting did have an effect. She told me that she was really excited when I wrote back the next morning.

The early messages are interesting to look back on, because they reveal so much about our mind-sets at the time. Both of us were anxious about the texts we were crafting, but we were oblivious to the fact that we were in the same boat.

As things progressed in the relationship (and in our messages), she talked about how much it meant to her when I sent some early loving texts saying that I missed her or was thinking about her.

When I read them, it took me back through all the excitement and fun we'd had during those times.

So although these new tools may cause us all stress and angst in the early parts of a relationship, the same technology has also given us all a new place to store, remember, and share our love for each other, and I'm glad we have it.

Don't think of online dating as dating—think of it as an online introduction service.

Online dating has probably been the single biggest game changer in the hunt for your soul mate. Remember: Between 2005 and 2012 *one-third* of all the couples who got married in the United States met on the Internet. By the time this book is out, that number undoubtedly will be higher and some new app or site will make Tinder or whatever is currently popular seem outdated.

Many online daters we spoke with were having success, but many were also frustrated and fed up with the scene altogether. However, most of the ones who were fed up seemed to be spending more time in front of their screens than in front of their dates in real life.

Online dating works best as a forum where you can meet people whom you'd never otherwise be able to meet. It's the ultimate way to expand the search beyond the neighborhood.

The key is to get off the screen and meet these people. Don't spend your nights in endless exchanges with strangers. Communicate with people you have some chance of liking, then, after a few messages—enough to figure out if there's something really, really wrong with them—just ask them out.

After a certain point, if you're still trading endless back-and-forth messages online, you're just wasting time. Have faith in your ability to size someone up in person.

The allure of online dating and its vast supply of potential dates can make staying in and clicking through profiles in your pajamas seem like a better option than heading out to a crowded bar or restaurant, but let's not forget another great source of potential mates—*the real world*.

Remember Arpan, the dude who was so burned out on online dating? We contacted him about a year after the focus group to see whether he was still meeting women online and taking them to the bowling alley (just for drinks, of course).

We were delighted to hear that his whole love life had taken a turn for the better. He had met someone special and been dating her for a few months, and he seemed genuinely happy, with way more energy than he had shown that sad Sunday morning with us.

Arpan met his new lady in real life, but he credited his online dating experiences with helping him meet new people. He explained that all those unanswered messages had reduced his fear of rejection and made him less apprehensive about approaching women.

He met his girlfriend at a bar, after seeing her at a distance and working up the courage to introduce himself. "I walked towards her group, said hello to all of her friends, looked this girl straight in the eye and said, 'I saw you from across the room and I just had to say hello.'" It was heartwarming to learn that Arpan had turned things around since we'd first met him, and it was fascinating to hear him trace his success in real-world romance to the things he learned while dating online.

With so many romantic options, instead of trying to explore them all, make sure you properly invest in people and give them a fair chance before moving on to the next one.

We have so many options and we're horrible at analyzing them. We go on boring dates and we're quick to move on to the next person.

Stack the deck in your favor. Go on interesting dates. Follow the "monster truck rally" theory, and do things that are going to help you experience what it's really like to be with this person. Don't just stare at each other across the table while sipping a beverage and making the same small talk you've made a thousand times about siblings, hometowns, and where you went to college.

Also, have faith in people. A person may seem just okay, but if you really invest time in the relationship, maybe they'll be greater than you assume.

Think about it in terms of the music of rapper Flo Rida.* When you hear his latest song, at first you think, *Goddamn it, Flo Rida. You're just doing the same thing again, song after song. This song is nothing special at all.* And by the tenth time you hear it, you're like, *FLO!!! YOU'VE DONE IT AGAIN! THIS IS A HIT, BABY!!!*

In a sense we are all like a Flo Rida song: The more time you spend with us, the more you see how special we are. Social scientists refer to this as the Flo Rida Theory of Acquired Likability Through Repetition.

The other thing that has stuck with me is how important it is to analyze options in the real world, not just on the screen. When I was finishing up this book, I got contacted by a woman who had been in the audience of a stand-up show I did in Michigan in September 2013. During the show I was discussing texting and asked if anyone had met someone recently and had been in a back-and-forth. This woman, who was sitting in the front, raised her hand, and I invited her to come up to the front of the stage and share her experience.

She told me she'd met the guy about a week earlier and had been messaging back and forth. She had met him through friends of friends at a bonfire. He lived in her apartment complex, and after

---

* "Shorty had them apple bottom jeans . . . boots with the fur . . . (with the fur!) . . . the whole club was looking at her . . . "

meeting her, he left her a note on her door that said, "Dinner tomor-row?" and his apartment number.

She wrote, "I'm busy," on the note and put it back on front of his door.

He then placed the note back on her door and wrote, "You're busy tonight? How about Monday, Wednesday, or Friday?"

She then took the conversation to Facebook and sent him a message that said:

> Hi Ron, I assume it's you not Sara sending me notes. 😊
>
> I think the idea of dinner is great, but things are kind of hectic right now in addition to a huge voice project that I'm working on all day, every day for the next two weeks. My brother in law's grandma won't be living much longer and I'm on call to babysit my niece and nephew if my sister has to be with her husband's family. Can I get back to you when things settle down? Thanks.

He responded: "No worries. Family always comes first."

As always, you can tell so much by these messages. Her ex-tended list of excuses, including that really intense one about the dying grandma, did not bode well for this would-be suitor. I asked the audience to clap if they thought she actually liked this guy and would go out with him when things "settled down." There was a smattering of claps. When I asked if people thought she didn't like him and they would never go out, there was massive applause. The audience knew this lady wasn't ready to go out with this guy.

After hearing this, she said, "Well, I've seen him around since and he's not terrible," and that she would "maybe" go out with him. It was the last I heard of this situation.

Then in September 2014, a year later, the woman was able to get in contact with me. She said that after we read through the messages, she realized she should give him a second chance. They started dating, and now, a year later, they were getting married!

It was pretty insane to hear.

And in the context of this book I think it's an important story to remember. With all our new tools for connecting and communicating, there's still nothing more useful than actually spending time with a person face-to-face.

Often, when you're out in the single world meeting people, you meet someone you like, get their number, and put it right in your phone, transforming them into an "option" that lives in your device. Sometimes you and that option engage in some phone-based interaction and you meet up in person. But sometimes that exchange never happens. That potentially cool, exciting person dies there, buried in your phone.

When I was actively dating, there was a woman I'd met in a bar. For whatever reason, our text conversation fizzled and we never met up after our initial meeting. We ran into each other at a mutual friend's party years later and really hit it off. I felt dumb. Why hadn't I ever followed up with this great person?

After writing this book, I think I know why. It's probably because I was busy chasing other options. I didn't text her and left her to die in my phone.

For me the takeaway of these stories is that, no matter how many options we seem to have on our screens, we should be careful not to lose track of the human beings behind them. We're better off spending quality time getting to know actual people than spending hours with our devices, seeing who else is out there.

Okay, well, I'm fucking done with my book!!! YEAH!!!

Before we part, though, I want to say one more thing about our current romantic conundrums. These days there are a lot of people out there saying that social media and all our new communications technologies are making it impossible for people to really connect with one another. There are an equal number of people saying that our new media makes things better than ever. By now I hope it's clear that I don't buy either of these extreme arguments.

Culture and technology have always shaken romance. When the plow came in and made women's labor value in the family unit drop, it was disruptive. When the car provided a means for people to travel and see people who lived farther away, that was disruptive too. Same with telegraphs, telephones, televisions, and whatever future inventions may come. Who knows, maybe some woman is reading this in the future and wondering, *Ummm. . . well at least dudes weren't teleporting dicks to your house on a regular basis! This sounds great.*

History shows that we've continually adapted to these changes. No matter the obstacle, we keep finding love and romance.

Now that I've finished this project, I have a much richer understanding of the new romantic landscape. And the main thing I've learned from all this research is that we're all in it together. I hope you feel this way too.

I wish you, and all the readers, the best of luck in modern romance.

And by best of luck, I mean I hope that one day you'll meet someone amazing, text them a thoughtful message, take them to a monster truck rally, and then hopefully at some point, after a bowl of delicious ramen, make love to them in a *Jurassic Park*–themed love hotel in Tokyo.

ACKNOWLEDGMENTS

This book is technically "by Aziz Ansari," but I cannot overstate what a group effort it has been on many levels.

To begin, I must thank Mr. Eric Klinenberg. If you are a renowned sociologist and best-selling author, teaming up with a comedian to write a sociology/humor book about modern romance is not necessarily a safe or logical bet. But Eric has believed in the project and me since day one. Over the past two years, we spent an insane amount of time working together, trying to conceive and execute this project. Working so closely and intensely with someone can be a grind sometimes, but with Eric it was always fun and interesting. It also helped that when it came to food, Eric was a maximizer as well, never questioning our extended lunch breaks or grueling research to find *the* best place to eat at that moment. Eric, a million thanks, sir.

Besides Eric, the other key to pulling off this book was our many interviews, which gave us real-world experiences to draw and learn from. The book would simply not have been possible without the hundreds of people all over the world who participated in these interviews and so graciously shared the most intimate parts of their lives. This also goes for everyone who took part in our online subreddit forum. I can't thank all of you folks enough.

We did a huge amount of research for this book, and we couldn't have done it without the help of our great collaborators and assistants.

Matthew Wolfe, aka the Wolfe Man, has been a superstar

research assistant and then some. Everything we threw at Wolfe was taken care of, no matter how weird. Whether it was tracking down classified personals from hundreds of years ago or finding someone to Photoshop pictures of Dwayne "The Rock" Johnson, he was on top of it. What's more, he did it all with the utmost professionalism and good cheer, which made working on the book a lot more fun and easy than it might have been. Wolfe Man, you killed it, and we thank you.

Shelly Ronen offered crucial assistance in the early stages of the project, helping us run focus groups in New York City and doing her own interviews as well as fieldwork in Buenos Aires. Kumiko Endo gave us great support in Tokyo, recruiting people for focus groups and tutoring us on the city's strange and fascinating romantic culture. Sonia Zmihi organized our focus groups in Paris. Gracias, arigato, merci.

Robb Willer, a sociologist at Stanford University and a fellow native South Carolinian, consulted with us throughout the research process, helping us analyze sophisticated data sets and appreciate the value of monster truck rallies in dating.

We benefited immensely from the contributions of scholars and dating experts who generously shared their time and ideas: danah boyd, Andrew Cherlin, Stephanie Coontz, Laurie Davis, Pamela Druckerman, Thomas Edwards, Eli Finkel, Helen Fisher, Jonathan Haidt, Sheena Iyengar, Dan Savage, Natasha Schüll, Barry Schwartz, Clay Shirky, and Sherry Turkle. These are all incredibly smart people and I feel lucky to have gotten to spend time with them and steal some of their wisdom.

I also want to give a special shout-out to a few people who were extremely helpful with our data. Christian Rudder, a cofounder of OkCupid, and Helen Fisher, an anthropologist and adviser to Match.com, offered us all kinds of original data from their dating sites and surveys. Victoria Taylor and Erik Martin at Reddit helped us set up the Modern Romantics subreddit, which proved to be an invaluable research tool. Michael Rosenfeld, of Stanford University, shared data from his amazing survey, "How Couples Meet and Stay

Together," and Jonathan Haidt of New York University allowed us to reproduce and take some liberties with his graphs.

Geoff Mandel is responsible for the amazing Photoshop work in the book and quickly addressed ridiculous e-mails from me that said things like "Hey Geoff, can we make the raptors in the Jurassic Park Honeymoon Suite 30% bigger and also put romantic candles on them?" Walter Green did the excellent graphs and layout. I must also give a huge thanks to Warren Fu and Crisanta Baker who helped with early concepts for the book jacket. The final jacket artwork was designed by Jay Shaw, with photography by Ruvan Wijesooriya. The limited edition's jacket was crafted by Dawn Baille and her team at BLT.

In New York City we got logistical help from Jessica Coffey, Siera Dissmore, Victor Bautista, Sebastien Theroux, and Matthew Shawver. In Los Angeles, Honora Talbot and Dan Torson kept us in gear. Also want to shout-out the Upright Citizens Brigade Theatre for helping provide venues for some of our larger focus groups, and the University Settlement for helping us arrange interviews with their seniors.

A small group of friends and colleagues read early drafts of the manuscript, and their comments helped us sharpen the final version. These folks include: Aniz Ansari, Siera Dissmore, Enrique Iglesias,[*] Jack Moore, Matt Murray, Kelefa Sanneh, Lizzie Widdicombe, Andrew Weinberg, Robb Willer, Harris Wittels, Jason Woliner, and Alan Yang.

Our agents and managers, Richard Abate, David Miner, and Dave Becky at 3Arts, Mike Berkowitz at APA (for Aziz), and Tina Bennett at William Morris (for Eric), were great advocates at every stage of the process. I also want to thank my publicist, Jodi Gottlieb, who, even though we technically have no clue what the press will be like for this project as I type this, I am so sure will work tirelessly to get the word out. I also need to thank David Cho, who does a lot of random shit very well on all fronts digital

---

[*] Numerous attempts to get a manuscript to Mr. Iglesias unfortunately were unsuccessful.

and is always down to get delicious Korean food with me. My lawyers, Jared Levine, Corinne Farley, and Ted Gerdes, who sent me awesome e-mails that said things like "You absolutely cannot say the old couple from the stock image site are 'fucking other people' unless you make it explicitly clear that they are *not* actually 'fucking other people.'"

Scott Moyers, our editor at Penguin, has been incredible every step of the way. He got the concept of this book immediately, always supported it, and never tried to make it something it was not. In addition to Scott, we need to thank Ann Godoff, Mally Anderson, Akif Saifi, Hilary Roberts, Jeannette Williams, and the rest of the team at Penguin Press, who always had our backs as well.

And finally, our greatest thanks go to our own partners in modern romance.

To Kate, who endured her husband's unexpected run as a spokesman for American singles, Eric hopes that this book has redeemed him.

To Courtney, if every person were lucky enough to have a partner as supportive, loving, caring, talented, and beautiful as you—I doubt there'd be a market for a book like this.

To Eric, this is Aziz. I hope I don't get you in trouble with your wife because I totally *destroyed* you in the "who wrote a sweeter note to their person" contest.

NOTES

Chapter 1: Searching for Your Soul Mate

1 James H. S. Bossard, "Residential Propinquity as a Factor in Marriage Selection," *American Journal of Sociology* 38, no. 2 (1932): 219–24.

2 John S. Ellsworth Jr., "The Relationship of Population Density to Residential Propinquity as a Factor in Marriage Selection," *American Sociological Review* 13, no. 4 (1948): 444–48.

3 William M. Kephart, "Some Correlates of Romantic Love," *Journal of Marriage and the Family* 29, no. 3 (1967): 470–74.

4 Stephanie Coontz, *Marriage, a History: How Love Conquered Marriage* (New York: Penguin, 2006), 7.

5 Elizabeth Rice Allgeier and Michael W. Wiederman, "Love and Mate Selection in the 1990s," *Free Inquiry* 11, no. 3 (1991): 25–27.

6 Esther Perel, "The Secret to Desire in a Long-Term Relationship," TED lecture, February 2013.

7 Casey E. Copen, Kimberly Daniels, Jonathan Vespa, and William D. Mosher, "First Marriages in the United States: Data from the 2006–2010 National Survey of Family Growth," *National Health Statistics Reports* 49 (2012).

8 These numbers come from a report on Internet trends by Mary Meeker of the venture capital firm Kleiner Perkins Caufield & Byers. The report

is available from the website *Quartz* at http://qz.com/214307/mary
-meeker-2014-internet-trends-report-all-the-slides/.

Chapter 2: The Initial Ask

1 The results of the survey, conducted by the communications company
   textPlus, are available at http://www.textplus.com/its-prom-party
   -time/.

2 Ibid.

3 The account of texting we tell here relies on Chris Gayomali, "The Text
   Message Turns 20: A Brief History of SMS," *The Week*, December 3,
   2012.

4 The 2010 data are reported in David Goldman, "Your Smartphone
   Will Run Your Life," CNN.com, October 19, 2010. The 2014 data
   come from Pew Research Center, "Device Ownership over Time,"
   Pew Research Internet Project, January 2014, http://www.pewin
   ternet.org/data-trend/mobile/cell-phone-and-smartphone-owner
   ship-demographics/.

5 Clive Thompson, "Clive Thompson on the Death of the Phone Call,"
   Wired, July 28, 2010.

6 George Homans established the classic sociological "principle of least
   interest," which holds that the person who is least interested in a relationship has the most power. See George Caspar Homans, *Social Behavior: Its Elementary Forms* (New York: Harcourt Brace Jovanovich, 1961).

7 Mike J. F. Robinson, Patrick Anselme, Adam M. Fischer, and Kent
   C. Berridge, "Initial Uncertainty in Pavlovian Reward Prediction
   Persistently Elevates Incentive Salience and Extends Sign-Tracking to
   Normally Unattractive Cues," *Behavioral Brain Research* 266 (2014):
   119–30.

8 Erin Whitchurch, Timothy Wilson, and Daniel Gilbert, " 'He Loves Me,
   He Loves Me Not . . .' Uncertainty Can Increase Romantic Attraction,"
   Psychological Science 22, no. 2 (2011): 172–75.

9 The survey, conducted by Hunter Public Relations, can be found at http://clientnewsfeed.hunterpr.com/category/Wine-Spirits-News .aspx?page=25.

Chapter 3: Online Dating

1 Christian Rudder, *Dataclysm: Who We Are (When We Think No One's Looking)* (New York: Crown, 2014).

2 Nathan Ensmenger, "Computer Dating in the 1960s," *The Computer Boys* (blog), March 5, 2014.

3 H. G. Cocks, *Classified: The Secret History of the Personal Column* (London: Random House, 2009).

4 This story is told in Jeff Kauflin, "How Match.com's Founder Created the World's Biggest Dating Website—and Walked Away with Just $50,000," *Business Insider*, December 16, 2011.

5 John T. Cacioppo, Stephanie Cacioppo, Gian C. Gonzaga, Elizabeth L. Ogburn, and Tyler J. VanderWeele, "Marital Satisfaction and Break-ups Differ Across On-line and Off-line Meeting Venues," *Proceedings of the National Academy of Sciences* 110, no. 47 (2011): 18814–19.

6 More of this data is here: http://data.stanford.edu/hcmst. The survey oversampled gays and lesbians to make sure there were sufficient numbers to draw meaningful conclusions.

7 Michael J. Rosenfeld and Reuben J. Thomas, "Searching for a Mate: The Rise of the Internet as a Social Intermediary," *American Sociological Review* 77, no. 4 (2012): 523–47.

8 Aaron Smith and Maeve Duggan, "Online Dating and Relationships," Pew Research Center, October 21, 2013.

9 Rudder, *Dataclysm*, 70.

10 Dan Slater, *Love in the Time of Algorithms: What Technology Does to Meeting and Mating* (New York: Current Books, 2013).

11　Christian Rudder, "The 4 Big Myths of Profile Pictures," *OkTrends* (blog), January 20, 2010, http://blog.okcupid.com/index.php/the-4 -big-myths-of-profile-pictures/.

12　Eli J. Finkel, Paul W. Eastwick, Benjamin R. Karney, Harry T. Reis, and Susan Sprecher, "Online Dating: A Critical Analysis from the Perspective of Psychological Science," *Psychological Science in the Public Interest* 13, no. 1 (2012): 3–66.

13　Laura Stampler, "Inside Tinder: Meet the Guys Who Turned Dating into an Addiction," *Time*, February 6, 2014.

14　Ann Friedman, "How Tinder Solved Online Dating for Women," *New York*, October 10, 2013.

15　Nick Bilton, "Tinder, the Fast-Growing Dating App, Taps an Age-Old Truth," *New York Times*, October 29, 2014.

16　Holly Baxter and Pete Cashmore, "Tinder: The Shallowest Dating App Ever?" *Guardian*, November 22, 2013.

17　Velvet Garvey, "9 Rules for Expats in Qatar," Matador Network, July 28, 2012.

Chapter 4: Choice and Options

1　Sheena S. Iyengar, Rachael E. Wells, and Barry Schwartz, "Doing Better but Feeling Worse: Looking for the 'Best' Job Undermines Satisfaction," *Psychological Science* 17, no. 2 (2006): 143–50.

2　Sheena S. Iyengar and Mark R. Lepper, "When Choice Is Demotivating: Can One Desire Too Much of a Good Thing?" *Journal of Personality and Social Psychology* 79, no. 6 (2000): 995.

3　On the age of first marriage by state, see Population Reference Bureau, "Median Age at First Marriage for Women (5-Year ACS)," http:// www.prb.org/DataFinder/Topic/Rankings.aspx?ind=133. On the rising divorce rate in small towns and rural areas, see Sabrina Tavernise and Robert Gebeloff, "Once Rare in Rural America, Divorce Is Changing the Face of Its Families," *New York Times*, March 23, 2011.

4   Donald G. Dutton and Arthur P. Aron, "Some Evidence for Heightened Sexual Attraction Under Conditions of High Anxiety," *Journal of Personality and Social Psychology* 30, no. 4 (1974): 510.

5   Arthur Aron, Christina C. Norman, Elaine N. Aron, Colin McKenna, and Richard E. Heyman, "Couples' Shared Participation in Novel and Arousing Activities and Experienced Relationship Quality," *Journal of Personality and Social Psychology* 78, no. 2 (2000): 273.

6   Paul W. Eastwick and Lucy L. Hunt, "Relational Mate Value: Consensus and Uniqueness in Romantic Evaluations," *Journal of Personality and Social Psychology* 106, no. 5 (2014): 728–51.

7   Paul W. Eastwick and Lucy L. Hunt, "So You're Not Desirable," *New York Times*, May 16, 2014.

Chapter 5: International Investigations of Love

1   Lindsey Galloway, "Living In: The World's Best Cities for Dating," BBC.com, June 16, 2014.

2   Abigail Haworth, "Why Have Young People in Japan Stopped Having Sex?" *Guardian*, October 20, 2013.

3   National Institute on Population and Social Security Research, "The Fourteenth Japanese National Fertility Survey," 2010.

4   An English-language summary of these findings can be found at "30% of Single Japanese Men Have Never Dated a Woman," *Japan Crush* (blog), April 3, 2013.

5   Roland Buerk, "Japan Singletons Hit Record High," BBC.com, November 28, 2011.

6   If you can read Japanese, see http://www.stat.go.jp/data/koku sei/2005/sokuhou/01.htm.

7   "Survey Finds Growing Number of Couples Turned Off by Sex," *Asahi Shimbun*, December 21, 2012.

8 Central Intelligence Agency, "The World Factbook," 2014, available at https://www.cia.gov/library/publications/the-world-factbook/ran korder/2054rank.html.

9 Linda Sieg, "Population Woes Crowd Japan," *Japan Times*, June 21, 2014.

10 A rundown of the Japanese government's marriage-support initiatives can be found in Keiko Ujikane and Kyoko Shimodo, "Abe Funds Japan's Last-Chance Saloon to Arrest Drop in Births," Bloomberg, March 19, 2014.

11 Kalman Applbaum, "Marriage with the Proper Stranger: Arranged Marriage in Metropolitan Japan," *Ethnology* 34, no. 1 (1995): 37–51. Also see David Millward, "Arranged Marriages Make Comeback in Japan," *Telegraph*, April 16, 2012.

12 Masami Ito, "Marriage Ever-Changing Institution," *Japan Times*, November 3, 2009.

13 Alexandra Harney, "The Herbivore's Dilemma," *Slate*, June 15, 2009.

14 National Institute on Population and Social Security Research, "Fourteenth Japanese National Fertility Survey," October-November 2011.

15 There's a totally fascinating video from *Vice* on the Japanese love industry that's available at www.vice.com/the-vice-guide-to-travel/the -japanese-love-industry.

16 If you're interested in hostess clubs, there's a whole anthropology book about them. Anne Allison, *Nightwork: Sexuality, Pleasure, and Corporate Masculinity in a Tokyo Hostess Club* (Chicago: University of Chicago Press, 1994).

17 The data on men's use of prostitution is assembled in "Percentage of Men (by Country) Who Paid for Sex at Least Once: The Johns Chart," ProCon.org, January 6, 2011. It can be found at http://prostitution .procon.org/view.resource.php?resourceID=004119.

18 The mayor's statements and the 60 percent figure can be found in Tara Brady, "'Women Who Say They Don't Like Cat-Calls Are Lying':

Buenos Aires Mayor Sparks Furious Backlash," *Daily Mail*, April 29, 2014.

Chapter 6: Old Issues, New Formats: Sexting, Cheating, Snooping, and Breaking Up

1 These statistics come from a few sources: The data on sending and receiving sexts are in Hanna Rosin, "Why Kids Sext," *Atlantic*, November 2014. The data on iPhone users versus Android users, on Tuesday-morning sexting, and on people in relationships sexting come from the Match.com survey we draw on throughout the book.

2 Jenna Wortham, "Everybody Sexts," *Matter*, November 11, 2014.

3 Rosin, "Why Kids Sext."

4 Oliver Tree, "'Stop Starin at My Weapon': Hilarious New Details of Weiner's Sordid Facebook 'Affair' with Blackjack Dealer Are Revealed," *Daily Mail*, June 8, 2011, http://www.dailymail.co.uk/news/article-2000386/Anthony-Weiner-Facebook-affair-blackjack-dealer-Lisa-Weiss-revealed.html.

5 The 2011 figure is reported in Sheelah Kolhatkar, "Cheating, Incorporated," *Bloomberg Businessweek*, February 10, 2011. The 2014 figure is on Ashley Madison's website. See https://www.ashleymadison.com/blog/about-us/.

6 Deni Kirkova, "You're Breaking Up with Me by TEXT?" *Daily Mail*, March 5, 2014.

7 Ilana Gershon, *The Breakup 2.0: Disconnecting over New Media* (Ithaca: Cornell University Press, 2011).

8 Rossalyn Warren, "A Girl Is Getting over Her Ex by Photoshopping Photos of Beyoncé Over His Face," BuzzFeed, July 29, 2014.

9 Irene Tsapelas, Helen Fisher, and Arthur Aron, "Infidelity: When, Where, Why," in William R. Cupach and Brian H. Spitzberg, *The Dark Side of Close Relationships II* (New York: Routledge, 2010), pp. 175–96.

10 Richard Wike, "French More Accepting of Infidelity Than People in Other Countries," Pew Research Center, January 14, 2014.

11 Frank Newport and Igor Himelfarb, "In U.S., Record-High Say Gay, Lesbian Relations Morally OK," Gallup.com, May 20, 2013.

12 Henry Samuel, "French Study Shows a Majority of Men and a Third of Women Cheat," *Telegraph*, January 21, 2014.

Chapter 7: Settling Down

1 Helen Fisher, "How to Make Romance Last," *O, the Oprah Magazine*, December 2009.

2 Philip N. Cohen, "Marriage Is Declining Globally: Can You Say That?" *Family Inequality* (blog), June 12, 2013.

3 Christina Sterbenz, "Marriage Rates Are Near Their Lowest Levels in History—Here's Why," *Business Insider*, May 7, 2014.

4 Andrew J. Cherlin, "In the Season of Marriage, a Question: Why Bother?" *New York Times*, April 27, 2013.

5 Mark Oppenheimer, "Marriage, with Infidelities," *New York Times*, June 30, 2011.

6 Mimi Valdes, "Do Open Relationships Work?" *Men's Fitness*, October 2007.

BOOKS CONSULTED

BAILEY, BETH. *From Front Porch to Back Seat: Courtship in Twentieth-Century America*. Baltimore: Johns Hopkins University Press, 1988.

BOYD, DANAH. *It's Complicated: The Social Lives of Networked Teens*. New Haven, CT: Yale University Press, 2014.

CHERLIN, ANDREW J. *Marriage, Divorce, Remarriage*. Cambridge, MA: Harvard University Press, 2009.

————. *The Marriage-Go-Round: The State of Marriage and the Family in America Today*. New York: Knopf, 2010.

COCKS, H. G. *Classified: The Secret History of the Personal Column*. London: Random House, 2009.

COONTZ, STEPHANIE. *Marriage, a History: How Love Conquered Marriage*. New York: Penguin Books, 2006.

DAVIS, LAURIE. *Love at First Click: The Ultimate Guide to Online Dating*. New York: Simon & Schuster, 2013.

DRUCKERMAN, PAMELA. *Lust in Translation: The Rules of Infidelity from Tokyo to Tennessee*. New York: Penguin Press, 2007.

DUNBAR, ROBIN. *The Science of Love*. Hoboken, NJ: Wiley, 2012.

FISHER, HELEN. *Anatomy of Love*: *A Natural History of Monogamy, Adultery, and Divorce*. New York: Simon & Schuster, 1992.

————. *Why Him? Why Her? Finding Real Love by Understanding Your Personality Type*. New York: Henry Holt, 2009.

HAIDT, JONATHAN. *The Happiness Hypothesis: Finding Modern Truth in Ancient Wisdom*. New York: Basic Books, 2006.

ILLOUZ, EVA. *Why Love Hurts: A Sociological Explanation*. Malden, MA: Polity Press, 2012.

IYENGAR, SHEENA. *The Art of Choosing*. New York: Twelve, 2010.

JONES, DANIEL. *Love Illuminated: Exploring Life's Most Mystifying Subject (with the Help of 50,000 Strangers)*. New York: HarperCollins, 2014.

KLINENBERG, ERIC. *Going Solo: The Extraordinary Rise and Surprising Appeal of Living Alone*. New York: Penguin Press, 2012.

LING, RICHARD SEYLER. *New Tech, New Ties: How Mobile Communication Is Reshaping Social Cohesion*. Cambridge, MA: MIT Press, 2008.

NORTHRUP, CHRISANNA, PEPPER SCHWARTZ, AND JAMES WITTE. *The Normal Bar: The Surprising Secrets of Happy Couples and What They Reveal About Creating a New Normal in Your Relationship*. New York: Harmony, 2013.

OYER, PAUL. *Everything I Ever Needed to Know About Economics I Learned from Online Dating*. Cambridge, MA: Harvard Business Review Press, 2014.

ROSENFELD, MICHAEL J. *The Age of Independence: Interracial Unions, Same-Sex Unions, and the Changing American Family*. Cambridge, MA: Harvard University Press, 2007.

RUDDER, CHRISTIAN. *Dataclysm: Who We Are (When We Think No One's Looking)*. New York: Crown, 2014.

RYAN, CHRISTOPHER, AND CACILDA JETHÁ. *Sex at Dawn: The Prehistoric Origins of Modern Sexuality*. New York: HarperCollins, 2010.

SCHWARTZ, BARRY. *The Paradox of Choice*. New York: Ecco, 2004.

SIMON, HERBERT A. *Models of Man: Social and Rational*. Oxford: Wiley, 1957.

SLATER, DAN. *Love in the Time of Algorithms: What Technology Does to Meeting and Mating*. New York: Current, 2013.

TURKLE, SHERRY. *Alone Together: Why We Expect More from Technology and Less from Each Other*. New York: Basic Books, 2012.

WEBB, AMY. *Data, a Love Story: How I Cracked the Online Dating Code to Meet My Match*. New York: Dutton, 2013.

Note: Page numbers in *italics* refer to illustrations and graphs.

brain scans, 214, 215

breakups, 191–95

Buenos Aires, 170–76
  aggressive culture in, 150,
    170–72
  casual sex in, 175–76
  dating culture in, 176
  flirting in, 175
  histérico/histérica in, 174–75
  living with parents in, 175
  love hotels in, 175–76
  Stop Street Harassment movement
    in, 171
  technology in, 173

Bullock, Sandra, 144

C

Cacioppo, John, 79, 80

Capilano River, Vancouver, 143–44

careers:
  and age of marriage, 17
  women and, 19, 24

cheating, 184–91, 203–5
  and ease of access, 188
  ending the affair, 190
  escalation in, 188
  and social media, 187, 195

Cherlin, Andrew, 21–22, 24
  The Marriage-Go-Round, 22, 221

choice, *see* options

Christmas ornaments, 128–29, 130

classified ads, 72–76, *73*

cliques, 135

cohabitation, 221

Cohen, Philip, 220

commitment, 134, 139, 218–19,
  223–24, 227

companionate love, 214–18

computer dating services, 71–72
  algorithms of, 79

connectivity, 251

control, need for, 58

conversation:
  face-to-face, 47, 107–9, 245
  phone vs. real-world, 47–48
  spontaneous, 41

Coontz, Stephanie, 225, 233
  Marriage, A History, 22–23, 224–25

cuddling cafés, 166

D

Dataclysm (Rudder), 88–89, 93, 97,
  101, 105

dating:
  best first dates, 141–42
  boring dates, 140–43, 145–47
  casual, 146
  effects of non-boring dates,
    143–45
  gokon (Japan), 165–66
  hanging out vs., 53–54
  initial ask, 33–37, *34*, 42
  machikon (Japan), 165
  mobile apps, 109–18, *110*
  online, *see* online dating
  past and present, 27–29
  quantity of dates, 145–47
  strategies for, 145–47
  tiring process of, 94

Davis, Laurie, *Love at First Click*, 108

deal breakers, 139–40

decoy stories, 86–87

Derek (OkCupid user), 88–91

digital devices, 29–32